Real Libertarianism Assessed

Also by Andrew Williams

THE IDEAL OF EQUALITY (*co-editor with Matthew Clayton*)

Real Libertarianism Assessed

Political Theory after Van Parijs

Edited by

Andrew Reeve
Professor of Politics
University of Warwick

and

Andrew Williams
Lecturer in Politics and Philosophy
University of Reading

First published 2003 by
PALGRAVE MACMILLAN
Houndmills, Basingstoke, Hampshire RG21 6XS and
175 Fifth Avenue, New York, N. Y. 10010
Companies and representatives throughout the world

PALGRAVE MACMILLAN is the global academic imprint of the Palgrave
Macmillan division of St. Martin's Press, LLC and of Palgrave Macmillan Ltd.
Macmillan® is a registered trademark in the United States, United Kingdom
and other countries. Palgrave is a registered trademark in the European
Union and other countries.

ISBN 0–333–91267–5

This book is printed on paper suitable for recycling and made from fully
managed and sustained forest sources.

A catalogue record for this book is available from the British Library.
A catalogue record for this book is available from the Library of Congress.

10   9   8   7   6   5   4   3   2   1
12   11   10   09   08   07   06   05   04   03

Printed and bound in Great Britain by
Antony Rowe Ltd, Chippenham and Eastbourne

Contents

List of the Contributors

Richard J. Arneson is Professor of Philosophy at the University of California, San Diego.

Brian Barry is Arnold A. Saltzman Professor in Philosophy and Political Science at Columbia University.

Thomas Christiano is Associate Professor of Philosophy at the University of Arizona.

John Cunliffe is a Senior Lecturer in the Department of Public Policy at the University of Central England.

Guido Erreygers is Professor in the Department of Economics at the University of Antwerp.

Andrew Reeve is Professor of Politics at the University of Warwick.

Hillel Steiner is Professor of Political Philosophy at the University of Manchester, and a Fellow of the British Academy.

Peter Vallentyne is Professor of Philosophy at Virginia Commonwealth University.

Robert J. Van der Veen is Lecturer in Political Theory at the University of Amsterdam.

Philippe Van Parijs is Professor of Economic and Social Ethics at the Université Catholique de Louvain.

Walter Van Trier is based at the Resource Centre for Labour Market Research at the Catholic University of Leuven, where he coordinates an interdisciplinary research team on the transition from school to work.

Stuart White is Fellow in Politics at Jesus College, Oxford.

Andrew Williams is Lecturer in Politics and Philosophy at the University of Reading.

Acknowledgements

For instructive discussion about the volume, the editors thank Matthew Clayton, John Cunliffe, Jeroen Knijff, Robert J. Van der Veen and Philippe Van Parijs. Work on the volume was funded, in part, by a Faculty Fellowship at the Center for Ethics and the Professions at Harvard University. Andrew Williams gratefully acknowledges the superb environment provided by the Center. Both editors also gratefully acknowledge the following permissions to reprint essays in this volume.

Peter Vallentyne, 'Self-Ownership and Equality: Brute Luck, Gifts, Universal Dominance, and Leximin' originally appeared in *Ethics* 107 (1997), pp. 321–43. Printed with permission of the author and the University of Chicago Press.

Brian Barry, 'Real Freedom and Basic Income' originally appeared in *Journal of Political Philosophy* 4 (1996), pp. 242–76. Printed with permission of the author and Blackwell Publishing.

Robert J. Van der Veen, 'Real Freedom and Basic Income: Comment on Brian Barry' originally appeared in *Journal of Political Philosophy* 5 (1997), pp. 274–86. Printed with permission of the author and Blackwell Publishing.

Andrew Williams, 'Resource Egalitarianism and the Limits to Basic Income' originally appeared in *Economics and Philosophy* 15/1 (1999), pp. 85–107. Printed with permission of the author and Cambridge University Press.

All editors' royalties from the sale of this book will be donated to Oxfam.

1
Introduction

Andrew Reeve

1.1 The reception of *Real Freedom for All*

In 1995, Philippe Van Parijs published *Real Freedom for All*, and was almost immediately greeted with considerable acclaim, as well as a great deal of critical attention.[1] Van Parijs's book has many merits, a number of which clearly contributed to its impact. First, Van Parijs's central contention is that justice demands that each individual receive a basic income unconditional upon his or her willingness to seek paid employment. There are few works that argue for the necessity of such a radical change in public policy in as original, and sophisticated, a manner as *Real Freedom for All*. Secondly, and connected with this first factor, Van Parijs draws upon, and illuminates, some of the most important debates within contemporary political philosophy. For example, he makes significant contributions to the growing literature on self-ownership, the relationship between liberty and equality, the currency of egalitarian justice and the nature of exploitation. Thirdly, as well as exploring these foundational issues, the book is also deeply concerned with how principles of justice are to be institutionalised, and draws freely on social science, including, in particular, economic theory. So, for example, Van Parijs discusses recent accounts of the microeconomics of the labour market, of aggregate demand management and of the behaviour of firms. Fourthly, Van Parijs's book is the fruit of many years' thought and defends itself against many objections that earlier versions of his argument provoked. As a result, it possesses considerable depth and continually challenges its readers to find additional objections to, or defects in, these new defences.

Acknowledging *Real Freedom for All*'s many virtues – its depth and originality, its contribution to major debates and its interdisciplinary appeal – is, of course, consistent both with outright rejection of its approach and with reservations about parts of the argument. It is, after all, a philosophical manifesto for a radical political position; and not everyone shares that radical impulse. As Van Parijs explains, he sets out from two convictions: 'One: Our capitalist societies are replete with unacceptable inequalities. Two: Freedom is of paramount importance' (p. 1). His book, he adds, 'is primarily addressed to those who share' these convictions with him. Not everyone does; but then they have to respond to his arguments accordingly. At the same time, many may indeed share those convictions, yet still be unpersuaded by the conclusions he draws from them, or by particular steps in his argument.

The contributors to this volume provide a searching assessment of the main claims advanced in *Real Freedom for All*. They range from those who believe that Van Parijs is, as it were, 'nearly right' to those who think he is more nearly completely wrong. Van Parijs replies to his critics in a final chapter, thus taking the debate forward. The purpose of this Introduction is to outline the structure and content of *Real Freedom for All* as a preliminary to the comments and criticism to follow. Before we proceed to consider Van Parijs's argument, however, some caveats are in order.

Although my task is not to provide a judgement on those arguments, or adjudicate about the debates in which he participates, it must be noted that even well-intentioned exposition amounts to interpretation, in part because of the need to be selective. *Real Freedom for All* contains 233 pages of main text, as well as 63 pages of footnotes. The majority of those notes provides additional argument, detail, nuance and caveat. It is clearly impossible to take all this into account in a brief summary. Secondly, interpretation of complex argument is often controversial and, as will become apparent, our contributors do not all read the book in the same way as each other, or as the author. Nevertheless, with these reservations in mind, I now turn to outline some of the main features of Van Parijs's book.

1.2 A brief overview

The structure of *Real Freedom for All* needs to be seen partly in the light of the question stated in its subtitle, namely, *What (if anything) can justify capitalism?* Van Parijs's title suggests that his main endeavour is to examine the rival merits of socialism and capitalism with respect to their capacity to instantiate a free society. A 'free society', for Van Parijs, is a just society – his *real libertarianism* conceives of justice in terms of distributing freedom. The distributive principle Van Parijs favours leads him to argue that a universal basic income should be paid to each member of society, at the highest sustainable level. In addition to the redistribution implied by the payment of a universal and unconditional basic income, Van Parijs also defends a second form of redistribution, which is targeted at those with particular disadvantages, and designed to achieve what he terms *undominated diversity*.

An argument for a just distribution, of course, requires a defence of not only the recipient's entitlements but also the legitimacy of any 'taking' involved in obtaining the resources to be distributed. Because of concerns with feasibility, the size of the pool of resources to be so distributed is highly important. Its size, however, will depend not only on economic performance but also on which assets are taken to be legitimate sources for revenue. One of Van Parijs's distinctive contributions to debates about (re)distribution is to add a new asset to the relevant pool: *employment assets*. His idea, as will become apparent, is that those who hold a job have appropriated a (social) asset, just as if they occupied a piece of land, and are required to pay a fair price for doing so. The question about the rival merits of socialism and capitalism from which he sets out then become refined: is the best version of capitalism superior to the best version of socialism in passing the test of providing a free society?

As Van Parijs explains, for a society to satisfy that test involves it meeting three conditions: securing 'formal freedom', respecting self-ownership, and ensuring the greatest real freedom for those who enjoy least freedom. This last condition, he goes on to argue, requires providing the highest possible sustainable basic income, subject to the satisfaction of what he terms *undominated diversity*. When optimal capitalism is compared to optimal socialism by this complex test, Van Parijs concludes that there is a strong presumption in favour of some form of capitalism allied with 'democratic scale lifting' and 'solidaristic patriotism'.

Before going on to explain these claims, it is worth quoting here Van Parijs's penultimate paragraph, for it illustrates the sense in which *Real Freedom for All* is a radical philosophical text, along with the structure, just summarised, which we shall proceed to unravel:

> The conclusion that emerges is that an earnest commitment to free-dom – appropriately understood as real-freedom-for-all – does nothing to warrant complacency with the inequalities of existing capitalism. Nor does it give us any good reason – on plausible factual assump-tions – to fight for socialism now ... Key issues for the future are rather whether, when, and how one should introduce an unconditional basic income, attribute redistributive powers to supranational authorities,

or constrain the organization of social life so as to nurture feelings of solidarity. These are the issues around which the crucial struggles of the future will be fought. It is the outcomes of these struggles that will determine the pace of progress towards more justice, towards greater real freedom for all.

(pp. 232–3)[2]

1.3   The nature of a free society

Having explained the overall structure of *Real Freedom for All*, and its author's answer to the question in its subtitle, we shall now look in more detail at the steps he takes to arrive at his conclusion. Since his initial question is 'If we wish for a free society, should we favour capitalism or socialism?', he naturally needs to tell his readers what they are to understand by 'freedom' and 'a free society'. But rather than provide these definitions, and then proceed to apply them to the workings of those rival socio-economic regimes, Van Parijs works towards an account of those terms by showing that there can be no a priori argument for either capitalism or socialism, and developing his account of freedom in the process.

The attraction of socialism as a fully democratic society is said to rest on confusing power with freedom; and worries are raised about the recognition of self-ownership in conditions of collective decision-making. Equally, *pace* those libertarians who would like to see capitalism as the necessary embodiment of a free society, Van Parijs claims that the libertarians who take that view suffer from 'rights-fetishism'[3] – they use a moralised notion of freedom, and require a rule about legitimate original appropriation which is eminently controversial.

For Van Parijs, a free society is one in which its individual members are free rather than merely participants in the power of collective decision-making. Furthermore, he also rejects conceptions of liberty that conceive it to be the freedom to do one's duty or to mean autonomy. Freedom, for Van Parijs, 'includes' self-ownership,[4] but he resists the cut-off between freedom and external resources emphasised by Hayek and others. Thus, while Hayek distinguishes the freedom to do something from the capacity to do it, Van Parijs wishes to make a connection between freedom and external objects by reference to the idea of opportunity, broadly construed. Although security and self-ownership are recognised by formal freedom, real freedom, he tells us, embraces opportunity as well. If all members of society are maximally free, we have a free society.[5] The list of freedom-reducing obstacles to opportunity is, radically, fairly all-embracing – whether such obstacles are internal to the person, whether they have been deliberately created, or whether they are either produced or removable by human action, they may still constitute restrictions on freedom.

As mentioned earlier, a free society is defined as one that meets three conditions. It provides security through properly enforced rights. It recognises self-ownership. Its structure of rights gives each person the 'greatest possible opportunity to do whatever she might want to do'. (It is important to note the 'might want' here.) This last condition raises a distributive issue because 'greatest possible' opportunity is to be provided to everybody. Van Parijs unpacks it not as maximum *total* freedom, nor *equal* maximum freedom, but as *leximin* freedom.[6] Thus, the opportunities of those with fewest opportunities are to be maximised. If the opportunities of the person next on the scale of opportunity-holders can be increased without diminishing those with fewer opportunities they should be; if not, they should not be. And so on.

In addition to the lexical priority in the distribution of opportunities of those who have least, there is also a weaker priority relation between the three conditions. Security has priority over self-ownership, which in turn has priority over the principle of leximin opportunity. Van Parijs proposes that there will be instances in which small violations of his second principle of justice would be acceptable, if the gains in satisfying the third were sufficiently large. The model, we are told, is more left-wing than liberal-egalitarianism, but is not strictly egalitarian, since it is fully consistent with the justice of undeserved, and unchosen, inequalities in opportunities. It is also claimed to embrace equal concern for persons, neutrality with respect to individuals' conceptions of the good, and to be a particular interpretation of the implications of a concern with liberty, equality and efficiency.

1.4 (Unconditional) basic income

We now need to consider what satisfying these conditions might involve. Van Parijs tells us immediately that they require the payment of an unconditional basic income to all members of the political society. In the remains of this section, I summarise what is meant by a basic income, and why Van Parijs thinks it is required by his conception of a free society.

A basic income is paid to each 'full member' of society without reference to that person's existing resources, willingness to work, household membership, or location. Such a payment is quite obviously different from standard welfare-state payments, which are often means tested, depend upon a person's availability and willingness to take employment, or relate to local considerations like levels of rent, or take into account the position of partners or others living in the household. It is a require-ment of justice, for Van Parijs, that the government should disburse such a basic income. This is because a free society is identified with a just soci-ety by real libertarianism. The relation between 'opportunity' and income is twofold. Inasmuch as we think about opportunities to consume, then the money available defines the bundles of goods that can be purchased by a particular person. Inasmuch as we think about opportunities to live as we might wish, an unconditional income (at least of a certain level) adds to our choice-set the opportunity to consider the choice between work and leisure in a way otherwise unavailable. The inclusion of the irrele-vance of willingness to work in the unconditionality, for Van Parijs, fol-lows from a genuine commitment to neutrality between conceptions of the good. Although there has been discussion about whether some form of basic income would be a desirable policy device in the conditions of the modern (European) welfare state, Van Parijs's claim, it also needs to be emphasised, is that the provision of the highest possible basic income financed by taxation on external resources is a requirement of any just society.

So far, of course, nothing has been said about the level of this basic income and, as if to emphasise the divergence in grounding between a Parijsian basic income and a welfare-policy-instrument basic income, he tells us that his own proposal might, depending on conditions, fall short of providing a subsistence level of income. Other issues also arise natu-rally enough, including how a basic income would impact on incentives. Since the basic income should be sustained across time – thereby raising problems of intergenerational justice, and demographic issues since we are dealing with a per capita income – Van Parijs modifies his require-ment to demand the maximum *sustainable* basic income for each full member, subject to respecting formal freedom and self-ownership. The concern with sustainability makes it necessary to identify the tax structure that gives the highest tax yield that can be maintained under whatever socio-economic regime we are assessing. Van Parijs's claim is that a real lib-ertarian should assess the rival merits of different socio-economic regimes by reference to the highest sustainable basic income each can provide (constrained by the prior principles already mentioned).

1.5 Measuring real freedom

Van Parijs's discussion thus far has been predicated on the assumption that each individual has the same talents and disabilities (or 'internal endowments'). However, he recognises that in our world this assumption is unrealistic. As with models in economic theory, we are invited to consider matters under simplifying assumptions, and then the consequences of relaxing them are examined.

Van Parijs's discussion of how to deal with variation in internal endowments appeals to the concept of undominated diversity. But before that discussion occurs, he addresses some of the critical responses directed against his conception of the justice-based requirement of a basic income in conditions of equal talent. As has already been mentioned, some key ideas contained in *Real Freedom for All* have been articulated in previous work by Van Parijs.[7] Perhaps this discussion reflects not only his own anticipation of difficulties but also the reaction of his various audiences.

First, Van Parijs addresses two aspects of the 'delivery' of the universal disbursement, and asks whether it should proceed in cash or in kind; for example, in the form of services free at the point of consumption, which may count as components of the universal disbursement. Here Van Parijs allows for a certain amount of paternalism – a willingness to override individuals' actual preferences (as they might translate into choices) in favour of what they would genuinely desire if better informed (and so on). Hence, there could be a justification for compulsory health insurance (independently of another consideration about compulsory universal health insurance being cheaper to put into effect) (pp. 41–5). The same paternalism is deployed to deflect another obvious point about delivery, namely, that a basic income might be delivered as a lump sum rather than as a cash flow (an issue which has been considered in previous centuries) (pp. 45–8).

Van Parijs next confronts the problem of measuring real freedom (pp. 48–51). This is an issue at two levels: if we are to take the notion of leximining real freedom on board, we must be able to compare the real freedom of different individuals. And if we are to use the notion of real freedom for all to assess the rival merits of different socio-economic regimes, we must be able to decide which regime is superior by that standard. It is, of course, true that many reasons have been advanced to suggest that freedom cannot be measured. If you are free to do some things I am not free to do, and vice-versa, we seem to require some judgement about the comparative importance of particular freedoms in order to decide which of us enjoys greater freedom. Many of these problems about measuring freedom arise in the context of conceptions of liberty far removed from that advocated by Van Parijs. But he acknowledges the problem just stated and two others that flow from his conception of real freedom as opportunity.

Clearly we could say that only if one set of opportunities is a subset of another set of opportunities, then the latter is superior, and this is evidence of inequality. This is rejected, however, as too forgiving of inequality. The other approach, again rejected, would focus on preference-satisfaction. We could identify inequality by judging the preference-satisfaction individuals achieve from their bundles of goods. Van Parijs rejects this *welfarist* metric by appealing to what has become known as the *problem of expensive tastes*,[8] which also recurs in his discussion of undominated diversity. The problem arises since a person with a particular set of 'expensive' tastes will find it harder to translate resources into welfare than someone who gains satisfaction from simple, inexpensive pleasures. This implies that more resources should be given to those with expensive tastes, and anti-welfarists, like Van Parijs, find that implication implausible.

So, the problem remains: how are we to measure real freedom (either interpersonally or as between socio-economic regimes like capitalism and socialism)? Van Parijs's own answer employs the idea of opportunity costs, at least under regimes of roughly competitive pricing. The weighting of any particular resource should reflect the cost to others of not being able to use it (p. 51). This argument has particular importance in relation to so-called job assets, as we shall see.

Though Van Parijs downplays this connection in his Reply, his approach has close affinities with a distributive principle known to economists as the *envy test*: equal freedom is not a matter of everyone having the same opportunities, but a matter of no individual preferring any other individual's opportunities. If there are properly competitive prices, and if nobody envies anyone else's bundle of external endowments, then there is equality. Departures from equality on the leximin principle would be justified by reference to this baseline (p. 53). (It must be remembered that the question of differential internal endowments is at present set aside.) For Van Parijs, if we can make a comparison between the real freedom a particular society can realise in two different states, we can compare two different socio-economic regimes.

1.6   Undominated diversity

The time has now come, in Van Parijs's argument, to abandon the assumption of equal internal endowments: talents differ, and some people suffer from handicaps, and so on. Recognising this point obviously means that a metric of external-goods-equality will no longer satisfy us. What is required, we are told, is a notion of distributive justice that goes beyond the narrow confines of external resources without falling prey to the problem of expensive tastes which besets welfare egalitarian proposals. Van Parijs reviews suggestions by Ronald Dworkin and Bruce Ackerman in particular, and concludes that the best test requires the achievement of undominated diversity. This condition is satisfied if, taking each individual's package of internal and external endowments – or *comprehensive endowment* – into consideration, it is not true that *everyone* comparing the endowments of any two individuals considers those of one to be preferable to those of the other. Van Parijs does impose some conditions on this test, including that the preferences of persons are genuine and are generally accessible. 'Generally accessible' (p. 77) requires that preference schedules should be based on some reasonable level of understanding, and that they should not be simply opaque to other members of society.

The issue is bound to arise as to whether this test of undominated diversity licenses too little or too much redistribution. Since it requires that redistribution to the 'disadvantaged' occur only up to the point where there is *someone* who considers that the pairwise comparison is on par, it may appear not to go far enough. Van Parijs, however, seems to worry about the other problem: that it will absorb too many of the resources available for redistribution. Hence, he relaxes the condition such that if everyone benefited from violating the condition (because of the resource implications) it would be right to do so. In other words, if sustaining undominated diversity required a set of transfers and taxes the absence of which would make everyone better-off (in terms of real freedom), then accepting the dominated pattern would be recommended (pp. 83–4).

By now the argument of *Real Freedom for All* has established two methods of redistribution: one, targeted benefits licensed by the principle of undominated diversity; two, a universal basic income. As we saw earlier, any proposal for redistribution (in this framework) requires not only an argument (from justice) that particular persons should be its beneficiaries but also a justice-based argument for taking the resources to be redistributed. This is the next question Van Parijs confronts. What is to be the source of the fund from which both types of payment are to be raised?

1.7 Funding basic income and job assets

We may note the obvious point, that for a given fund, the greater redistribution required to secure undominated diversity the less is available for distribution as a basic income. Once again, Van Parijs distinguishes the situation when internal endowments are equal from the situation in which they are not. The starting point is very wide and, for that reason, bears quotation. As Van Parijs explains,

> What is relevant, from a real-libertarian standpoint, in this situation in which internal endowments are assumed to be equally distributed, is of course the whole set of external means that affect people's capacity to pursue their conceptions of the good life, irrespective of whether they are natural or produced. External endowments, in other words, include whatever usable external object in the broadest sense individuals receive access to. Such material objects as factories and stamp collections, private houses and public bridges, such immaterial objects as nursery rhymes and computer programmes, the work ethic and nuclear technology constitute external assets on a par with beaches, pumpkins and parrots. The relevant pool coincides with the external assets with which people are endowed.
>
> (pp. 100–1)[9]

It would seem to follow, says Van Parijs, that taxation at the level of 100 per cent on all bequests and gifts is justified. But there are reservations, the most important of which is that the aim of maximising the tax yield is unlikely to be secured by confiscatory measures. And, in any case, Van Parijs cites empirical evidence to suggest that the yield on inheritance and gift taxes is very small (p. 102).

Van Parijs circumvents this apparently depressing conclusion about the size of the pool to be redistributed as basic income by focusing on the 'existence of a type of asset that has been overlooked so far' (p. 113). Correcting the oversight, Van Parijs argues that everyone should have a tradeable entitlement to an equal share of the value of *job assets*, and that a tax should therefore be levied on the wages of those in paid employment. More specifically, the tax system should recoup job-holder's *employment rents*, or 'the difference between the income (and other advantages) the employed derive from their job, and the (lower) income they would need if the [labour] market were to clear' (p. 108).

As has been emphasised, this argument has so far rested on the idea that talents (skills) are equal. But, of course, they are not. Nor are talents equivalent to skills, since skills can be acquired and, presumably, talents are in-built. Van Parijs's next move is to assimilate jobs to external assets, rather than to internal endowments, so they are not covered by the undominated diversity provisions that apply to internal endowments. The problem of acquired skills is handled not by differential taxation (differentiating, that is, between *natural* talent and *acquired* skill) but by the stability of the tax regime (so that those who set out to acquire a skill, leading to a higher paid job, know in advance where they stand). The upshot is a stable (through time) system of income taxation for job-holders.[10]

1.8 Exploitation

Van Parijs's penultimate chapter, before we return to the assessment of the relative virtues and vices of socialism and capitalism, deals with exploitation. This issue is clearly highly germane, for two reasons. First, one of the main criticisms of capitalism has been – and remains – that it exploits people (whereas socialism does not). *If* this is so, it will obviously have to be weighed in the final reckoning of the claims of those socio-economic regimes. Secondly, the provision of a basic income subject to the satisfaction of the condition of undominated diversity may raise the charge of exploitation in a society characterised by real freedom for all – that the idle exploit the industrious by receiving an income generated (*inter alia*) by the activity of those who choose to work.

To consider these points, Van Parijs confronts the various theories of exploitation that have been offered. Having accepted a rough account of 'exploitation' as taking unfair advantage of someone else's work, Van Parijs embarks on an exploration of the notions of 'unfair', 'work', 'someone' and 'advantage' in that characterisation. Van Parijs considers five proposals to limit the range of what counts as exploitation: that workers are entitled to the full fruits of their labour (otherwise they are exploited); that the creator of a product should be entitled to keep it (otherwise s/he is exploited); that exploitation consists in the appropriation of surplus value; that exploitation is a violation of the principle 'to each according to his/her efforts'; and the game theoretic approach of John Roemer, which tries to determine whether exploitation exists by reference to the distribution of assets. He finds fault with all these formulations, but settles on a conception of exploitation akin to Roemer's in that it suggest that (suitably modified) asset-based inequality arguments about exploitation will assess capitalism and socialism in a similar way to the test of real freedom for all.

1.9 A world of basic income?

And so, in his final chapter, Van Parijs moves to make that assessment. I have already quoted his conclusion, and I hope now to have explained how he reaches it. But we need to explore a little further the arguments of that final chapter, because they touch upon two more important issues: the geographical scope of the real libertarian principle of justice, and problems which arise from what is now known as *globalisation*.

A world market, even for socialist regimes, puts competitive pressure on all those involved in the (world) division of labour. There is thus a problem (discussed in a section called 'Steering Clear of Penguin Island') arising from these competitive pressures: it might be that by the standards of real-freedom-for-all a society was just, but that it contained great inequalities and very little by way of state welfare provision. This might arise because, under all the circumstances, including international competitive pressure, it was providing the maximum sustainable basic income (subject to the usual constraints). Some of the effects of this competitiveness, Van Parijs hopes, might be mitigated by the development of 'solidaristic patriotism' – a reluctance to take opportunistic advantage of one's right to migrate based upon pride in the collective project of sustaining a just society. Some others might be mitigated by 'democratic scale-lifting' – moving democratic decision-making to a level at which it was able to control the rules of trade, etc., rather than being hamstrung by the pressures of competition. Ideally, then, a democratic world government; and, ideally too, a world society of real freedom for all. Van Parijs is clear that the imperatives of leximin real freedom are not extinguished at national borders. Given the remoteness of either democratic world government or world leximin real freedom, however, he also sees merit in regional, trans-national arrangements.

1.10   The search for social justice

It was claimed at the beginning of this Introduction that Van Parijs has addressed fundamental concerns – for example, the nature of justice and the rival appeals of capitalism and socialism – and contributed to the literature on important debates in contemporary political philosophy – for example, the nature of self-ownership and the nature of exploitation. The aim of this Introduction was to set out the structure of *Real Freedom for All*, and to show how, for this reader, his answers to the fundamental concerns relate to his positions on those debates. As the critical essays in this volume illustrate, his argument invites searching assessment at many points. It is also likely to generate differences in interpretation. Van Parijs, in his Reply, has an opportunity to examine those interpretations and to respond to his critics. As he there makes clear, the debate on the merits of real libertarianism continues – and so does political activity directed at securing its introduction. There can be no doubt that one of the central projects of political philosophy (conceived as a collective endeavour) in the last generation – determining what, exactly, is required by a commitment to social justice – is both exemplified and carried forward by his contribution. The reader is invited to join in that endeavour by engaging with the debates that follow.

Notes

1. See *Real Freedom for All: What (if Anything) Can Justify Capitalism?* (Oxford: Clarendon Press, 1995). Unless specified otherwise, all unmarked page numbers refer to this book. More recently, in 2001, Van Parijs received Belgium's most prestigious academic award, the Franqui Prize.
2. The excluded sentence reads: 'In the process of reaching this conclusion, the focus of discussion has moved away from the traditional question with which this book started – the choice between capitalism and socialism – towards other dimensions along which socio-economic regimes may vary.'
3. 'Libertarians should rather be called rights-fetishists, and their alleged freedom-based case for capitalism, pure or otherwise, is worth no more than the freedom-based case for socialism rejected in the previous section' (p. 15).
4. Self-ownership is a notoriously slippery notion. Van Parijs thinks that self-ownership does not preclude income taxation (pp. 115–17, p. 254 n. 17), and he seems willing to limit the right to strike (pp. 213–14). Van Parijs discusses 'self-ownership' in sections 1.1 and 1.8 in particular, and acknowledges (p. 9) that 'Self-ownership is not a perennial idea. It is a modern idea, and one that remains controversial.'
5. Van Parijs's discussion begins on p. 25. The explication of the notion of a maximally free society is complex. He writes: 'I take it for granted that this leximin (or "lexicographic maximin") formulation is better than either a purely aggregative formula (for example, in terms of the opportunities of society's average member) or a more egalitarian formula (for example, in terms of maximum equal opportunities) to express the idea that the members of a (maximally) free society are *all* as free *as possible*.'
6. The inspiration for the idea of leximin freedom is, of course, John Rawls's difference principle. Like the principle of leximin opportunity, the difference principle is subordinate to prior principles, which, in the Rawlsian case, require an equal distribution of basic civil liberties, and a fair opportunity to acquire jobs, or other positions of authority and influence. The difference principle itself requires that the basic structure be arranged so that inequalities maximally advantage the least advantaged representative individual.
7. Examples of such previous work are: Robert Van der Veen and Phillippe Van Parijs, 'A Capitalist Road to Communism', *Theory and Society* 15/5 (1986), pp. 635–56, reprinted in P. Van Parijs, *Marxism Recycled* (Cambridge: Cambridge University Press, 1993), ch. 8; Van Parijs, 'Why Surfers Should Be Fed: the Liberal Case for Basic Income', *Philosophy and Public Affairs* 20 (1991), pp. 101–31; and Van Parijs, 'Basic Income Capitalism', *Ethics* 102 (1992), pp. 465–84.
8. For classic discussion, see Ronald Dworkin, *Sovereign Virtue* (Cambridge, MA: Harvard University Press, 2000), ch. 1, esp. section viii. For further discussion,

see also Mathew Clayton and Andrew Williams, 'Egalitarian Justice and Interpersonal Comparison', *European Journal of Political Research* 35 (1999), pp. 445–64, esp. pp. 448–50.

9. See also Bert Hamminga, 'Demoralizing the Labour Market: Could Jobs Be like Cars and Concerts?' *Journal of Political Philosophy* 3 (1995), pp. 23–35.

10. The thought then occurs that if individuals are taken to possess a right of access to external assets like jobs, it is not clear whether there might not be potentially embarrassing analogies with access to personal relationships – an issue which Van Parijs appears to take seriously, on the ground that rationing implies the presence of rent, albeit in this case a rent not likely to be worth trying to obtain. (This is because a 'scarcity rent' has to be 'sufficiently sizable and seizable to be worth chasing – a condition unlikely to be met in the case of partnerships' (p. 130).)

2
Basic Income: Pedigree and Problems

John Cunliffe, Guido Erreygers and Walter Van Trier[1]

2.1 Introduction

In *Real Freedom for All*, Philippe Van Parijs claims to provide a principled justification of a substantial unconditional basic income. At least four objections have been advanced in response to this claim. The most basic objection questions whether real freedom requires basic income. The second argues that an unconditional basic income licenses exploitation. The third concerns the level and sources of the proposed basic income. And the final set of worries has to do with the global or local scale of the scheme. We show that several of these current objections were anticipated in some of the earliest formulations of the idea of basic income, which were until recently completely neglected: the *guaranteed minimum*, put forward by Joseph Charlier initially in 1848; and the state bonus scheme, proposed in 1918 by Dennis and Mabel Milner. In this respect, we demonstrate the remarkable continuities between the old and the new debates on basic income, irrespective of their different contexts. Yet we do not claim that the modern debate is nothing more than a case of old wine in new bottles; in this paper we stress the similarities, but we are well aware of the fact that there are also important differences. In Section 2.2 we briefly elaborate the four problems mentioned initially. In Sections 2.3 and 2.4 respectively we show that Charlier and the Milners already confronted similar problems, and explain how they dealt with them. In Section 2.5 we present an assessment of the strategies used in the three cases.

2.2 Objections to *Real Freedom for All*

Since many of the questions raised in the debate on Van Parijs's work are dealt with at length in other contributions to this book, we confine ourselves to a rough sketch of what is at stake.

2.2.1   Validity

Brian Barry divides arguments for basic income into two categories: pragmatic and principled.[2] Pragmatic arguments provide instrumental justifications for basic income as the best mechanism for achieving certain social policy objectives in modern welfare states. Principled arguments provide intrinsic justifications for basic income by appealing to rights or entitlements derived from principles of social justice. When considered within this framework, Van Parijs's principled justification is based upon a real libertarian conception of justice, which in his view determines the nature and form of the particular basic income scheme. Similarly, though Charlier and the Milners also outlined many pragmatic advantages of their schemes, both appealed unambiguously to principles of justice, which for them generated an unconditional entitlement to a basic income. Whether real libertarianism actually requires basic income is discussed elsewhere in this volume, and whether Charlier or the Milners were any more successful in deriving basic income from their respective principles of justice is also arguable.

2.2.2   Soundness

The most influential objection to an unconditional basic income is that it enables able-bodied idlers to live off the labour of their hard-working fellow citizens in a way which violates some fundamental principle of reciprocity.[3] The existence of widespread exploitation might also be considered politically unattractive and to put at risk the sustainability of basic income through time. Van Parijs considers several variants of this objection, and either rejects them because they are based on indefensible conceptions of social justice or argues that they do not call into question the legitimacy of an unconditional basic income.[4] From the very outset, Charlier recognised and responded to this exploitation objection; similarly, the Milners immediately appreciated the objection and sought to counter it.

2.2.3   Level

The exploitation objection is connected to disputes over the composition and extent of the common pool of resources from which basic income is to be financed. One of the novelties of Van Parijs's position is that in his case the pool is composed of three layers of external assets: pure natural resources, inherited produced wealth and above all job assets. If the pool were restricted only to the first two layers, then the exploitation objection might be easier to defuse, but only a relatively low level would be feasible. Alternatively, once job assets are included, the exploitation objection becomes particularly pressing, but a more generous basic income would be possible.[5] Charlier argued that the basic income had to be funded from the competitive rent of pure natural resources, and that this would provide a subsistence level grant which was all that was required by his conception of justice. In contrast, the state bonus scheme drew on a proportional tax on all incomes, but again this would finance only the subsistence level needed within the view of justice held by its advocates.

2.2.4 Scope

The final set of queries relates to the scope of Van Parijs's proposal at the level of ideal theory. He argues unambiguously for a global implementation of real libertarianism that requires real freedom quite literally for *all* human beings. This entails the introduction of redistributive mechanisms not only on a national scale but also between different countries. From the viewpoint of principled justifications, this global perspective might be quite legitimate, even if it raises formidable pragmatic difficulties. Charlier shared this global perspective and fully appreciated the difficulties. The Milners, however, seemed to limit their proposal to the national level.

2.3 Charlier

2.3.1 Charlier's life and work

Joseph Charlier was born in Brussels on 20 June 1816, and died there on 6 December 1896. He advocated basic income in four key works:

- *Solution du Problème Social ou Constitution Humanitaire, Basée sur la Loi Naturelle, et Précédée de l'Exposé de Motifs* (1848, 106 pp.). This introduced the scheme for a 'guaranteed minimum' funded from the socialisation of rent. Charlier explained in detail why he proposed the scheme, and presented it in the form of a 'humanitarian constitution'.
- *Catéchisme Populaire, Philosophique, Politique et Social* (1871, 88 pp.). Here Charlier refined the core theme of the guaranteed minimum under the new form of 'the system of territorial dividend'.
- *La Question Sociale Résolue Précédée du Testament Philosophique d'un Penseur* (1894, 252 pp.). This is Charlier's most substantial work. He reproduced the relevant sections of the *Catéchisme* on territorial dividend, included a scheme for pension provision initially suggested

in 1887, and introduced another 'humanitarian constitution' which was similar, but not identical to, the 1848 version, together with a set of justifying 'interpretative remarks'.

- *L'Anarchie Désarmée par l'Équité. Corollaire à la Question Sociale Résolue* (1894, 35 pp.). This summarised the diagnosis and solution of social issues presented immediately before in *La Question Sociale Résolue*.

Apart from these texts, we have very little to work with. Despite our sustained attempts to discover more information, Charlier remains something of a mystery, and his exact profession is unknown. Although he classified himself as a 'juriste',[6] his occupation is variously described in successive population registers as 'writer', 'accountant' and 'merchant'.[7] Passing references to him occur in many of the standard sources on the history of socialism in Belgium; in one of these references Charlier is designated as a 'Fourierist'.[8] There is, however, no substantial study of either his life or work.[9]

2.3.2   Charlier's basic income scheme

Charlier adopted the familiar jurisprudential contrast between natural and produced resources. He argued that a creators–keepers principle did not justify individual property rights in land itself, but only in assets resulting from human labour.[10] Giving that familiar distinction a new dimension, he maintained that natural resources were intended by God to provide a guarantee for the 'vital needs' of all persons. Produced assets, by contrast, were destined to meet the 'acquired needs' of each person.[11] Only 'vital needs' generated an absolute right: because every human being had the right to live, each person had a right to a share of the fruits of the earth sufficient to provide subsistence.[12] The essential role of the state consisted in guaranteeing these individual rights to the produce of the common patrimony by ensuring that all were included and none excluded.

This role would be realised through the provision of a 'guaranteed minimum', that is, a basic income. Charlier stressed that the right to a basic income was equal and universal, in that it was possessed by each individual from birth. On a more practical level, the problem to be resolved was the introduction of a basic income in a setting where there was private land ownership, especially in a concentrated form. Although Charlier emphasised that private land ownership was incompatible with the notion of a common natural patrimony, he also insisted that current legal titles to land had to be respected. The proposed resolution hinged on a system of mutual compensation, mediated by the state, between the minority of current landowners and the landless majority. Landowners would be compensated, at least partly and temporarily, for any loss resulting from the reassertion of the collective right to the land. The landless majority would be compensated permanently through the disbursement of a basic income. In Charlier's view, only this mechanism could remedy the injustice of private land ownership without introducing another injustice by a forced dispossession of legal titles. He claimed that his 'humanitarian constitution' provided a 'mathematical solution' to the problem.[13]

Charlier did not limit himself to a general description of his scheme. Following his own injunction against impractical plans, he worked it out in great detail and added calculations to show that it was financially sound.[14] As the sole landowner, the state would receive all the existing land-rents. In compensation for the loss of their land, owners would not receive its capital value, but instead would be entitled to an annual revenue equal to the estimated loss of land-rent income. The revenue would be an increasing function of the capital value of the land, whereas the ratio between revenue and capital would be a decreasing function of it.[15] Moreover, it would diminish through time according to the number of intergenerational transfers: with each transfer the revenue would decrease by a quarter of its original amount.[16] The difference between the rent revenues of the state and its compensation payments to the original landowners would be the amount available for basic income.

With intriguing minor variations, this diagnosis and the corresponding prescription remained constant throughout all of Charlier's subsequent works in social theory over nearly 50 years. Two of these variations were the change in terminology from 'guaranteed minimum' to 'territorial dividend', and the increase in the frequency of payment from quarterly to monthly.

2.3.3 From Charlier to Van Parijs

In Charlier's reflections on his basic income scheme many and varied pragmatic benefits were suggested. These ranged from a reduction in religious rivalries, and a fall in robberies and begging, to a decrease in legal disputes, and so forth. Indeed, the claimed advantages were so many and various that the scheme resembled a panacea. Undoubtedly, however, Charlier's major defence of the scheme was the principled one that it secured the natural right to subsistence central to his conception of social justice. So, quite apart from pragmatic advantages in terms of social policy, basic income alone could secure the fundamental entitlment that constrained all other policy objectives. Insofar as this entitlement was secured, Charlier argued consistently that personal independence and dignity would be enhanced, because all individuals would consider themselves as citizens and not as exploited subjects.[17] They would be liberated from personal dependence on others, especially for the satisfaction of basic needs,[18] and workers in particular would be elevated from the status of 'wage slaves' to that of equal partners with capitalists in production.[19]

As well as providing the positive defence for basic income, Charlier anticipated precisely the objection that it licensed exploitation. In doing so, he considered the claim that a guaranteed minimum would constitute 'une prime d'encouragement à la paresse'[20] [an incentive to be lazy] which would create a new class of 'rentiers'.[21] He recognised the possibility that some individuals might be content to survive on the basic income alone. Charlier presented two responses to that concern. The first *principled* response was to accept without reservation that this was indeed their right:

> Tant pis pour les paresseux: ceux-là resteront réduits à la portion congrue. Le devoir de la société ne va pas au delà: assurer à chacun sa juste participation à la jouissance des éléments que la nature a mis à son service, sans usurpation des uns au préjudice des autres.[22]
>
> [Too bad for the lazy: they will have to get by with the minimum allowance. The duty of society does not go beyond this: to assure to everyone his fair share in the enjoyments of the elements that nature has put at his disposal; without usurpation by some people to the detriment of others.]

The second *pragmatic* response was that only a minority would act in this manner and that, for the majority, the basic income scheme would actually be an incentive to labour. The security derived from the guarantee of basic needs would allow individuals to concentrate on satisfying the expanding domain of their acquired wants, which could be achieved only through labour itself.

Unlike some present-day advocates, Charlier did not worry in the least that exploitation would be a threat to the sustainability of basic income levels through time. However, he did consider the possibility that the provision of a basic income would act as an incentive to population growth, reducing the per capita level of payment below a subsistence rate.[23] According to him, this would not be the case: population increase would continue to follow its 'normal course'. Apart from endorsing the familiar appeals to divine providence, he argued rather unpersuasively that a guaranteed minimum would have no effect on parents' calculations (if any) about family size.

Charlier also tackled in detail the issue of the level of payment that could be achieved through a scheme apparently based on the market value of natural resources only. The suspicion was that the aggregate flow of land-rent revenue would be insufficient to cover the basic needs of all through a basic income, especially after the deduction of the compensation payments to the original landowners.[24] Charlier readily accepted that the initial dividend level would be 'necessarily minimal' and probably insufficient to satisfy basic needs. But what about the level once the transitional compensation payments had fallen significantly? In most of his calculations Charlier did not restrict that patrimony to pure natural resources, that is, to land in its original condition before any changes resulting from human labour. Without offering any explicit justification, he increased the pool considerably by identifying it with 'real estate'.[25] This category included not only land in its improved form as a result of labour but also buildings and other fixtures. With one possible exception, no attempt was made to separate the revenue attributable to the original site from the total.[26]

This increased pool would arguably provide funds not only for basic income but also for the provision of further services for especially vulnerable groups, as required by Charlier's views on the duties of the state. Children would be entitled to education, and the old and the infirm to special care. This implied that the state would have to provide institutions for these purposes.[27] On efficiency grounds he made a particularly strong case for the public provision of free and universal education.

The final set of issues relates to the possibility of very different levels of basic income between countries. In the first instance, Charlier accepted that the level of basic income would be determined by the ratio between resources and population within each country. This raised the possibility that in some countries the per capita land-rent revenue might be too low to meet vital needs. However, Charlier believed that on a global scale the dividend generated by the common patrimony would be more than enough to satisfy the vital needs of *all* people. Leaving aside the formidable practical difficulties, he insisted that ultimately humanity would form one universal society and that this global calculation would actually be implemented. In the meantime, various transitional arrangements would be devised to promote this universal perspective.[28]

2.4   State bonus

2.4.1   The origins

Dennis Milner was born in 1892 in Hartford, Cheshire, and died in 1956. He initially presented his scheme for a state bonus in 1917.[29] In the following year, Milner and his wife, Mabel Milner, published the scheme in the form of a brief pamphlet.[30] With the help of Bertram Pickard, another young Quaker, a league was set up to advocate the scheme. The league was short-lived and no traces of its existence can be found after 1921. The scheme was advocated in the following three works:

- E. Mabel Milner and Dennis Milner, *Scheme for a State Bonus* (Kent: Simpkin, Marshall & Co, 1918), 16 pp.
- Bertram Pickard, *A Reasonable Revolution: Being a Discussion of the State Bonus Scheme – a Proposal for a National Minimum Income* (London: George Allen & Unwin, 1919), 78 pp.
- Dennis Milner, *Higher Production by a Bonus on National Output: a Proposal for a Minimum Income for All Varying with National Productivity* (London: George Allen & Unwin, 1920), 127 pp.

In addition to the pamphlet and the two books, both Milner and Pickard published a series of articles in Quaker journals (*The Ploughshare, The Friend*) and in the daily and weekly press.

The scheme had a limited immediate response. It was referred to in the writings of, among others, G. D. H. Cole, Eleanor Rathbone, Paul H. Douglas and Hugh Dalton. And it was discussed at Annual Labour Party conferences on at least two occasions (1920 and 1921). After that, however, it seems to have been ignored in virtually all subsequent debates.[31]

2.4.2   The state bonus scheme

At first sight, the main justification of the state bonus scheme was the pragmatic one of providing a simple but comprehensive solution to *the* two pressing issues of the time: the problem of reconstruction and the social problem. At a deeper level, however, this solution was founded on the familiar principle 'that every human being has a moral right to the bare necessities of life'.[32] This right itself was linked to a broad conception of liberty in which individual economic security was central.[33] The remedy proposed in the state bonus literature is clearly one of a universal and unconditional basic income in the modern sense.[34] The claimed superiority of basic income to alternative mechanisms for securing livelihoods was that it alone could do so without 'pauperising the recipients and undermining existing incentives'.[35] Since minimum wages or poor law relief would have precisely these consequences, they were rejected accordingly.

The level of the basic income was determined by the requirement that it should be just sufficient to maintain life and liberty. 'It follows...that it will have to be based on the primal needs of individuals (which are nearly the same for all), namely food, shelter, and a minimum of recreation....'[36] To finance the scheme, it was proposed to deduct, at source, a fixed percentage of all income, earned and unearned. In order to secure a decent basic income to every man, woman and child within Britain, it was estimated that this fixed percentage should be set at 20 per cent.[37] Basic income would be paid on a weekly basis and it would replace all existing monetised benefits such as old-age pensions. Other benefits, notably education, might still be provided through public services.

2.4.3 From state bonus to Van Parijs

Milner and Pickard claimed many pragmatic advantages for the state bonus scheme ranging from scientific wage setting to a cost-efficient remedy to poverty. Although not always explicitly, they also pointed to a wide range of principled justifications; these included the promotion of equality, liberty, self-development and human dignity. Apparently, they did not consider the possibility of tensions between those principles. Consequently, no clear ordering of them is presented.

The criticism that the proposed basic income scheme might be exploitative or promote 'slacking' is a recurrent theme in the state bonus writings. Milner immediately conceded that there was nothing new about the problem of slackers; they existed now, just as they had done throughout history, and would continue to do so in the future. The question was whether the state bonus would either increase or reduce their number, and whether it mattered that much anyway. The advocates of the state bonus confidently expected that the scheme would reduce the number of slackers by an appropriate balance of positive and negative incentives, which would increase both the capacity and willingness to work. Even if that expectation turned out to be ill-founded, in the last resort slackers could not be forced to work 'at the point of the bayonet of starvation'.[38] Milner and Pickard counted on the prospect that slackers would be subject, nevertheless, to social pressures and moral regulation. In other words, 'the only alternative is to educate them into a desire to work'.[39] Ultimately, however, because the state bonus was the monetised equivalent of the right of universal access to land, the recalcitrant slacker, like any other member of society, could not legitimately be deprived of the entitlement to it. Since at present this right was clearly denied, 'it would seem only reasonable for Civilisation to give in exchange the cash equivalent of what a man could grow with very little effort. Obviously giving the equivalent in cash is a great deal simpler than reorganising our whole land system!'[40]

Rather naively, the Milners and Pickard believed that problems of sustainability would not occur. On several connected grounds, they argued that the benefits of the scheme would exceed its costs. Even with higher taxes, they expected at the very least a neutral and probably a positive effect on labour supply. In addition, they confidently anticipated a spectacular increase in productivity that would lead to a much higher production level.[41]

Despite their general endorsement of an internationalist perspective, Milner and Pickard seemed to assume that the scheme could be implemented only within the framework of existing countries. On the assumption that the state bonus was introduced in Britain, 'the Scheme would only apply to British subjects whose permanent residence was in Britain. Foreigners would not be admitted until fully naturalised. Irishmen would only be admitted after a qualifying residence of, say, six months (i.e. the period qualifying for a vote).'[42] If these nationality or residence criteria were met, the basic income would be absolutely inalienable and free from all legal obligations. Neither Milner nor Pickard explicitly mentioned any of the complications arising from the introduction of a basic income scheme in more than one country, such as different levels of allowance and the temptation of benefit migration.

2.5   Conclusion

The most striking finding that emerges from this excursion into the history of basic income is the remarkable continuity in the difficulties which have been thought to beset the idea in three quite different contexts. We have categorised these difficulties as concerning (1) validity, (2) soundness, (3) level and (4) scope objections to basic income. In relation to validity, just as it is disputed whether real libertarianism requires basic income, so it might be argued that the principle of the right to subsistence, endorsed by Charlier as well as by the Milners, does not uniquely favour basic income rather than, for example, a statutory right to work or extensive public services. The early advocates of basic income were aware of this and rejected the alternatives by appealing both to principles (such as human dignity) and to pragmatic arguments (such as excessive state intervention). The second category of objection claims that unconditional basic income itself is unjust, and not merely inadequately defended, and should be rejected because it licenses exploitation. In response, Charlier and the proponents of the state bonus scheme ultimately counter-asserted that justice-based entitlements conferred the right not to work. But they also considered the problem of exploitation relatively unimportant for two reasons. First, the basic income would be fixed at the bare subsistence level required by their conceptions of justice; and, secondly, at that level, they thought that an unconditional basic income would not eliminate the incentive to labour. By contrast, Van Parijs explicitly rejects any justification of the level of basic income by reference to 'real needs'.[43] Instead, what real freedom requires is the highest sustainable level of basic income, which might either fall short of or substantially exceed subsistence.[44] Finally, with respect to scope, Charlier, unlike the Milners, did explicitly consider the tensions which could be created by differences in basic income between countries. Ultimately, however, he defended a universalist or cosmopolitan position close to the one defended by Van Parijs.

Notes

1. We are grateful to Andrew Reeve, Tom Schatteman, Robert van der Veen and Andrew Williams for many helpful discussions.
2. See B. Barry, 'Real Freedom and Basic Income', *Journal of Political Philosophy* 4 (1996), pp. 242–76.
3. See S. White, 'Liberal Equality, Exploitation, and the Case for an Unconditional Basic Income', *Political Studies* 45 (1997), pp. 312–26.
4. See P. Van Parijs, 'Reciprocity and the Justification of an Unconditional Basic Income: Reply to Stuart White', *Political Studies* 45 (1997), pp. 327–30.
5. See White's paper, as well the reply by Van Parijs.
6. See J. Charlier, *La Question Sociale Résolue Précédée du Testament Philosophique d'un Penseur* (Bruxelles: P. Weissenbruch, 1894), p. 10.
7. This information has been provided to us by Maryline Van Parijs. We are very grateful to her for her extensive archival searches.
8. See V. Serwy, *La coopération en Belgique* (Bruxelles: Les Propagateurs de la Cooperation, 1952), vol. 4, p. 110, which described him as 'Publiciste, poète, fouriériste'.
9. For more details, especially on the Fourierist background of Charlier's work, see J. Cunliffe and G. Erreygers, *The Enigmatic Legacy of Fourier: Joseph Charlier and Basic Income* (Antwerp: University of Antwerp, UFSIA, Faculty of Applied Economics, Department of Economics, Research Paper 99-022, 1999).
10. 'Le sol à personne, mais le fruit à tous. Telle est la grande, la véritable maxime sur laquelle repose le salut de la société humaine et dont nous allons démontrer

la légitimité intrinsèque et les bienfaits' [The land to nobody, but the fruit to all. That is the great, true maxim on which the faith of human society rests and of which we will demonstrate the intrinsic legitimacy and benefits]. See Charlier, *Solution du Problème Social ou Constitution Humanitaire, Basée sur la Loi Naturelle, et Précédée de l'Exposé de Motifs* (Bruxelles: Chez Tous les Libraires du Royaume, 1848), p. 23.

11. We use the expression 'vital needs' for Charlier's 'besoins absolus', 'besoins naturels' or 'besoins naturels et vitaux', and 'acquired needs' for his 'besoins relatifs', 'besoins artificiels' or 'besoins acquis'.

12. 'L'homme en naissant apporte avec lui le droit de vivre; de ce droit inhérent à son être et que personne à coup sûr n'osera lui contester, découle comme conséquence obligée le droit de demander au sol, patrimoine commun des hommes, sa part dans les fruits nécessaires à son existence' [When he is born man brings with him the right to live; from this right, which is inherent to his being and which surely nobody will dare to contest, follows as a necessary consequence, the right to demand from the land, the common patrimony of men, his share of the fruit that he needs for his existence]. See Charlier, *Solution du Problème Social*, p. 20.

13. See Charlier, *Solution du Problème Social*, p. 21.

14. The calculations applied to Belgium; he arrived at the conclusion that in the first year the scheme would yield an income of about 50 francs per head. For more details, see Charlier, *Solution du Problème Social*, pp. 47–50.

15. See Charlier, *Solution du Problème Social*, p. 105.

16. 'La valeur de ces biens sera, après l'estimation cadastrale, ou toute autre mode d'appréciation à déterminer, convertie en rentes viagères au profit des propriétaires et leurs descendants jusqu'à la quatrième génération et par amortissement d'un quart par génération' [Based upon survey estimates or any other valuation method to be decided, the value of these goods will be converted into annuities to the benefit of proprietors and their descendants, and this until the fourth generation and by depreciation of a quarter per generation]. See Charlier, *Solution du Problème Social*, pp. 40–1.

17. See Charlier, *Solution du Problème Social*, p. 38. See also Charlier, *La Question Sociale*, p. 54; and Charlier, *L'Anarchie Désarmée par l'Équité. Corollaire à la Question Sociale Résolue* (Bruxelles: P. Weissenbruch, 1894), p. 25.

18. See Charlier, *La Question Sociale*, pp. 54–5.

19. See Charlier, *La Question Sociale*, pp. 222–3 and 246.

20. See Charlier, *Solution du Problème Social*, p. 35.

21. See Charlier, *Catéchisme Populaire, Philosophique, Politique et Social* (Bruxelles: Typ. De Ch. et A. Vanderauwera, 1871), p. 51.

22. See Charlier, *La Question Sociale*, p. 56.

23. See Charlier *Solution du Problème Social*, pp. 73–4; Charlier, *Catéchisme Populaire*, pp. 64–5; Charlier, *La Question Sociale*, pp. 241–2.

24. See Charlier, *Solution du Problème Social*, pp. 76–7; Charlier, *Catéchisme Populaire*, pp. 44–5; Charlier, *La Question Sociale*, pp. 211–12 and 226–7.

25. He moved from 'la propriété foncière' to 'la propriété immobilière'.

26. 'La propriété immobilière produit: A. Les fruits civils, comprenant les loyers pour l'usage du fonds; B. Les fruits industriels, c'est-à-dire tout ce que l'homme peut, par son travail, en obtenir ou extraire.

Les premiers appartiennent, de droit primordial, aux usufruitiers du fonds commun, en vertu de leur droit sui generis d'usage. Ici, point de propriété personnelle sur le fonds.

Les seconds appartiennent à ceux qui les ont produits; ils constituent dans leur chef le droit d'en disposer selon leur volonté et leur intérêt. Ces produits donnent donc lieu à un droit de propriété absolu en leur faveur' [Real estate produces: A. Civil benefits, including the rents for the use of the fund; B. Industrial benefits, that is to say everything that man, by his own labour, can obtain or extract from it.

The first belongs, by fundamental right, to the usufructuaries of the common fund, by virtue of their sui generis right of use. In this case, there is no personal property in the fund.

The second belong to those that have produced them; they constitute in their opinion the right to dispose of them according to their wishes and interests. These products create an absolute property right in their favour]. See Charlier, *L'Anarchie Désarmée par l'Équité*, pp. 17–18.

27. See Charlier, *Solution du Problème Social*, pp. 64–73 and 82–6.
28. See Charlier, *Solution du Problème Social*, pp. 75–80; and Charlier, *Catéchisme Populaire*, pp. 63–4.
29. More details on the state bonus proposal can be found in W. Van Trier, 'Every One a King' (Louvain: K. U. Leuven, Faculteit Sociale Wetenschappen, Departement Sociologie, unpublished Ph.D. thesis, 1995, pp. 29–142).
30. More precisely, it was presented in February and June at two meetings of the War and Social Organisation Committee of the Yearly Meeting of the Society of Friends. The first version of the proposal was published by the War and Social Organisation Committee (1918).
31. In the vast literature on the history of British social policy, only one book mentions the state bonus scheme very briefly as part of the context in which the real debate on Family Allowances started in the mid-1920s. See J. Macnicol, *The Movement for Family Allowances, 1918–45: a Study in Social Policy Development* (London: Heinemann, 1980).
32. See B. Pickard, *A Reasonable Revolution: Being a Discussion of the State Bonus Scheme – a Proposal for a National Minimum Income* (London: George Allen & Unwin, 1919) p. 20.
33. '[T]he Bonus would bestow greater economic freedom upon that very large section of the community to whom the fear of destitution is an ever-present reality. It is easy to see how this new-found freedom would increase the bargaining power of the "worker", and how this power would be used to reinforce, not only his demand for a larger share in the fruits of industry, but also for a greater control of the machinery of Production itself'. See Pickard, *Reasonable Revolution*, p. 33.
34. It proposes '(a) That every individual, all the time, should receive from a central fund some small allowance in money which would be just sufficient to maintain life and liberty if all else failed. (b) That everyone is to get a share from this central fund, so everyone who has any income at all should contribute a share each in proportion to his capacity.' See E. M. Milner and D. Milner, *Scheme for a State Bonus* (Kent: Simpkin, Marshall and Co, 1918), p. 7.

35. See D. Milner, *Higher Production by a Bonus on National Output: a Proposal for a Minimum Income for All Varying with National Productivity* (London: George Allen & Unwin 1920), p. 112.
36. See Milner and Milner, *Scheme for a State Bonus*, p. 7.
37. This would be in addition to existing taxes. The Milners calculated that in 1917 the revenue thus raised would be sufficient to pay each individual a state bonus of 5 shillings per week.
38. See Pickard, *Reasonable Revolution*, pp. 36–7.
39. See D. Milner, *Higher Production by a Bonus on National Output*, p. 86.
40. See Milner and Milner, *Scheme for a State Bonus*, p. 14.
41. Here is a typical example of their trust in the positive effects on production: 'An increase in production. If this reaches so little as 25 per cent and if the advantages are distributed in proportion to present incomes, it will leave absolutely every individual better off than he or she is at the present moment.' See Milner and Milner, *Scheme for a State Bonus*, p. 124.
42. See D. Milner, *Higher Production by a Bonus on National Output*, p. 28.
43. See P. Van Parijs, *Real Freedom for All: What (if Anything) Can Justify Capitalism?* (Oxford: Clarendon Press, 1995), p. 35.
44. See A. Williams, 'Resource Egalitarianism and the Limits to Basic Income', *Economics and Philosophy* 15 (1999), pp. 85–107 (89).

3
Self-Ownership and Equality: Brute Luck, Gifts, Universal Dominance and Leximin[1]

Peter Vallentyne

3.1 Introduction

During the last twenty years or so, egalitarian political theorists have been reexamining the role of freedom and responsibility in their theories. Increasingly, they are endorsing the view that at a fundamental moral level autonomous agents are (initially, at least) self-owning in the sense of having moral authority to decide how to live their lives (within the constraints of the rights of others). As will be explained below, this leaves open whether agents are entitled to the full benefits of their choices and of their natural personal endowments (e.g., intelligence, strength, or agility) and whether or how they own parts of the natural world (e.g., land). Important aspects of this issue have been developed by Ronald Dworkin, G. A. Cohen, Hillel Steiner, Amartya Sen, John Roemer, Richard Arneson, Eric Rakowski, Will Kymlicka, various economists working on envy-free allocations of wealth (e.g., Hal Varian, Marc Fleurbaey, and Christian Arnsperger, to mention but a few), and others.[2]

Philippe Van Parijs's *Real Freedom for All* is a state-of-the-art contribution to egalitarian liberalism. Van Parijs is a Belgian political philosopher who is extremely well versed in the relevant economics literature. He is also a member (along with G. A. Cohen, Hillel Steiner, John Roemer and others) of the highly innovative September Group, which meets annually to discuss issues in egalitarian political theory. Van Parijs's book, which builds upon his earlier work, makes clear that he is among the leading contemporary political theorists.[3]

Van Parijs defends a theory of justice that has three main components. First, he holds that each autonomous agent is *self-owning*, at least in the weak sense that he or she (and not society or someone else) has the moral authority to control the use of his or her body in various ways. Van Parijs articulates and defends a more specific, and stronger, notion of self-ownership, which will be examined carefully below. Second, he holds that *compensation* is owed to those who are *disadvantaged* for non-choice-related reasons in their endowments. More specifically, he holds that justice requires that no one's situation be so bad that someone else's situation is preferred to it by every single member of society. Third, subject to these two constraints, wealth is to be distributed in society so as to maximize the minimum sustainable level of real opportunities for a good life. Although I agree with his general egalitarian liberal approach, I shall challenge several of his specific claims.

Using this theory, Van Parijs argues that in contemporary Western countries justice requires that each citizen receive a fairly high unconditional basic income (independent of need or willingness to work). He also uses his theory of justice to argue that the best feasible forms of capitalism are more just than the best feasible forms of socialism, and he discusses and evaluates different notions of exploitation (especially those of John Roemer). Although Van Parijs is full of insight on these interesting and important issues, my discussion will be limited to his theory of justice.

3.2   The egalitarian liberal framework

Van Parijs's approach is a form of Egalitarian Liberalism. It is liberal in that it endorses a form of self-ownership and thereby protects certain liberty rights of agents. It is egalitarian in that it endorses a form of social ownership of natural resources and in that it calls for social wealth to be spent on promoting a form of equality. (Here and below, I use 'equality' loosely to include both equality of distribution and priority for the worse off.)[4] More specifically, Van Parijs endorses:

> Egalitarian liberalism: Subject to the (nonempty) constraints imposed by a plausible conception of self-ownership, equality should be efficiently promoted.[5]

This leaves open what exact constraints a plausible conception of self-ownership imposes, what the equalisandum is, and how equality is to be promoted. It makes clear, however, that the demands of self-ownership on some suitable construal are prior to the demands of equality.

Van Parijs is right to endorse egalitarian liberalism.[6] In the remainder of this section, I shall flesh out the part of Van Parijs's conceptions of self-ownership and of equality that I endorse. In the following sections I shall criticize the parts I disagree with.

Let us start by considering the conception of self-ownership that Van Parijs endorses. To keep things simple, I'll make three assumptions. First, I'll assume that in some relevant sense normal adult human beings are psychologically autonomous and make genuine choices. Second, I'll assume that an essential part of oneself is one's *body*, and thus that self-ownership includes ownership of one's body. This is a plausible assumption if necessarily selves occupy exactly one body. It becomes doubtful if selves are not necessarily embodied (e.g., as in free-floating souls) or if necessarily embodied selves can move easily among different bodies (so that bodies are like clothes). Finally, I'll assume that there are no beings with moral standing that are not full agents (fully psychologically autonomous). I'll pretend, for example, that there are no nonagent animals and that agents pop into existence 'overnight' (and so no children). This is obviously unrealistic, and dealing with the claims of such beings is an important problem. But there are enough problems for us to worry about without taking on here the claims of nonagent beings.

At the core of the idea of self-ownership is the idea that agents have the moral authority to control the use of their bodies. More carefully stated, the idea is the following:

Control self-ownership: In the absence of any previous commitments or wrongdoings by the agent, each psychologically autonomous agent has the moral right to control the use of his or her body.[7]

Spelling this out fully requires more space than I have, but the rough idea has two parts. First, if an agent has made no relevant previous commitments, and has neither committed nor is about to commit any relevant wrongs, then it is wrong for others to make use of the agent's body without his or her permission. Without permission, it is wrong, for example, to kill, torture, assault, or physically constrain that person, and wrong to remove bodily organs for the benefit of others. Second, if the agent consents to having someone use his or her body in various ways, and doing so violates no other rights, then it is permissible for that person to make such use.

Van Parijs doesn't explicitly discuss Control Self-Ownership in these terms, but it is reasonably clear that he endorses something like control self-ownership (chap. 2). Although this condition is extremely weak, it rules out all standard forms of teleology or consequentialism (since they deny that agents have any sort of strong rights at a basic level). It also rules out rights approaches (which no one today would defend) that allow some autonomous agents to be nonvoluntarily enslaved by others (either by individuals or by society). Finally, it rules out Hobbesian (but not clearly Lockean or Kantian) contractarianism, since agents are not self-owners in even the weak sense in a Hobbesian state of nature.

Control self-ownership has no implications for the legitimacy of various tax policies, since tax policies concern rights to income, not control of one's body. Van Parijs endorses, however, another element of self-ownership that does impose some such constraints (p. 64):

Leisure self-ownership: No wealth tax on the value of *personal* endowments (e.g., skills and abilities) is legitimate.

To see the plausibility of leisure self-ownership, consider a model where each person is taxed each year an amount equal to the maximum competitive value of goods and services that he or she could produce during that period. The tax is not based on what is actually produced, but rather on what one could produce. It is an asset tax (a tax on the ability to produce) rather than a production (or income) tax.[8]

Although this model is compatible with control self-ownership, it is not, as Van Parijs makes clear, compatible with a plausible self-ownership in the context of egalitarian liberalism. For it leads to effective (although not formal) slavery of the talented: agents with highly productive capacities would have to work more hours (and thus have less leisure) to pay their taxes than individuals with less productive capacities. This follows because the tax owed is equal to the maximum competitive value that the agent could produce during the tax period. Thus, before the division of the social pot, all agents have to work all day in their most productive capacity in order to pay their taxes. The returns from the social pot, however, can be used to pay taxes for the next period (and thus purchase some leisure time). Assuming that the social pot is divided so that disadvantaged individuals get no less (and presumably more) than advantaged individuals, the net result of this approach is that advantaged agents will have less leisure than disadvantaged ones. For a given dollar amount will cover a lower percentage of the taxes owed (and thus free up less leisure time) for the advantaged than for the disadvantaged (because the former owe higher taxes). Indeed, it can easily lead to scenarios in which the most advantaged individuals must work all day every day at jobs they absolutely hate in order to pay their taxes, and slightly disadvantaged individuals do not need to work at all. This effective slavery of the talented is incompatible with a plausible conception of self-ownership.

Of course, instead of having a tax equal to the maximum possible production, the tax could be some positive percentage of maximum production. But this would only reduce, and not eliminate, the problem. Agents with higher-than-average productive capacities would still have less leisure time than the less productive.

Given the problem of the effective slavery of the talented, leisure self-ownership is a compelling principle. It is not legitimate to tax human capital. That leaves open, however, whether it is ever legitimate to tax income. Income, of course, can be generated in a variety of ways. As we shall see below, Van Parijs rejects a conception of self-ownership that includes the right to the (untaxed) income from brute luck (e.g., unforeseen gifts, unforeseen natural events, or favorable genetic endowments). He is, however, committed to a conception of self-ownership that includes the right to the income generated by one's *choices* in cases where there is no differential brute luck among agents.

To help focus our thoughts, consider a world with just two identically endowed agents (same skills, wealth, etc.) and with natural resources being abundant relative to their desires. Suppose that each agent knows that to remain healthy he or she must regularly exercise and eat nutritiously. One of the agents, Prudence, chooses to forgo some of the short-term pleasures of leisure and more exciting food for the long-term benefits of good health, whereas the other agent, Imprudence, chooses the short-term pleasures. As a result of these choices and nothing else (nothing unforeseeable happens), after several years Prudence is in good health and Imprudence is not. Does justice require that Prudence in some way compensate (e.g., by providing food to) Imprudence for his disadvantage?

Van Parijs rightly answers no to this question (pp. 90, 99). Prudence has no duty of justice to compensate Imprudence for his current disadvantage. By assumption, Prudence's advantage over Imprudence is solely attributable to their respective choices, and it would be unfair to make Prudence bear the burdens of Imprudence's choices in such a situation.

In this example, we assumed that natural resources were abundant. As we shall see below, Van Parijs holds that where natural or other kinds of social resources are scarce, agents who appropriate them owe rent (a kind of tax) for the appropriation. The point and significance of this rent will be made clear below, but for the moment we simply need to note that, whatever rights to income Van Parijs holds are protected by self-ownership, they do not preclude the collection of rents on scarce social resources.

Van Parijs is, I believe, committed to:

> Non-brute luck income self-ownership: Redistributive taxation of choice-generated income is illegitimate except perhaps to the extent necessary to eliminate inequalities in brute luck (or where it is for the rent owed for the appropriation of scarce social assets).

Although Van Parijs explicitly endorses the content of this claim, he does not explicitly consider it a part of his conception of self-ownership. This is because he conceives (e.g., p. 183) of the demands of equality as limited to compensating for bad brute luck (e.g., as limited to equalizing *initial* endowments plus adjustments for later brute luck), and thus there is no need for the above constraint. In order to highlight Van Parijs's rejection of the equalization of any purely choice-generated inequalities, it will nonetheless be useful for the purposes of this paper to include the above element as part of Van Parijs's conception of self-ownership.

Van Parijs, then, rightly endorses the above three self-ownership conditions. For ease of reference, let us give their conjunction a name:

> Limited self-ownership: Control self-ownership, and leisure self-ownership, and non-brute luck income self-ownership.

The assumption of limited self-ownership leaves open who morally owns the rest (the nonagent part) of the world. (Throughout, the ownership involved is moral, not legal, ownership.) In particular, it leaves open who owns the natural resources (in their unimproved state, before being transformed into artifacts). Van Parijs rightly holds the following:

> Social ownership of natural resources: All natural resources (land, oil, etc., in their natural state) are socially owned.

The idea is that, because natural resources were not created by agents, they belong to everyone. There are, of course, a great variety of forms that social ownership can take, ranging from joint ownership in the sense that all decisions of use are made collectively (e.g., by voting) to common ownership in the sense that everyone is free to use a given resource as long as no one else is using it and the user doesn't reduce the value of the resource.

Van Parijs rightly endorses (roughly speaking at least; pp. 99–101) the following form of social ownership of natural resources, proposed many years ago by Thomas Paine, Herbert Spencer and Henry George:[9]

> Georgist social ownership of natural resources: Each person is entitled to use a given natural resource that is not already claimed by someone else as long as he or she pays society for any reduction in market value that the use involves. Furthermore, a person may claim exclusive use of a natural resource not already claimed by someone else, as long as he or she pays society the market rent value of those rights.

The idea is that, in the absence of private property claims, everyone is free to use the natural resources as long as they pay the costs of any value-reducing activities. Private appropriation is allowed, but only in a weak sense that makes exclusive control conditional upon the regular payment of rent to society for the right of exclusive control. Thus, there is no joint ownership of natural resources (requiring collective decision making), just common ownership modified by quasi-private appropriation.

This, of course, is only a sketch of a highly controversial position. Here I shall neither develop nor defend it, but rather simply assume it as the part of Van Parijs's framework that I accept.

Let us turn now to a more detailed look at Van Parijs's conception of self-ownership.

3.3 Self-ownership and the limits of taxation

Van Parijs holds that, subject to the constraints imposed by limited self-ownership, tax policy should be set so as to promote equality efficiently. I shall suggest in this section that limited self-ownership fails to incorporate some important and plausible elements of self-ownership. As a result, Van Parijs endorses, I claim, illegitimate taxation.

In what follows we shall consider what sorts of redistributive taxation are compatible with the rights of self-ownership. Two points should be kept in mind. First, we shall be concerned only with redistributive taxation, and not, for example, with taxation for externalities or for public goods. Second, as Van Parijs emphasizes, the fact that people do not have *the right* to the income from certain sources does not entail that it should be taxed at 100 percent. For it may be that on efficiency grounds the *total* amount of tax revenue generated from these sources will be maximized if tax rates are less than 100 percent. For example, even if people have no right to gift income, taxing gifts at 50 percent rather than 100 percent may generate more gift tax revenues. All the following discussions are about whether self-ownership permits taxation, not about the level at which they should be taxed.

3.3.1   Good brute luck

Brute luck is luck (good or bad) that no reasonable person could have taken into account in past choices, whereas option luck is luck the chances of which reasonable people could take into account in their past choices. The completely unpredictable discovery by accident of oil on one's property or the completely unpredictable increase in pay for one's professional services are examples of good brute luck to the extent that one could not have reasonably anticipated these events to be possible outcomes of one's choices. Winning the lottery is an example of good option luck (since reasonable agents would know that such an event is a possible outcome of their choice to buy a ticket). The benefits of option luck are attributable to one's choices, whereas the benefits of brute luck are not.

In discussing brute luck, it is often useful to distinguish brute luck in *initial* endowments (as a starting adult) from *adult* brute luck (after the start of adult life).[10] The initial endowment of an agent consists of his or her (internal, nontransferable) *personal endowment* (capacities, vulnerabilities, etc.) and (external, transferable) *situational endowment* (wealth, situational opportunities, etc.) at the onset of adulthood (psychological autonomy).

Within the framework of egalitarian liberalism, strongly egalitarian views hold that the benefits of good brute luck are socially owned (and thus taxable at up to 100 percent) and not owned by those who happen to be in the right place at the right time,[11] whereas strongly libertarian views hold that, as a consequence of self-ownership, the benefits are owned (and thus not taxable) by those fortunate to be in the right place.[12] Van Parijs (pp. 107, 281, nn. 86, 88) endorses the strongly egalitarian view and rejects the view that a plausible conception of self-ownership includes the right to the benefits of one's good brute luck.

Although I shall suggest that a plausible conception of self-ownership includes the right to the benefits of certain kinds of brute luck, there is one type of brute luck where I agree that self-ownership entails no right to the benefits thereof. Consider a case where the natural resources that one 'owns' (subject to paying rent to society) undergo completely unpredictable increases in value (e.g., because someone else accidentally discovers a use for the oil on one's land). Here I agree with Van Parijs that the benefits of the brute luck are socially owned. Because natural resources are socially owned, so are the benefits associated with that ownership. The level of the rent owed by the appropriators of natural resources depends on what rights they claim and are recognized by society. If the rights claimed include a right to income from good brute luck relating to the natural resource, then the rent will be higher than if no such right is claimed. Because this is largely a matter of conventional legal rights, this can be handled either by charging a higher rent and recognizing the appropriator's right to the income from brute luck or by charging a lower rent with the benefits of good brute luck reverting to society. All that matters is that society get the competitive value of the right claimed (including the value of any right to the benefits of good brute luck). So, with respect to this sort of brute luck, I agree with Van Parijs.

Because ownership of personal endowments (skills, etc.) and artifacts (creations, such as cars, assuming the rent has been paid for the raw natural resources) is not conventional in this way, the issue cannot be dealt with so easily in these cases. The question is whether the owners of such assets are entitled to the benefits of good brute luck. Are roofers entitled to the increase in pay that their services command after a completely unpredictable hailstorm? Is the owner of an antique car entitled to the increase in market value after a completely unpredictable series of events destroys all the other similar cars?

Although I shall not pursue the issue at length here, I would argue that a plausible conception of self-ownership includes the right to the benefits of one's good brute luck relating to one's personal endowments and artifacts. Defending this claim would involve appealing to some deep normative (not metaphysical) separateness of persons that places limits on the extent to which one person is required to share in the unchosen burdens of others. Of course, strong egalitarians will rightly insist that differences due to brute luck are morally arbitrary, but once some form of self-ownership is recognized as a legitimate constraint on the demands of equality (as on Van Parijs's view), then it is recognized that equality is not the only morally relevant demand. It then becomes a question of what the various relevant moral demands are and of how they relate to each other. I would argue that (pace various monisms) there are several independent moral demands, that they include both a demand for self-ownership and a demand for equality, and that a very strong form of self-ownership (one that includes the right to the benefits of one's good brute luck) constrains the demands of equality.[13]

I should emphasize, however, that I agree with strong egalitarians that those who suffer *bad* brute luck have a claim for compensation. The social pot (e.g., from rents on natural resources and the gift taxes discussed below) should be spent on those disadvantaged by bad brute luck. The issue here is different. With Van Parijs, I hold that the demands of self-ownership are prior to the demands of equality. The question concerns how strong those demands are. I claim that they preclude taxing the benefits of *good* brute luck. The issue, that is, is whether self-ownership permits the benefits of good brute luck to be a legitimate source of compensation for bad adult brute luck (and not whether those suffering bad brute luck have a legitimate claim for compensation).

The issue is obviously extremely complex, and I won't attempt to provide an argument here. But I will at least sketch a defense of a weaker claim of self-ownership that Van Parijs (along with all strong egalitarians) rejects. We need, I claim, to distinguish between comparative and noncomparative brute luck. For both, brute luck concerns the net impact of factors that one could not reasonably have taken into account in one's choices. The difference concerns the standard of comparison. One experiences good *comparative* net brute luck during a given time period just in case one's net brute luck during that period is better than that of specified *others* (e.g., some particular individual or the societal average). One experiences good *noncomparative* net brute luck during a given time period just in case the net brute luck experienced was good compared to its absence. If, for example, nothing happens to a given agent during a given time period that she could not have reasonably anticipated as a possibility, then she experiences no noncomparative brute luck. But compared to someone who did experience some bad noncomparative net brute luck, she experiences good comparative brute luck.

Consider, now, two agents who started with equally valuable endowments, Neutral, who later experiences no noncomparative brute luck, and Unlucky, who later experiences bad noncomparative net brute luck. According to Van Parijs (and the standard strong egalitarian view), it is legitimate to tax Neutral to compensate Unlucky for her bad brute luck. The rationale is that Unlucky had worse comparative net brute luck than Neutral. But from Neutral's perspective at least, this looks suspiciously like confiscation of his purely choice-generated income. After all, they had equal initial endowments, and Neutral experienced no later net noncomparative brute luck. Why should he have to part with any of his income? Wouldn't a plausible conception of self-ownership entitle him to his income under these circumstances?

Strong egalitarians will, of course, question the relevance of noncomparative brute luck. After all, they will rightly insist, brute luck with respect to *initial* endowments has to be understood in comparative terms (since there are no antecedent agent expectations to compare them with). So surely, they will claim, it is comparative brute luck that is the relevant notion.

This is a legitimate challenge that must be met if the suggested claim of self-ownership is to be defensible. And even if the suggested claim is defensible, it does not establish that one has a right to the benefits of good noncomparative brute luck or a right to the benefit of good comparative brute luck in initial endowments. I hope, however, that I've said enough to give at least some plausibility to a form of income self-ownership that is stronger than the one that Van Parijs endorses.[14]

3.3.2 The right to make gifts

Van Parijs holds (pp. 90, 101) that gifts (*inter vivos* gifts and bequests) are legitimately 100 percent taxable. I shall briefly mention two sources of doubt.

First, gifts are typically partly good option luck and partly good brute luck. Typically, gifts are made at least in part in response to the prior choices made by the donee. An attentive daughter may receive more gifts from her parents than her neglectful brother. Gift income attributable solely to the choices of the donee (and not to any differential brute luck) is, I would argue (and most egalitarian liberals would agree), fully owned by the donee. So at best it is only the brute luck component of gifts (e.g., a gift from a great aunt of whom one was never aware) that is 100 percent taxable.

Second, even if a plausible conception of self-ownership does not include the right to the benefits of one's good brute luck, it does not follow that brute luck gifts may be taxed at 100 percent. For, unlike *natural* brute luck, gifts involve two agents: the donor and the donee. Although it may not violate the donee's rights of self-ownership to tax gifts at 100 percent, it may violate the donor's rights of self-ownership. Gift giving is typically an important part of the good life for most people. Most people care quite a bit about certain others, and to deny them the opportunity to give benefits to such others would be to deny the benefactors something important. So, consideration for the rights of the donor make 100 percent taxation of gifts more problematic than 100 percent taxation of natural brute luck.

Indeed, I would argue that a plausible conception of self-ownership includes the right to transfer by gift without taxation any wealth that is purely *donor generated* (as opposed to received by gift or by natural brute luck). If, for example, all agents had equal initial endowments, and there has been no later brute luck, then they are fully entitled to the wealth they generate through their choices. This entitlement includes, I would argue, not only the right to spend it on themselves but also the right to transfer it (undiminished) to others.

This is *not* to claim that those who receive gifts have the right to transfer that wealth by gift to someone else without taxation. For wealth that one receives as a brute luck gift is not wealth that one has generated through one's choices. The rights transferred by gift may include the right to consume the wealth, but they need not include the rights to further transfer that wealth by gift. Indeed, given that an unrestricted right to transfer by gift can lead to wealth dynasties that radically undermine equality-of-life prospects, it is very doubtful that a plausible conception of self-ownership includes the right to transfer by gift wealth that one gained by brute luck.[15]

3.4   Social spending on the disadvantaged

Van Parijs holds, and I agree, that subject to the constraints imposed by a plausible conception of self-ownership, equality should be efficiently promoted as much as possible. Above I suggested that Van Parijs's conception of self-ownership is too weak in that it allows taxation of brute luck and of gifts of donor-generated wealth. I fully agree, however, that the social pot, derived from the rent from natural resources and taxes on gifts of brute-luck-generated wealth, should be spent to compensate those disadvantaged by brute luck.[16]

There are, of course, many approaches to measuring, and compensating for, inequality. Van Parijs discusses and effectively refutes Rawls's approach and Dworkin's two insurance approaches.[17] He also insightfully discusses envy-free approaches (which in the technical sense require that no one prefer the endowment of someone else to his or her own). Given that envy-free allocations are not always possible when there are different personal (nontransferable) endowments, he develops a less demanding approach in the same general spirit of envy-freeness.

According to Van Parijs, justice requires that the social pot be spent so as to *leximin* the value of the opportunities open to each member of society, that is, to maximize the value of the least valuable opportunity set, and where there are ties to maximize the value of the second least valuable opportunity set, and so on. Leximinning requires not that everyone's opportunity set have the same value, but only that the least valuable set be as valuable as possible. Although leximinning is more plausible than requiring strict equality, I shall criticize it as giving too much priority to the worst-off members of society when resources would provide greater benefits to other disadvantaged members. I shall also question Van Parijs's views about how the value of opportunities is measured.

3.4.1 Evaluating endowments: universal-dominance and transferable wealth

Van Parijs holds that, subject to the constraint of limited self-ownership and the constraint that no one's endowment is universally dominated by another (i.e., such that everyone prefers the latter to the former), transferable wealth is to be leximinned. Although Van Parijs doesn't put it in these terms, his theory of justice can usefully be reformulated as requiring that, subject to the constraint of limited self-ownership, the value of endowments be leximinned, where one endowment is more valuable than another just in case (1) it universally dominates the other (i.e., everyone prefers it to the other) or (2) it is not universally dominated by, and has more transferable wealth than, the other. This reformulation simply moves the constraint against universal dominance inside the metric of value.[18]

In this subsection I shall raise some doubts about this conception of value of endowments by contrasting it with a competing conception of value, namely, one that evaluates endowments in terms of their opportunity for welfare. For simplicity, in this section I assume that we are concerned only with evaluating *initial* endowments, so that we don't have to worry about adjusting for later brute luck.[19]

Start by contrasting Van Parijs's metric with a simple version of the opportunity-for-welfare metric: with a given endowment, each agent has an array of possible life paths. Which path agents follow depends in part on their choices and in part on factors beyond their control. Each life path produces a certain level of well-being for the agent. By assuming that each agent makes the best choice (in terms of well-being) at each point of choice, and appealing to the probabilities for factors beyond the agent's control, we can evaluate an agent's endowment in terms of the best achievable (by choice) expected level of well-being.[20]

This version of the approach evaluates endowments on the assumption that agents make the best choices they are capable of at each point. Because this may be an implausibly high level of accountability, other assumptions might be made instead. One might assign probabilities that reflect how likely agents in that situation are to make the various choices (a sort of weighting for reasonableness) and evaluate endowments based on these probabilities. There are a host of important and difficult issues here, but I shall leave open exactly how they are addressed.[21]

To be plausible, this approach must defend a plausible account of individual welfare (happiness, preference satisfaction, etc.) so as to make clear the importance of promoting the opportunity for such welfare. The account of welfare must also be such that levels of welfare are interpersonally comparable.

Van Parijs writes as if he objects to the opportunity-for-welfare approach on the grounds that it fails to hold people responsible for their preferences. The core idea is that there is no reason why someone who cultivates expensive tastes (e.g., for expensive wines) should receive more resources than an otherwise identical person who does not cultivate such tastes. This core idea is right, and it is a powerful objection against standard utilitarianism, but it is not applicable to equality of opportunity for welfare. For the most plausible version of equality of opportunity for welfare gives agents equal initial endowments and then holds agents responsible for their choices. No adjustment in resources is made if one of them chooses to develop expensive tastes and thereby achieves less welfare than the other. That's a personal matter.[22]

The equality-of-opportunity-for-welfare approach does, however, compensate people who have expensive *initial* welfare dispositions (tastes, preferences, etc.). For such dispositions are unchosen. Of course, agents may be able to alter their welfare dispositions, and, if they are, equal opportunity for welfare holds them responsible for their choices. It insists, however, that otherwise identical initial endowments are unequal if it is more costly to achieve welfare with one initial welfare disposition than with the other. It holds that disadvantageous initial welfare dispositions are just as eligible for compensation as initial physical disabilities. Van Parijs, however, seems to treat initial welfare dispositions as ineligible for compensation. He seems (e.g., pp. 50, 71, 80–2, 93, 96) to hold that people are responsible not only for their chosen preferences but also for their unchosen ones. I shall argue, however, that Van Parijs cannot consistently object to compensation for initial disadvantages in welfare disposition.

To see this, let us, following Van Parijs (p. 80), consider a case where initial endowments are identical except for preferences, and where preferences are uniformly malleable in the sense that, although people may start with different preferences, the range of preferences that a person can choose to adopt is the same for everyone, and such adoptions can be done easily and quickly without any cost in welfare. In this case, equal opportunity for welfare judges all endowments as equal. For, given the (very strong and unrealistic) assumption of uniform malleability of preferences, everyone has equally valuable opportunities for welfare. So there is no disagreement with Van Parijs in this case.

In real life, of course, initial preferences are not uniformly malleable. Some people have access to, and even have, preferences that are not accessible for others. And even where two people have access to the same preferences, the costs associated with adopting different ones are typically different (e.g., because they start with different preferences). The central question here is whether disadvantages in initial (unchosen) welfare dispositions are a source of inequality. I claim that they should be treated just like any other (unchosen) disadvantage in initial endowment (e.g., physical disability).

To see this, let us focus on a second extreme sort of case. Suppose that initial preferences are unalterable. Nothing an agent can choose has any effect on the preferences, although choices can affect other aspects of the world. Consider now a world with two agents who are initially identically endowed except that one has difficult-to-please (expensive) preferences. To start, let us suppose that both agents prefer the initial endowment of the agent with the easier-to-please preferences (since welfare is easier to achieve). In this case Van Parijs agrees that compensation is owed, since there is universal dominance. So, in this case at least, compensation is owed to those with disadvantageous initial preferences.

The same conclusion holds if we relax the assumption of unalterability. As long as all agents prefer one welfare disposition to the other, there will be universal dominance, and Van Parijs's approach agrees that compensation is owed for disadvantaged preferences.

So, Van Parijs should drop his objection that equality of opportunity fails to hold people accountable for their preferences. It does hold them accountable to the extent they can influence what preferences they have. And it, like Van Parijs's approach, rightly holds that disadvantages in initial welfare dispositions may be compensable sources of inequality.

Van Parijs's real objection to the opportunity-for-welfare approach is, I believe, that it implausibly presupposes that welfare – understood as a measure of the good life – is fully interpersonally comparable. The only plausible account of welfare, he might claim, is one based on people's preferences (what they care about). Any other account of welfare is perfectionist and fetishistic (as Van Parijs's Hippie/Yuppie example on p. 81 makes clear). Now, if everyone had the same extended preferences, this would provide a full basis for interpersonally comparable welfare (since extended preferences rank endowments that people may have). But people do not have the same extended preferences. And since, it might be plausibly argued, the only basis for interpersonal comparisons of preference-based welfare is intersubjective agreement, there is no full comparability of welfare. So, it might be concluded, the opportunity-for-welfare approach described above is a nonstarter.

Not all is lost, however. The opportunity-for-welfare approach can hold that one endowment is less valuable than another if everyone prefers (extendedly) one to the other. And that is just to say that one endowment is less valuable than another if the latter universally dominates the former.[23] This is a fairly weak principle, since, given the variability in people's extended preferences, it will leave many pairs of endowments unranked. If, however, one endorses equality of opportunity for welfare, as well as the premises of the above argument criticizing the presupposition that welfare is fully interpersonally comparable, one may well be inclined to accept the view that the requirement to promote equality is not as demanding as one might have thought.[24]

Van Parijs, however, takes a different approach. He claims that universal dominance is sufficient but not necessary for one endowment to be more valuable than a second. He holds that, where neither endowment universally dominates the other, the one with more transferable wealth is more valuable. This produces a much more robust (and, indeed, complete) ranking of endowments and thus a more demanding conception of equality.

Van Parijs defends this approach by claiming that it measures real freedom, which he understands as the extent to which agents have the means to do whatever they might want to do. Where personal endowments are the same, transferable wealth measures the means to do whatever one might want to do. Where personal endowments are not the same, however, transferable wealth does not capture the differences in the means to do whatever one wants that come from personal endowments (e.g., skills). These differences are, Van Parijs argues, captured by holding that an endowment that universally dominates another is more valuable.

Although, as Van Parijs points out (p. 75), there is more than one way to appeal to transferable wealth to obtain a complete ordering of endowments by expanding upon the universal dominance criterion, Van Parijs's way is arguably the most plausible. It's not clear, however, that it is plausible to expand the universal dominance criterion into a complete ordering. For doing so invokes considerations of value that are not grounded in people's preferences. Universal dominance captures everything that people agree about. For typical preference profiles, it ensures that, where personal endowments are the same, an endowment with more transferable wealth is more valuable than one with less. But it says nothing about two endowments where the personal endowments are *unequal*, and some people prefer the first while others prefer the second. To hold, of two endowments neither of which universally dominates the other, that the one with greater transferable wealth is more valuable is to import a questionable value judgment that is not solely grounded in people's preferences.

A particularly striking way of illustrating this point is to note that Van Parijs's metric is incompatible with envy-freeness as a criterion of equality. Suppose there are just two agents, one of whom is initially endowed with a poor singing voice but lots of money and the other of whom is endowed with a good singing voice (which we will suppose has no market value) but little money. Suppose that each prefers her own endowment to that of the other (since the first cares little for singing and a lot for money and the second cares a lot for singing and little for money). In this case there is no envy, and so it is very plausible that there is no inequality. The universal dominance principle is silent here, since there is no universal dominance. But Van Parijs's metric judges the endowment with more money as more valuable than the other, since where there is no universal dominance he ranks endowments on the basis of transferable wealth. But this is surely implausible. Envy-freeness may not be a necessary condition for equality (since it is not always possible), but it is surely a sufficient condition.

The issue is of course complex, and in the end the view that value is grounded solely in people's preferences may not be defensible. But if Van Parijs wishes to have a theory of value grounded solely in people's preferences, he needs to reject the appeal to transferable wealth and appeal solely to envy-freeness, to the universal dominance, or to other preference-based criteria.

3.4.2 Efficiently promoting equality: the worst off versus the greatest beneficiary

Van Parijs holds that justice requires that, subject to the constraints imposed by self-ownership, the value of endowments should be lexi-minned (i.e. that the value of the least valuable endowment should be maximized, and, if there are ties, the value of the second least valuable endowment should be maximized, etc.). A standard objection to theories that endorse social spending on equalization of some sort is that under certain conditions they require spending almost all the social pot on a small number of difficult-to-help disadvantaged individuals. I shall discuss how Van Parijs deals with this objection and suggest that a different approach is needed.

Because of decreasing marginal benefits and related matters, all else being equal, a worse-off individual will get more benefit from a given amount of resources than a better-off individual. But typically all else is not equal. First, the worse-off person, but not the better-off person, may be in circumstances that are particularly expensive to improve (e.g., some hopeless medical condition). Second, the thesis of decreasing marginal benefit in its standard form is *not interpersonal*. It only says that, for a given person, the less a person has of a given good, the more he or she will benefit from a given additional allocation. It is compatible with different people having different marginal benefit schedules. It is compatible, for example, with my getting one unit of benefit from $100, when I have $1,000, and your getting a hundred units of benefit in the same situation. It is also compatible with my getting one unit of benefit from $100 when I'm the worst-off person, and your getting ten units of benefit from $100 when you're much better off.

A worse-off person may not get the greatest benefit from a given amount of resources. Indeed, the worst-off person may be in such a hopeless condition that he or she would benefit only slightly from enormous allocations of resources. Nonetheless, leximin and several other standard approaches to equalization require that resources be so allocated in such cases. This is deeply counterintuitive and a problem that egalitarian spenders, and Van Parijs in particular, must address.

A first step to limiting this problem is to impose a strong conception of self-ownership as a constraint on legitimate taxation. This at least limits the demands that can be placed on others to deal with the problem. Egalitarian theories with no such constraints are extremely vulnerable to this objection. Van Parijs, as we have seen, endorses limited self-ownership, and that goes some way to limiting the demands of equality. Still, if he endorsed a stronger conception of self-ownership, that would provide further plausible protection.

Van Parijs has, nonetheless, a number of ways of alleviating the problem (pp. 83–4). First, his conception of value (universal dominance or non-universal dominance and more transferable wealth) is much less demanding in the resources required to benefit the least well-off than a full-blown equality of opportunity for welfare (and various other conceptions of equality as well). This is because, given the variety of extended preferences, universal dominance will hold only for extreme cases, and, where it doesn't hold, Van Parijs's principle evaluates endowments on the basis of their transferable wealth (as opposed to subjective welfare). Second, he qualifies his general principle that requires the elimination/reduction of inequality so as to ignore cases where the beneficiary gets only a small benefit and it is at a great cost to others.

I shall argue nonetheless that Van Parijs's appeal to leximinning is mistaken because of its (well-known) monomaniacal concern with the worst off. Suppose that there are 3 billion people who are below average in life prospects, all but one of whom are moderately poorly off (e.g., bare subsistence with a moderate amount of pain) and one of whom is extremely poorly off (e.g., bare subsistence with lots of pain). Suppose that with the resources available for equalization one could either improve the lot of the worst off so that his lot is equal to that of the other poorly off people (whose situation is not improved) or improve the lot of all the other below-average people so that they are moderately well off (a significant improvement) and leave the worst-off person unimproved. A leximin approach to equalization requires that resources be allocated to benefit the one worst-off person rather than significantly benefiting the other 3 billion less one people. Even Van Parijs's qualification about ignoring small benefits to the least well off when the costs to others are great is inapplicable here, since this is a significant benefit to the least well off.

I agree that equality should be efficiently promoted, but I reject the leximin conception thereof. It is crazy to hold that one should help one person moderately instead of helping many other needy people even more. The problem with leximin is that it gives absolute priority to the worst-off person(s). A more plausible view would agree that a worse-off person has some priority over a better-off person without claiming that this priority is absolute in the sense that any benefit (no matter how small) to a worse-off person has priority over any benefit (no matter how great) to a better-off person.

A plausible approach to egalitarian spending must give some consideration to how much benefit individuals will get and not merely be based on how poorly off they are.[25] I will mention a few such approaches to illustrate how this could be done.

One approach would be to assign finite weights to each person, with larger weights assigned the worse off a person is. One could then hold that, for a given unit of resource to be allocated, a person with a greater weighted marginal benefit has priority over a person with a lesser weighted benefit. Thus, if a worse-off person with a weight of four would get one unit of benefit, but a better-off person with a weight of two would get four units of benefit from a given unit of resources, then the better-off person would have priority. A defect of this approach, I think, is that it gives priority to the person with the greater weighted marginal benefit – no matter how many people with slightly smaller weighted marginal benefits could be helped instead. This approach, like leximin, is nonaggregative. This problem could be overcome by holding that one should maximize the total weighted marginal benefit. This is like utilitarianism, but with weights for how poorly off the person is.[26] Another approach would be to hold that (like utilitarianism) total (unweighted) marginal benefit should be maximized, but to count marginal benefits only up to the societal average (so that marginal benefits to those who are above average count for nothing).

Obviously, the question of egalitarian spending priorities is a complex issue. But it's reasonably clear, I think, that the absolute priority to the worst-off person accorded by the leximin approach is not plausible. Equality can be efficiently promoted, in the sense that matters, by giving moderate benefits to enough disadvantaged people instead of even a significant benefit to the most disadvantaged. So, Van Parijs should replace his leximin conception of inequality reduction with a more plausible approach. His qualification of leximin for costs to others compared with the benefits to the worst off already moves in this direction, but it doesn't go far enough.

3.5   Conclusion

Van Parijs rightly holds that equality should be promoted, subject to the constraints of a plausible conception of self-ownership. He rightly denies that self-ownership includes a right to appropriate natural resources without paying competitive rent to a social pot, or a right to make untaxed gifts drawn from wealth one was given. I have suggested, however, that his conception of self-ownership is not strong enough in that it fails to give agents a right to the benefits of their good brute luck and in that it fails to give agents the right to make untaxed gifts of wealth that they generated. I have also questioned Van Parijs's conception of value (based on universal dominance and transferable wealth) and criticized his appeal to leximin (instead of an approach that is significantly sensitive to marginal benefits).

Despite the above questionable features of Van Parijs's theory of justice, this is clearly an important work in political theory. It's superbly written and argued, and full of insights from economic theory. More important, it is, broadly speaking, right.

Notes

1. A review of Philippe Van Parijs, *Real Freedom for All: What (if anything) can justify Capitalism?* (Oxford: Clarendon Press, 1995), pp. ix + 330. All parenthetical references in the text are to this work. I'm indebted to Richard

Arneson, Tony Ellis, Brad Hooker, Trenton Merricks, Gene Mills, Arthur Ripstein, Hillel Steiner, Philippe Van Parijs, Stuart White and Andrew Williams for helpful comments.
2. Ronald Dworkin, 'What Is Equality? Part 1: Equality of Welfare', *Philosophy and Public Affairs* 10 (1981), pp. 185–345, and 'What Is Equality? Part 2: Equality of Resources', *Philosophy and Public Affairs* 10 (1981), pp. 283–345; G. A. Cohen, 'Self-Ownership, World Ownership, and Equality', *Social Philosophy and Policy* 3 (1986), pp. 77–96, 'On the Currency of Egalitarian Justice', *Ethics* 99 (1989), pp. 906–44, 'Self-Ownership, Communism, and Equality', *Proceedings of the Aristotelian Society* suppl. vol. 64 (1990), pp. 25–44, and *Self-Ownership, Freedom, and Equality* (Cambridge: Cambridge University Press, 1995); Hillel Steiner, 'The Natural Right to the Means of Production', *Philosophical Quarterly* 27 (1977), pp. 41–9, 'Slavery, Socialism, and Private Property', *Nomos* 22 (1980), pp. 244–65, 'Liberty and Equality', *Political Studies* 29 (1981), pp. 555–69, 'Capitalism, Justice, and Equal Starts', in Ellen Frankel Paul, Fred D. Miller, Jeffrey Paul and John Ahrens (eds), *Equal Opportunity* (Cambridge, MA.: Blackwell, 1987), pp. 49–71, and *An Essay on Rights* (Cambridge, MA.: Blackwell, 1994); Amartya Sen, *Commodities and Capabilities* (Amsterdam: North Holland, 1985); John Roemer, 'Equality of Talent', *Economics and Philosophy* 1 (1985), pp. 151–87, 'The Mismarriage of Bargaining Theory and Distributive Justice', *Ethics* 97 (1986), pp. 88–110, 'Public Ownership and Private Property Externalities', in Jon Elster and Karl Ove Moene (eds), *Alternatives to Capitalism* (Cambridge: Maison des Sciences de l'Homme and Cambridge University Press, 1989), and 'A Pragmatic Theory of Responsibility for the Egalitarian Planner', *Philosophy and Public Affairs* 22 (1993), pp. 146–66; Richard Arneson, 'Equality and Equal Opportunity for Welfare', *Philosophical Studies* 56 (1989), pp. 77–93, 'Liberalism, Distributive Subjectivism, and Equal Opportunity for Welfare', *Philosophy and Public Affairs* 19 (1990), pp. 158–94, and 'Lockean Self-Ownership: Towards a Demolition', *Political Studies* 39 (1991), pp. 36–54; Eric Rakowski, *Equal Justice* (Oxford: Clarendon Press, 1991); Will Kymlicka, *Contemporary Political Philosophy* (New York: Oxford University Press, 1990); Hal Varian, 'Distributive Justice, Welfare Economics, and the Theory of Fairness', *Philosophy and Public Affairs* 4 (1975), pp. 223–47; Marc Fleurbaey, 'L'absence d'envie dans une problematique "post-welfariste"', *Recherches Economiques de Louvain* 60 (1994), pp. 9–41, 'On Fair Compensation', *Theory and Decision* 36 (1994), pp. 277–307, 'The Requisites of Equal Opportunity', in W. A. Barnett, H. Moulin, M. Salles and W. Schofield (eds), *Advances in Social Choice Theory and Cooperative Games* (Cambridge: Cambridge University Press, 1995), pp. 37–53, and 'Equal Opportunity for Equal Social Outcome', *Economics and Philosophy* 11 (1995), pp. 25–55; Christian Arnesperger, 'Envy-Freeness and Distributive Justice', *Journal of Economic Surveys* 8 (1994), pp. 155–86.
3. Philippe Van Parijs, 'Equal Endowments as Undominated Diversity', *Recherches Econmiques de Louvain* 56 (1990), pp. 327–55, 'Why Surfers Should Be Fed: the Liberal Case for an Unconditional Basic Income', *Philosophy and Public Affairs* 20 (1991), pp. 101–31, and 'Competing Justifications of Basic Income', in Philippe Van Parijs (ed.), *Arguing for Basic Income* (New York: Verso, 1992), pp. 3–43.

4. See Derek Parfit, 'Equality or Priority', Lindley Lecture (Kansas: Department of Philosophy, University of Kansas, 1991), for the distinction and discussion of its significance.

5. Although the names and formulations of this and other displayed principles come from me, it is clear from the text that Van Parijs endorses them (or something close to them).

6. Strictly speaking, I reject egalitarian liberalism as formulated. For I hold that the demands of self-ownership and of equality do not impose constraints on what is just but, rather, determine a welfare baseline such that justice requires (1) that no one be worse off than on that baseline and (2) that welfare be promoted in a mutually beneficial manner from that baseline. Thus, violations of self-ownership and inequality are allowed, indeed required, when they benefit all in an appropriate manner relative to the welfare baseline. (I defend this view in my 'Rights-Based Paretianism', *Canadian Journal of Philosophy* 18 [1988], pp. 89–101.) So, strictly speaking, I endorse egalitarian liberalism as setting the welfare baselines, not as imposing any constraints. For simplicity, however, I shall ignore this point and write as if I endorse the principle as stated.

7. See John Christman, *The Myth of Property* (New York: Oxford University Press, 1994), for important and insightful discussion of the centrality of control self-ownership, as distinct from the ownership of the income that one generates in making choices. For discussions of the notion of ownership in general, and self-ownership in particular, see also Arneson 'Lockean Self-Ownership'; Anthony Fressola, 'Liberty and Property', *American Philosophical Quarterly* 18 (1981), pp. 315–22; Gerald Gauss, 'Property Rights and Freedom', in Ellen Paul, Fred Miller and Jeffrey Paul (eds), *Property Rights* (New York: Cambridge University Press, 1994), pp. 209–40; James Grunebaum, *Private Ownership* (New York: Routledge & Kegan Paul, 1987); Attracta Ingram, *A Political Theory of Rights* (Oxford: Oxford University Press, 1994); Eric Mack, 'Self-Ownership and the Right of Property', *Monist* 73 (1990), pp. 519–43; Stephen Munzer, *A Theory of Property* (Cambridge: Cambridge University Press, 1990); Frank Snare, 'The Concept of Property' *American Philosophical Quarterly* 9 (1972), pp. 200–6; Judith Jarvis Thompson, *The Realm of Rights* (Cambridge, MA.: Harvard University Press, 1990); and Jeremy Waldron, *The Right to Private Property* (Oxford: Clarendon Press, 1988).

8. This approach treats initial personal endowments as socially owned. Each person owes competitive rent on the personal resources that he or she is managing. Dworkin's extended auction (including the auction of talents) and income-fair approaches to allocation have this general form.

9. Thomas Paine, 'Agrarian Justice', *The Thomas Paine Reader*, (ed.) Michael Foot and Isaac Kramnick (1795; Harmondsworth: Penguin, 1987); Herbert Spencer, *Social Statics* (New York: Augustus M. Kelley, 1851); Henry George, *Progress and Poverty* (New York: Robert Schalkenbach Foundation, 1879), and *A Perplexed Philosopher* (New York: Robert Schalkenbach Foundation, 1892).

10. Note that sometimes initial endowments are understood to be the endowments at conception or birth, whereas I am understanding them to be at the beginning of full autonomy. Recall also, that we are assuming for simplicity that agents pop into existence with full psychological autonomy.

11. See Dworkin, 'What Is Equality? Part 1', and 'What Is Equality? Part 2'; Rakowski; Arthur Ripstein, 'Equality, Luck, and Responsibility', *Philosophy*

and Public Affairs 23 (1994), pp. 3–23; and Jules Coleman and Arthur Ripstein, 'Mischief and Misfortune', *McGill Law Journal* 41 (1996), pp. 61–130, for enlightening discussions of this issue.

12. Traditional libertarians include, of course, Robert Nozick, *Anarchy, State, and Utopia* (New York: Basic, 1974), and Jan Narveson, *The Libertarian Idea* (Philadelphia: Temple University Press, 1988). Roughly speaking, my approach is what is called 'left-libertarianism' which, with traditional libertarianism, endorses a strong conception of self-ownership but which has a more egalitarian conception of natural resources and perhaps gifts. The two most influential authors on left-libertariansim are Cohen (who rejects it) and Steiner (who develops and defends it).

13. Van Parijs has some very interesting discussion about an often ignored source of brute luck. Where, for a given good or service, the market price is greater than the price at which the market would clear (with demand equalling supply), the sellers of the good or service receive a clearance rent, understood as the income above that which they would receive at the clearance price. Van Parijs denies that agents are entitled to clearance rents, since this is a form of brute luck income. This view is far more plausible than the view, defended by David Gauthier in *Morals by Agreement* (London: Oxford University Press, 1986), that agents are not entitled to any producer surplus, understood roughly as anything beyond the minimum needed to induce them to sell their service or good (which is implausibly sensitive to the preferences of the agent). See Cohen, *Self-Ownership, Freedom, and Equality*; and Philippe Van Parijs, 'Free Riding versus Rent Sharing: Why Even David Gauthier Should Support a Basic Income', in F. Farina, F. Hahn and S. Vanucci (eds), *Ethics, Rationality, and Economic Behaviour* (Oxford: Clarendon Press, 1996), pp. 159–81, for superb analyses of this issue.

14. For an excellent discussion of Nozick's Wilt Chamberlain example and the issue of the ownership of good brute luck, see Barbara Fried, 'Wilt Chamberlain Revisited: Nozick's "Justice in Transfer" and the Problem of Market-Based Distribution', *Philosophy and Public Affairs* 24 (1995), pp. 226–45.

15. The distinction between the right to make gifts of donor-generated wealth and the right to make gifts drawn from brute luck income (at least if from previous gifts) has been made by Eugenio Rignano. *The Social Significance of the Inheritance Tax* (New York: Knopf, 1924) (see Ronald Chester, *Inheritance, Wealth, and Society* [Bloomington: Indiana University Press, 1982], for useful discussion of the Rignano plan); and by Robert Nozick, *The Examined Life* (New York: Simon & Schuster, 1989), ch. 3. See also the discussion of inheritance in D. W. Haslett, 'Is Inheritance Justified?' *Philosophy and Public Affairs* 15 (1988), pp. 122–55.

16. Steiner, *Essay on Rights* (and elsewhere), like George in *Progress and Poverty* and *Perplexed Philosopher*, argues that the social pot should be divided equally with no compensation made for bad brute luck, whereas I agree with Van Parijs that the social pot should be spent to promote equality. I've recently discovered that the view that the rents on natural resources should be used to promote equality has already been held by Peter Brown, 'Food as National Property', in Peter Brown and Henry Shue (eds), *Food Policy* (New York: Free Press, 1977), pp. 65–78; and Rolph Sartorius, 'Persons and Property?', in R. G. Frey (ed.), *Utility and Rights* (Minneapolis: University of Minnesota

Press, 1984), pp. 196–214. A very different, but loosely related approach, is defended in Baruch Brody, 'Redistribution without Egalitarianism', *Social Philosophy and Policy* 1 (1983), pp. 71–87. Some of my early thinking about compensation of disadvantages in initial endowments is in Peter Vallentyne and Morry Lipson, 'Equal Opportunity and the Family', *Public Affairs Quarterly* 3 (1989), pp. 29–47.

17. John Rawls, *A Theory of Justice* (Cambridge, MA.: Harvard University Press, 1971); Dworkin, 'What Is Equality? Part 2'.

18. The idea of appealing to universal dominance is a generalization of an idea (applied to genetic endowments) of Bruce Ackerman, *Social Justice in the Liberal State* (New Haven, CT: Yale University Press, 1980).

19. Benefits and burdens from choices might be factored out by focusing on initial endowments only and making some adjustment later for brute luck experienced. Exactly how this should be done, however, is not clear, and is an important problem. See Roemer, 'Pragmatic Theory of Responsibility for the Egalitarian Planner', for an important approach to this problem.

20. See Arneson, 'Equality and Equal Opportunity for Welfare' and 'Liberalism, Distributive Subjectivism, and Equal Opportunity for Welfare'; and Cohen, 'On the Currency of Egalitarian Justice', for a full statement and defense of this approach. Cohen defends an equal opportunity for advantage, where this is not understood solely in welfare terms.

21. See, e.g., Rakowski, for discussion of some of these issues.

22. Arneson in 'Equality and Equal Opportunity for Welfare' and 'Liberalism, Distributive Subjectivism, and Equal Opportunity for Welfare'; and Cohen in 'On the Currency of Egalitarian Justice' make this point. I address the problem of expensive tastes in the context of welfare from illegitimate sources (e.g., malice) in my 'The Problem of Unauthorized Welfare', *Nous* 25 (1991), pp. 295–321.

23. Van Parijs, in *Real Freedom for All*, recognizes the deep similarity between his approach and the equal opportunity for welfare approach on p. 81.

24. A natural supplement to the universal domination criterion of when one endowment is more valuable than another is, I would argue, the envy-free principle according to which all endowments of an endowment profile (one endowment for each person) are equally valuable if no one prefers someone else's endowment to his or her own.

25. See Dennis McKerlie, 'Egalitarianism', *Dialogue* 23 (1984), pp. 223–38; Parfit, 'Equality or Priority'; and Larry Temkin, *Inequality* (Oxford: Oxford University Press, 1993), for important discussions of related issues. For simplicity I have assumed that marginal benefits are fully interpersonally comparable. The ideas apply (although with less force) even if they are only partially comparable.

26. Paul Weirich, in 'Utility Tempered with Equality', *Nous* 17 (1983), pp. 423–39, advocates such an approach.

4
Real Freedom and Basic Income[1]

Brian Barry

4.1   Some difficulties in the measurement of real freedom

The full title of Philippe Van Parijs's book is *Real Freedom for All: What (if anything) can justify capitalism?* The themes announced in the title and subtitle are linked in the following way. What real freedom for all requires is the highest sustainable basic income. Because capitalism is more productive than socialism, it makes possible a higher sustainable basic income. On condition, therefore, that its productive energies are harnessed to the provision of the highest possible basic income, capitalism is justified.

The choice between economic systems plays a secondary role in Van Parijs's analysis, as it does in Rawls's theory of justice. For Rawls, economic systems are to be assessed primarily by their impact on the socio-economic prospects of the worst off; for Van Parijs, the criterion for judging between them is how high a basic income they can sustain. I shall therefore focus on the argument for this criterion, which is very simple. Van Parijs asserts that social justice requires the minimum level of real freedom to be as high as possible, and then claims that a society will satisfy this condition if it provides the highest sustainable level of basic income to its members. In short, social justice entails maximin real freedom, which requires maximum basic income.[2]

The key concept in Van Parijs's argument for basic income is 'real freedom'. What is real freedom? Your real freedom, according to Van Parijs, is the extent of your ability to do things you might want to do, regardless of whether or not (given your actual preferences) you would ever want to do any of them and regardless of the reason for your not being able to do them. This definition has some strange implications. I am not free (I lack the real freedom) to swim across a lake even if there is nobody and nothing to stop me except the fact that 'my lungs or my limbs would give in before reaching the other side' (RFA, 23). Indeed, 'even stating that I am not free to travel faster than light is only slightly odd, if at all' (RFA, 23). Other people's linguistic intuitions may well lead them to differ from Van Parijs on this: mine certainly do. However, I do not intend to engage with the literature on the definition of freedom. I am content to let Van Parijs appropriate the notion of 'real freedom' for his own purposes.

A natural interpretation of real freedom as 'the opportunity... to do whatever one might want to do' (RFA, 23) might be that you have real freedom to the extent that you are able to do the things you actually want to do and some other things besides. This would throw the focus on being able to do what you actually want to do. And why not? It has been said of Norman Douglas that he 'thought... that the chief business of life was to enjoy oneself, by which he meant to be able to do what one wants to do'.[3] Despite the fact that many of the things Norman Douglas wanted to do (and did) were illegal, immoral or fattening, the general idea seems to me hard to fault. The only reason for being concerned about being able to do things you do not want to do is that you might change your mind.[4] In contrast to this, Van Parijs's way of interpreting the definition implies that getting what you want has *no value at all*. It may on the face of it seem bizarre to build an entire social philosophy around a definition of freedom that has this implication. But Van Parijs constantly emphasizes that the definition of real freedom does not give any privileged status to the agent's actual wants as against wants that the agent might have had but does not in fact have. Any alternative to this, he says, would entail the introduction of irrelevant 'welfarist' considerations.[5]

Let me illustrate the way in which this indifference to actual wants works out. Suppose the thing I want at the moment is an ice cream and the only thing available is spinach, which I do not care for at the best of times and would especially not enjoy as a substitute for ice cream. I shall be told by Van Parijs that my real freedom in this situation is just as great as that of somebody who loves eating spinach at every opportunity. For I might have had the tastes of that person. Yet my disappointment at the unavailability of ice cream is surely not likely to be much assuaged by the thought that I might have been very pleased with spinach. Nor is it any consolation to be told that there exist people who are very pleased with spinach. What matters to me is that I am not of their number.

On the definition of real freedom given by Van Parijs, it necessarily follows that two people who face identical choice sets enjoy equal amounts of real freedom. The root idea is thus the same as that informing

Julian Le Grand's definition of equity as identical choice sets. However, Le Grand has recognized the difficulty that this conception of equity runs into (though I think he underestimates its intractability).

> Suppose, [he writes] there are two individuals, one of whom likes oranges but hates apples while the other detests oranges but is rather partial to the occasional apple. Each is given a bowl of fruit that, because of factors beyond either's control, contains the same number of apples, but no oranges. Both people have equal choices; but nevertheless the orange-lover might regard the outcomes as inequitable.[6]

Obviously, this could be so only in some sense of 'equity' that is not 'equal choice sets'.[7]

Having now explained what real freedom is, I want to devote the rest of this section to its measurement. In particular, I shall be concerned with two questions: (1) In a given situation, how do we establish who has the least real freedom? And (2) how can we establish which of two different situations has a lower minimum level of real freedom? I shall begin by assuming away the first problem. I shall stipulate that everybody in a given state of affairs faces the same choice set. Even then, as we shall see, it is often going to be impossible to say that everybody in one state of affairs has more or less real freedom than everybody in another.

It is instructive to compare the problem of commensurability in relation to real freedom with the problem of commensurability that is created by the criterion for a Pareto improvement. The Pareto criterion stipulates that one state of affairs x is better that another y if and only if at least one person prefers x to y and nobody prefers y to x. It is notorious that the Pareto criterion is extremely prone to generate the conclusion that x is not better than y, nor is y better than x, nor are they equally good. Rather, they are incommensurable. All we need for this to happen is that at least one person should prefer x to y and another person y to x.

Figure 4.1 illustrates this for a case with two goods I and II, amounts of which are represented on the vertical and horizontal axes respectively. The two situations x and y are defined by the two solid lines, which depict the budget constraints in the two situations. The slopes of the lines x and y give us the relative prices of good I and good II. If the society shifts from state x to state y, this means that good I becomes more expensive relatively to good II: more of good I has to be sacrificed to gain a given additional amount of II. The society consists of three people: A, B and C. A and B are fond of II, so they like the change from x to y since (as the arrows show) they can buy more of both I and II in y

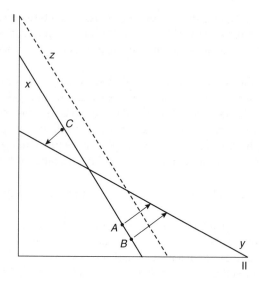

Figure 4.1   Incommensurability under the Pareto criterion

than they chose to buy (given their tastes) in *x*. C, however, is very keen
on good II, so he loses from the change from *x* to *y*. His most preferred
mix of the two goods in *x* and *y* (shown by the origin and terminus of the
arrow) has him consuming less of both I and II in *y*. The Pareto criterion
can deliver no verdict, therefore, on the relative merits of *x* and *y*.

Now suppose that C drops out of the society, leaving only A and B, or
that C is replaced by somebody else whose tastes are the same as those of
A or B. Then the Pareto criterion will tell us that *y* is better than *x*. What
this shows is that, where the budget constraints intersect, the Pareto criterion requires information about actual preferences in order to be
applied. This is another way of saying that it is 'welfarist'. Indeed, it was
put forward as an attenuated form of utilitarianism that did not require
interpersonal comparisons of utility, so its 'welfarist' roots are evident.

Now contrast real freedom with the Pareto criterion. The implication
of its not being 'welfarist' is that information about the actual preferences of the members of the society is irrelevant. What real freedom is
concerned about is the preferences they *might* have. Therefore, even if
everybody in the society actually had the preferences of A and B (or preferences in the neighbourhood of A and B), the sheer possibility that
there *might* be a C is enough to drive us to the conclusion that *x* and *y*
are incommensurate in terms of real freedom.

In general, then, changing prices will frustrate commensurability. So long as prices stay the same, however, there is no problem in comparing different budget constraints, since one will necessarily lie wholly outside the other. Thus, in Figure 4.1 the dashed line z shows a budget constraint that provides more real freedom than x: everyone has a higher income, in the only sense of 'higher income' that is completely unambiguous.[8] We may notice that z has this characteristic: it is Pareto-superior to x whatever the preferences of the people in the society may actually be. Thus, real freedom is, we may say, 'welfarist' at one remove: one situation contains more real freedom than another if and only if it would be Pareto superior under any distribution of preferences.

There is, I must now add, one respect in which Van Parijs has an advantage over Pareto. This arises not from the definition of real freedom itself but from the stipulation that we are interested, for the purpose of comparing alternative states of affairs, only in maximin real freedom. The Pareto criterion, in contrast, has to ask about each person's gains and losses. The 'welfarist' equivalent of maximin real freedom would be maximin utility. We would (assuming we knew how to do it) compare the utility of the worst-off person in x and the worst-off person in y and, regardless of the utilities of anybody else, pronounce the winner to be the state of affairs in which the worst-off person was better off.

Unfortunately, however, the criterion of maximin real freedom does not simplify comparison between different situations as much as (leaving aside the problem of measurement) would maximin utility. This is for two reasons. First, we shall generally find it impossible to discover who is the worst-off in terms of real freedom in a given situation. And second, even if we could do that for each of two different situations, we would still generally find it impossible to say that the person with the least real freedom in the one situation had more real freedom than the person with the least in the other. I have already demonstrated the second point, so I shall now take up the first.

I can illustrate it by reference to Figure 4.2, in which the lines in Figure 4.1 are relabelled. Instead of x and z representing everybody's budget constraint in one situation and everybody's budget constraint in another, let us now think of x and z as the budget constraints of two people in a given state of affairs. Say that x is D's budget constraint and z is E's budget constraint. D and E face the same prices, so the lines are parallel. We can therefore assert that E has more real freedom than D in this situation. We may imagine more lines out beyond E's budget constraint corresponding to yet higher incomes. If D's line is the one closest to the origin, he is the person with the least freedom in this situation. Now let us add

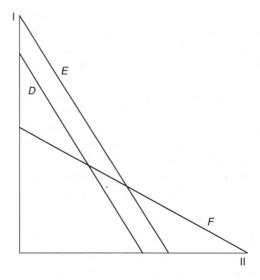

Figure 4.2   Incommensurability of real freedom

somebody, F, with a budget constraint corresponding to *y* in Figure 4.1. We can compare F's real freedom in this situation with that of anyone who has a budget constraint parallel to his. But because the budget constraints of D and F intersect, we cannot say that D has more real freedom than F or vice versa (or that they have the same amount).

I should emphasize that the talk here of 'budgets' and 'prices' can be treated figuratively. The general case is one of choice sets – whatever the elements in these choice sets may be. Stated in these terms, the conclusion is that, in our search for the person with the least real freedom, we can eliminate all those whose choice sets contain all the elements in somebody else's choice set and more. But when we have done that, we can go no further. All those who are left are candidates – not equal in real freedom but incommensurable.

Clearly, the first and second problems of measurement work together to make it unlikely that we shall be able to say that a change from one state of affairs to another increases or decreases minimum real freedom, barring some sort of catastrophic decline or almost miraculous improvement, between the two situations.

4.2   Real freedom as real income

Van Parijs offers a solution to the problem of incommensurability that solves it for the case in which what has to be compared is the set of commodities available to people in two different situations. It does not – or so I shall argue in the next section – get anywhere with heterogeneous choice sets, such as those (crucial to comparing a basic income regime with alternatives) in which there are intersecting sets containing leisure as well as goods. But it would, given the gloomy conclusion of the previous section, be quite a triumph to ensure the commensurability of all situations in which different baskets of goods are available. The proposed solution is therefore worth attention in its own right. In the course of discussing it I hope to shed some new light on the much-controverted question of 'the currency of egalitarian justice'.

According to Van Parijs, then, if we hold other things (for example, leisure) constant, real freedom increases monotonically with real income. This is, of course, a conclusion that I have already reached, but only on a criterion of increased real income that excludes intersecting budget constraints. Yet this, as we have seen, offers a very weak basis for comparison. Van Parijs cuts the Gordian knot by stipulating that real income can be compared across price changes so long as prices reflect the opportunity cost to society of the goods. There is, in any given situation, in principle only one correct set of prices: the one that reflects relative scarcity in the case of goods whose supply is fixed (for example, plots with access to the seashore) or cost of production in the case of others. So long as the prices in situation x and the prices in situation y are market equilibria, we can compare them for real income and hence real freedom.

Treating income at market prices as a true measure of real freedom is a heroic solution to the problem of the incommensurability of choice sets. But I want to argue that it cannot plausibly do the job assigned to it. This is not to say that income at market prices might not be a measure of fair distribution, on some reasonable view of what fair distribution requires. Indeed, I shall argue later in this section that there is a plausible notion of fairness from which this follows. But it is not a view that articulates with Van Parijs's notion of real freedom.

I contend that Van Parijs's solution fails in its own terms. For, as soon as we depart from the conception of real income that I set out towards the end of section 4.1, we cannot avoid introducing a 'welfarist' conception that violates the whole idea of real freedom as defined by Van Parijs. We can see the problem by asking precisely how the real income in one situation is to be compared with that in another. Suppose that the basic income is fifty pounds per week in situation x and one hundred pounds per week in situation y. Has real income represented by the basic income gone up or down? The criterion for a change in real income that I put forward earlier required non-intersecting budget constraints. So long as relative prices remain the same, this condition will be met. Thus, let us suppose that the doubling of money incomes has been associated with a more than twofold increase in prices across the board. Then we can say that real income has decreased, because the new budget constraint lies wholly within the old one. But what if relative prices have changed? How do we reduce these changes to a single index number for overall change in prices so as to establish how real income has changed?

As is well known, the method used by economists is to consider a certain 'basket' of goods and ask how much it would cost to buy it in situation x and situation y. If it costs twice as much money to buy this basket in situation y as in situation x, the price level is said to have doubled, and so on. There are, unfortunately, serious difficulties of a logical nature in constructing an index number in this way. For we want our 'basket' to be composed in a way that is representative of average purchases. But we must anticipate that the quantities of the commodities that people buy will change as the prices change: normally, they will buy more of what costs relatively less and less of what costs relatively more. How, then, are we to choose the basket of goods the cost of which is to be compared in the two situations? Taking a representative basket reflecting the pattern of purchases with the earlier prices seems as arbitrary as taking a representative basket reflecting the pattern of purchases with the later ones; yet attempts to combine them generate contradictions.

These logical problems do not, of course, prevent price indices from being constructed; and we might swallow our doubts if real income measured in the way I have described could properly be regarded as a proxy for real freedom. But it cannot. For it is too 'welfarist' to constitute a measure of changes in real freedom. What it tells us about is the fate in the two situations of somebody who buys a certain basket of goods in both. Real freedom, however, turns on what people *might* want to do; and it is obvious that people might (and, indeed, almost certainly will) want to buy goods in different proportions from those represented by the standard basket. Suppose, for example, that all prices rise but the price of necessities rises faster than that of luxuries. Suppose, also, that everybody's money income increases by the same amount. Applying a standard deflator to money incomes in the second situation, it may be that 'the real income of the society' has increased. But this means only that somebody who buys a basket of goods representative of the pattern of purchases in the society as a whole has gained. It is quite consistent with this that poor people (who spend a larger proportion of their incomes on necessities) have lost.

Economists could respond to this (and they do) by suggesting that a separate index of prices should be constructed for the poor using a representative basket of goods purchased by them. For Van Parijs's purposes, however, this is at once to go too far and not far enough. It goes too far to suit his official theory that everyone must be assumed to face the same set of prices. But it does not go far enough to produce a measure enabling us to compare the minimum level of real freedom in the two situations. For one of the poorest people in the first situation might have even more unfortunate tastes than the average poor person, buying almost exclusively those goods whose prices have gone up the most. Only if there is no conceivable pattern of expenditure such that the person with the smallest income in the first situation could not buy more in the second situation can we say that minimum real freedom has increased.

The underlying problem is that the rationale for taking the stuff of justice to be real income (measured in this way) is completely alien to that which gives rise to a concern for real freedom. We can best see this by taking a look at the best-known argument for taking the currency of egalitarian justice to be resources: this entails treating real income at ideal market prices as the appropriate measure of material resources. The argument is the one put forward by Ronald Dworkin in 'What Is Equality?'[9] I believe, at any rate, that the argument I shall present is in essence Dworkin's. But if I depart from it, let it be understood to be my argument.

We start, then, from the historic liberal position with respect to rights. This is that a fair distribution of rights cannot be challenged on the ground that it bears more hardly on some than others. For the rationale of a just system of rights makes no reference to any resultant distribution of satisfaction with it. Thus, let us take the paradigmatically liberal claim that rights with respect to religion are fairly distributed if each person can worship unimpeded in accordance with his own beliefs. Clearly, this suits very well those whose beliefs commit them anyway to religious tolerance, whereas it inhibits the pursuit of religiously-derived ends on the part of those who believe that a certain orthodoxy should be imposed on everybody. But this cannot be deployed by the latter as a ground for claiming unfair treatment.

Rights (like other resources, such as income) are, of course, important for what they let people do: if people did not want to exercise them, there would be no point in having them. But the fairness of the set of rights is to be established independently of any consideration of the pattern of want-satisfaction to which it is liable to give rise. Thus, suppose we say that equal freedom to worship is an intrinsically fair way of distributing religious rights, because it in some sense treats everybody equally. There is no suggestion that this kind of equal treatment is intended to generate equality of welfare (that is, want-satisfaction). It cannot therefore be a valid objection that it fails to do so, except in the obvious sense that one might propose equality of welfare as an alternative criterion of equal treatment and hence (at any rate in this kind of situation) fairness. The crucial point is that there is no problem for the 'equal rights' criterion *in its own terms* if it has a different impact on different people (or groups) according to their beliefs, tastes or aspirations.

In terms of the now customary vocabulary, we might say that those who wish to suppress the freedom of others to worship have an 'expensive taste'. It is expensive in the sense that they could be satisfied as well as others only if they were given an unfair share in respect of rights to worship. The same analysis can be applied to ordinary legislation that establishes the relative rights of (say) racists, rapists, paedophiles and their respective victims. Assuming the law gives an absolute priority to the interests of the potential victims, this will cause great frustration among those who are strongly attached to racial abuse and discrimination, rape or paedophilia as a way of life. Yet they have no claim to either a modification of the law better to accommodate their desires nor to compensation for the frustration it causes them. They may, indeed, have a reasonable claim to free medical treatment if they sincerely wish to extinguish their antisocial desires – but that is a quite different matter.

Racists, rapists and paedophiles have an expensive taste, in that a fair share of rights fails to satisfy desires important to them. For (I am assuming) a fair distribution of rights is one that gives everyone freedom from their attentions. In the present context, there is no need to press the question further back and ask why this is a fair distribution. The point is simply that, if we say that it is fair for such people not to be accommodated or compensated, we are not saying that the law that makes them suffer produces a fair distribution of welfare (in the sense of want-satisfaction). For the rationale of the law does not mention any resultant distribution of welfare.

Thus, for example, we are not obliged in order to justify the outcome to say that racists, rapists and paedophiles could change their beliefs and desires if they chose to. Perhaps they could not. This does not affect the case for saying that the law making the exercise of their proclivities a criminal offence assigns rights fairly as it stands, and for denying that it needs to be either modified or accompanied by compensation. We might say: it is a fundamental liberal principle that nobody can offer difficulty in compliance as a valid ground for complaint against a law that can be shown on independent grounds to be just. This principle is not derived as a theorem from some other distributive principle, except perhaps some general characterization of justice. That is what is meant by calling it a fundamental principle.

The same line of thought can be extended to economic resources. Suppose we have determined that a fair share of resources is one that gives everyone an equal real income, calculated in prices that reflect the opportunity cost to the society of each good. Then nobody can say that this distribution of resources is unfair on the ground that he requires more income than most to achieve an equivalent standard of satisfaction. This statement will require some qualification in section 4.4 to deal with special needs. But the point here is that an expensive taste – an inability to enjoy cheap wine, for example – does not count as a valid reason for demanding more as a matter of fairness.

It is easy to see why Van Parijs regards Dworkin as an ally, since both are committed anti-welfarists. This congruence of view is, however, somewhat misleading. For the form taken by their anti-welfarism is quite different. Van Parijs, as we have seen, is still concerned with want-satisfaction; what makes him anti-welfarist is simply that his interest lies in potential want-satisfaction as against actual want-satisfaction. What matters is the range of things people *might* do if they had preferences that led them in this direction or that. Thus, 'giving more resources to those with expensive tastes... depresses the real freedom of those with cheaper tastes to do whatever they might want to do' (RFA, 70).

The sense in which Van Parijs is a crypto-welfarist is dramatically demonstrated by his assumption that some reason has to be given for saying that it is fair to take account of what people *might* want and not at all of what they *do* want. This reason is provided by 'the principle that people should be held responsible for their preferences' (RFA, 71). This means that, if you have an expensive taste, you cannot complain about getting less satisfaction than others from a given allocation, because your tastes are your responsibility. Clearly, the principle enunciated here is a highly disputable one, and we might reasonably expect a good deal more explication than we get – which is scarcely any at all. What does the claim about responsibility amount to? Is it a (remarkably implausible) empirical claim about the ability of people to shape their tastes, aspirations, religious beliefs (and so on) at will? (But then it would be odd to call it a principle.) Alternatively, it could be construed as a metaphysical claim. But is it then any more than a restatement in fancy form of the conclusion it is supposed to underwrite: that allocations otherwise adjudged fair cannot be challenged by those with expensive tastes? There is no need to settle that here. The point is that Van Parijs thinks that some such premise is required.

It has been argued that Dworkin must implicitly be basing his case on exactly the same premise as the one stated explicitly by Van Parijs. Thus, G. A. Cohen has suggested that Dworkin's division between compensable and noncompensable disadvantage comes in the wrong place.[10] According to him, Dworkin gets the right answer in relation to expensive tastes for which people can properly be held responsible; but he should accept that expensive tastes for which they cannot be held responsible are in principle a valid basis for a claim to a greater share of resources. As Cohen concedes, it would be impossible to devise feasible public policies that could be counted on to make the right discriminations, so acceptance of the principle would have little practical effect. But why should we accept the principle?

Cohen seems unable to conceive that Dworkin could really have meant what he said: that a fair share of resources is a fair share of resources (measured in social opportunity costs) and that is all there is about it. Cohen's criterion for an equal distribution is (in the respects that concern us here) the same as that proposed by Richard Arneson: equal opportunity for welfare.[11] And this is also the underlying criterion of Van Parijs. The differences in their conclusions stem from different ideas about what we may legitimately say constitutes an opportunity to extract utility from an element in the choice set.

The significance of Van Parijs's stipulation that people are fully responsible for their desires is that people can be said to have an opportunity to derive utility from all the elements in their choice sets. If there is anybody who can enjoy spinach then it is axiomatic that everybody can. If in spite of this it turns out that somebody cannot, all we can say is that it is his fault or at any rate his responsibility – if that means something different in this context.

The opposite extreme is to say that people are not responsible for their desires at all. This is compatible with holding them responsible for their actions, so long as we do not assume that people are blind utility-maximizing machines. But it does mean that if they gain little satisfaction from the most attractive element in their choice set, we have to say that this is bad luck. We cannot say that they are responsible for not having desires better articulated with what is available, for they have no responsibility for their desires. The implication of this view is that the criterion of equal opportunity for welfare reduces to the criterion of equal welfare. For we are now in effect supposing that people have an opportunity to enjoy only what they actually do enjoy.

Finally, there are intermediate positions, represented by Arneson and Cohen. According to these, not all elements of a person's choice set are accessible in a form that constitutes an opportunity for that person. Clearly, this is different from the line taken by Van Parijs. But it does not deny that people can be held responsible for some of their desires. The implication is that some expensive tastes do not reduce opportunity for welfare even though (given that the person actually has them) they reduce actual welfare. Thus, equal opportunity for welfare does not reduce to equal welfare, as it would if people were held responsible for none of their desires.

I hope that this illustrates the point that Van Parijs's conception of real freedom belongs to a family of ideas about 'the currency of egalitarian justice' that is (we might say) welfarist at one remove – and indeed reduces to straight welfarism on a certain assumption about responsibility. I hope I have also shown that the whole approach is entirely alien to that followed by Dworkin (as represented by me, anyway) in his proposal that the relevant currency is resources measured in social opportunity costs. It therefore follows, I believe, that Van Parijs cannot appropriate Dworkin's conclusion and claim it as the implication of his own conception of real freedom. To put the contrast in a nutshell: Dworkin's is a supply-side conception whereas Van Parijs's is one of a family of demand-side conceptions.

There is some textual evidence to suggest that Van Parijs himself is uneasily aware of the lack of congruence between his measure of real income (as he defines real income) and his conception of real freedom. For in the section of his book that announces the solution to the problem of incommensurability, he says that this provides for 'a *fair* distribution of external-resource-based real freedom' (RFA, 51, my emphasis). As I have suggested, a good case can be made for saying this. But the conception of fairness to which it appeals is one foreign to the logic of Van Parijs's 'real freedom'.

4.3   From real freedom to basic income

Let us, for the sake of argument, accept the claim that the equation of real income at market prices with real freedom solves the indeterminacy problem in a fair way. We can then move on to examine Van Parijs's case for the proposition that maximin real freedom requires the maximum sustainable basic income. The intuition underlying this is, contrary to his official theory, a 'welfarist' one. For it involves a comparison between the situations of actual people distinguished from one another solely by their having different structures of preference. (See especially RFA, 92–8.) The way this goes is that those with a weak taste for money and a strong taste for leisure are discriminated against by any scheme of contingent benefits in comparison with those who have a strong taste for income and are prepared to work to get it.

At this stage of his discussion, Van Parijs is assuming that everyone is equally talented, which implies that everybody has the same ability to transform leisure into income. (I shall take up the case of differentiated talents in the next section; but, as we shall see there, Van Parijs claims that it does not materially affect the conclusions already reached.) If all the members of a society are equally talented and are subject to the same rules, it follows that they all have the same amount of real freedom in any given situation. For they all face the same choice set with respect to income and leisure. Thus, what we have to compare is not the real freedom of different people in the same situation but the real freedom of everybody in different situations. Let us reconstruct the argument for basic income in these terms.

We can follow Van Parijs in reducing the different types of people in our model society to two. There are those with a relatively strong taste for leisure as against income (Van Parijs calls them 'Lazies') and those who value leisure relatively little in relation to income (Van Parijs even-handedly calls them 'Crazies'). The invalid (because 'welfarist') move would be to say that a system of contingent benefits is hard on Lazies because it denies them the possibility of the life of leisure they would like and could achieve with a basic income scheme. What we have to say is, rather, that somebody (anybody) might be a Lazy, and would then be frustrated by the unavailability of an unconditional income. We can then conclude that the lack of this possibility reduces real freedom for everybody, Lazies and Crazies alike, since anybody might have Lazy preferences. This is how the argument for basic income must be formulated to conform with Van Parijs's definition of real freedom in terms of the preferences people might have, and not in terms of the preferences that they actually do have.

It may have occurred to an acute reader that there is a certain difficulty in reconciling any such line of argument with the idea that Van Parijs relied on to underwrite the desired conclusion in the previous section: the idea that people are totally responsible for their preferences. If we can tell people with expensive tastes that they might have had cheap tastes, and we regard that as a sufficient reason for denying them additional resources, why cannot we tell Lazies that they might have been Crazies, and that that is a sufficient reason for not caring whether or not they can satisfy their taste for leisure? Why cannot we say that leisure is an expensive taste?

I do not have a good answer to this question. But what is clear to me is that carrying through the notion of responsibility for preferences in the way implied by that move would undermine the whole concept of real freedom. It is perfectly coherent to define 'real freedom' in terms of the extent of choice sets. It will then of course follow that real freedom has nothing to do with 'welfare' (that is, utility), since two people faced with the same choice sets may derive very different amounts of utility from them depending on their tastes. We can if we like say with Van Parijs that real freedom so defined is a matter of 'the opportunity... to do whatever one might want to do' (RFA, 23). But this does not have to be understood as conveying any suggestion that preferences are malleable: as far as that definition goes, it is consistent with the view that they are completely fixed. We can construe it simply as a (potentially misleading) way of talking about choice sets. It will then follow straightforwardly enough that adding elements to the choice set increases real freedom because it increases the opportunities to do things one might want to do.

It is the further premise that people are wholly responsible for their preferences that causes the trouble. This avoids the objection (if it is an objection) that the same choice set may have a very different value for different people because of their different tastes. For it tells us that their different tastes are of no ethical significance: they are the personal responsibility of the people concerned. Hence, every choice set necessarily holds the same opportunity for welfare for everybody, not merely in the sense that everybody *might* have had the same preferences but in the far stronger sense that everybody *could* have had the same preferences. But the price paid for this new premise is not only its gross implausibility but its undermining the connection between real freedom and the size of the choice set. For it is anybody's guess whether or not adding an element to the choice set will increase the opportunity for welfare. It would seem to depend on whether or not the utility of somebody with the best-adapted preferences would go up.

Fairly clearly, what Van Parijs needs to be able to say, if he is to rescue the connection between the extent of real freedom and the range of choice, is that a situation in which only spinach is available is one in which there is not much real freedom and that the addition of ice cream makes for a significant increase in the amount of real freedom. The rationale, stated in terms of opportunities to get what one might want, should surely be as follows. While it is true that the ice-cream-lover might have craved spinach, it is equally true that the spinach-lover might have hated it. This permits the conclusion that both of them have their real freedom enhanced by the addition of ice cream to the menu. For both, the reasoning goes, might have had pro-ice-cream tastes, and then the availability of ice cream would have enabled them to do something they wanted to do. Thus, in assessing the amount of real freedom in some state of affairs, we have to take account of all the preferences that people might have, including preferences that mesh poorly with the choices that are actually on offer.

This is manifestly a more sensible way of talking about real freedom than the alternative one that counts only the maximum possible welfare achievable in the situation, and it is the one that I shall rely on in this section. The point of the excursus has been simply to ask how this interpretation of real freedom can be reconciled with the way in which the axiom of personal responsibility is used by Van Parijs to shoot down claims for extra resources based on expensive tastes. And my conclusion is that there is an unresolved tension between them. This problem will return to haunt us in the next section, where Van Parijs deploys the idea of responsibility for tastes in an especially counter-intuitive way.

With that by way of prologue, let me now return to the argument that maximin real freedom requires basic income at the highest sustainable level. I can show what is wrong with it fairly easily. For the argument has to be that basic income adds an option, enabling those who place a high value on leisure to get what they want. The counter-argument is that, while this is so, we cannot say that it constitutes an unambiguous increase in real freedom because that is not the only change that occurs in a move to basic income from a regime of conditional benefits. It may be that those who continue to work the same amount will finish up with less income, or (to put it another way round) those who want to achieve a certain net income have to work harder to get it. There are thus liable to be gainers and losers, which makes the comparison of the two kinds of regime indeterminate.

We can truly say that an unconditional basic income provides combinations of income and leisure that would be unobtainable if benefits for able-bodied adults were conditional on willingness to work. But it is equally true that the taxation required to pay for the basic income is virtually certain to foreclose other combinations of income and leisure obtainable under a system in which benefits are conditional on willingness to work. Anybody who chooses to work a lot will almost certainly find that the net income derived from a given effort will be less. Thus some gain and some lose, according to their relative tastes for income

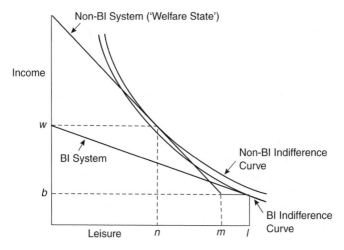

Figure 4.3　The 'Welfare State' and Basic Income compared

and leisure. The implication is therefore that we cannot say that one situation has more real freedom in it than the other. The point is in essence the one made in section 4.1: with two independent goods, we cannot say that real freedom has increased unless the new choice set includes all the elements in the old one and more besides.

Van Parijs seems to assume that anybody who would choose to live on a basic income must prefer that to having to work. But Figure 4.3 shows that this need not be so.[12] Here we can see the choice facing someone with a given earning capacity under two regimes. One is a conventional welfare state and the other a system with a basic income. Both establish a minimum income *b*, but in the first case this is conditional upon willingness to work while in the second case it is unconditional. The welfare state withdraws its benefits on a pound-for-pound basis until earnings reach the amount *b*. The implication is that working an amount of time (*l–m*) does not increase final income, and that it is better to be unemployed than earn less than *b*. Under the basic income regime, all earnings increase final income above the amount *b*, thus avoiding the 'poverty trap' characteristic of welfare states. However, the tax rate required to pay for the basic income is assumed to be higher than that required to finance the welfare state. Hence, the slope representing post-tax income is less steep in the basic income regime than in the welfare state regime, since giving up an hour of leisure produces more final income in the latter than the former. As well as showing the income–leisure trade-off for our representative individual, Figure 4.3 also shows indifference curves for various combinations of income and leisure.

In each situation, we suppose that the chosen combination of work and leisure is the one that gets our individual on to the highest attainable indifference curve. It will be seen that in the welfare state regime this person chooses to work an amount $(l–n)$ and finish up with a post-tax income w, whereas in the basic income regime he cannot do better than do no work and live on the basic income. It may be seen, however, that the first combination of income and leisure puts this person on a higher indifference curve than the second. Thus, resistance to basic income may come not only from people who object to others living off their labours but also from people who are living on the basic income yet would prefer to be in a situation in which work was a more attractive alternative to leisure.

None of this shows, I hasten to add, that basic income is not a good idea. I have argued on pragmatic grounds that there is indeed a great deal to be said for it. But if my argument here is correct, it cannot be justified on the ground that it brings about maximin real freedom. The concept of real freedom is too weak to do what is required to make the relevant comparisons. But even if the case could be made, why should we accept that maximin real freedom is what is required by social justice? Van Parijs tells us that a 'free society' is one that has maximin real freedom (RFA, 25).[13] He also asserts that 'a just society [is] a free society in this sense' (RFA, 27). Putting these two together gives us the conclusion that 'real freedom-for-all [that is, maximin real freedom] is all there is to social justice' (RFA, 5). But what is justice? Van Parijs does not tell us. Instead he immediately moves on to a brief discussion of the extent to which justice has priority over other values. The answer given is that it has 'soft lexicographic priority', which means that it should normally prevail over competing values but allows for the possibility that at the margin some other value (for example, fraternity) might modify the wholehogging pursuit of justice. (However, Van Parijs offers the view that it is not likely that justice will actually conflict with other important values.)

But what – to repeat – is justice? I suppose Van Parijs might intend us to understand him as simply identifying 'justice' with 'the most important value' – whatever that might be. In this case saying that justice is realized by maximin real freedom would simply be saying that maximin real freedom is the most important value. But we would still need a supporting argument for that proposition. The only possible alternative requires 'justice' to have some independently definable content in virtue of which it can be seen to be the most important value. Once the meaning of 'justice' has been specified, we need some chain of argument leading to the conclusion that maximin real freedom is the best realization of justice. Since we are offered none of this, I have to say that we lack any reason for accepting that maximin real freedom 'is all there is to social justice'.

I am inclined to think that the closest we ever get to some general principle making a connection between maximin real freedom and justice is a sentence towards the end of the book (RFA, 232) which talks about equal respect for people's conceptions of the good life and equal respect for their interests. This firmly places Van Parijs on what Will Kymlicka has called the 'egalitarian plateau'.[14] But there are, notoriously, many paths on this plateau, leading to different destinations. It is true that Van Parijs locates himself in the region where rights and resources are not differentially allocated on the basis of some view of the desirability of the way of life they will be used to pursue ('neutrality'). But I think that he greatly overestimates the extent to which this narrows down the possibilities. In particular, he frequently suggests that anybody who objects to the voluntarily idle getting an income must be motivated by disapproval of idleness as a way of life. But this is not so.

Opportunities may legitimately be limited not on the ground that their exercise is intrinsically undesirable but on the ground that their exercise would place an unfair burden on others. Thus, smoking may be prohibited in public places not on the basis of any belief in the moral turpitude of smokers (which would just as well be a basis for prohibiting it in private) but simply on the ground that the conflict of interest between those who want to smoke and those who want to breathe smoke-free air should, as a matter of fairness, be resolved in favour of the latter. Similarly, it might be claimed that the voluntarily idle represent an unfair burden on the productive members of the society. There is no need to bring in any notion of the intrinsic undesirability of idleness.

It would indeed be quite possible to regard a life of leisure as intrinsically admirable, but nevertheless hold that an arrangement permitting it to anybody who chose it would be unfair to those whose work sustained it. This shows clearly that opposition to basic income (and maximin real freedom as a criterion of social justice in as far as it implies basic income) does not have to rest on any disparagement of a life of leisure, considered in itself. It may be regarded as a genuine good, but one that should have to be earned rather than offered unconditionally.

4.4   Some further problems with real freedom

Van Parijs devotes a good deal of space to the rebuttal of claims that it is unfair to provide everyone with a uniform unconditional income. We might think of this as an indirect way of arguing for basic income as what justice demands. But it seems to me that this is liable to be question-begging. Thus, Van Parijs notes that a possible objection to a uniform basic income is that it is hard on people who have grown up in the capital, and have friends and relatives there, if the basic income is not enough to live on in the capital though it would be enough to live on in other parts of the country. Van Parijs does not deny that the objection is valid, in the sense that this really does constitute a hardship for some people. He simply says that it is a 'welfarist' objection, and that maximin real freedom (which takes account of what people might want to do and not what they actually want to do) requires a uniform rate of basic income, without any variation to take account of the expense of living in different parts of the country.

The snag with this response is that anybody with a tendency to be moved by the objection in the first place will presumably be sympathetic to 'welfarism' to that extent, and will therefore be inclined to regard the demonstration of the implications of maximin real freedom as providing a good reason for not embracing it as the criterion of social justice. What is needed here to convince the objector is not a mere reiteration of the move from premise to conclusion but an argument designed to persuade someone prone to 'welfarist' thoughts to abandon them. This Van Parijs does not provide, and I am not at all sure that a general argument of the required kind could be given. This scepticism reflects my view that there is no single 'currency of egalitarian justice'.

In this section, I shall look at Van Parijs's replies to two objections to basic income: that it does not take account of special needs and that it does not build in compensation for those with limited talents. I shall argue that Van Parijs's responses to these objections are of the same potentially counter-productive nature as his peremptory dismissal of the 'welfarist' objection to a uniform level of basic income in all parts of the country. That is to say: Van Parijs's demonstration that maximin real freedom gives short shrift to the needy and the untalented is liable to lead those concerned for their welfare to reject it as a criterion of justice. Worse, it seems to me that Van Parijs's way of manipulating the concept of real freedom in order to arrive at his results suggests that it is too arbitrary to be of any ethical value.

Van Parijs makes the criterion of justice the maximization of the smallest amount of real freedom that anybody has. And the measure of real freedom is the ability to do things you might want to do, whether you actually want to do them or not. Now it might seem obvious that (other things being equal) people who are blind, deaf or unable to walk must have less real freedom than other people to the extent that their disability prevents them from being able to do many things that others are able to do. Whether or not a certain disabled person actually wants to play tennis, paint pictures, or listen to music, the relevant point is that he might want to. Maximizing the minimum level of real freedom would thus seem to require compensation for disabilities on a very large scale indeed, since even the sedentary person who loses a toe might have a keen interest in tennis, and should be compensated as if he had. (We cannot, of course, confine the compensation to the actual tennis players, because that would be 'welfarist'.)

Such a basis for compensation might reasonably be regarded as excessively generous. But Van Parijs's proposed alternative is quite extraordinarily parsimonious. According to him, no compensation should be due for a disability if it is possible that the person suffering from it would not have minded having it. Thus, people who lose their sight normally experience this as resulting in a major reduction in their ability to do things they want to do. But it is conceivable that they might have had the preferences of Brentano, who is reputed to have said that he was grateful for the blindness that afflicted him late in his life because it enabled him to concentrate more effectively on his philosophical thinking. On the basis of this possibility, then, it would seem that we can deny any claims by blind people for special treatment.

I should add that Van Parijs hedges this stark position a bit, though I find it hard to decide quite how he thinks the concessions are supposed to be implemented. Thus, having told us that claims of special need are negated if we can find somebody who takes a positive view of the disability, he adds the proviso that the view must be 'available', which he glosses as follows: 'people could feasibly adopt [it] – and hence could fairly be held responsible for failing to adopt [it]' (RFA, 80). Later on the same page, he substitutes 'accessible' for 'available' and says that accessible preferences are those that one has the capacity though not the desire to acquire. But this proviso does not render the move acceptable.

The root objection is that it is unreasonable and unfair to make state provision for special needs depend on the (actual or possible) views of people with idiosyncratic preferences. It should be related to what the great majority of people want, and that includes enjoying the faculties of sight, hearing and physical mobility. Whether or not people exist, or could exist, who would not regret the loss of these faculties should be regarded as completely irrelevant. Adding the proviso that such peculiar preferences should be ones that a person has the capacity to acquire, even if this is not accompanied by any desire to acquire them, does not get round the underlying objection. What people have a reasonable claim on their fellow citizens for is the means to live a normal life, to the extent that that is achievable. It is not acceptable to say that they should be denied these means if they have the capacity to adapt so as to value an abnormal life.

What emerges from this is that any discussion of special needs has an ineliminable reference to a normal level of activity. This level is subject to some sort of collective determination and may be expected to vary, within certain limits, from one society to another. Thus, in any society there are certain key activities that should be open to physically disabled people, and it is the responsibility of public authorities to ensure, by regulation and where appropriate by financing the required works, that buildings are suitable to provide the disabled with access. Obvious examples in contemporary society are places of work, worship and entertainment, shops, museums and art galleries, and educational institutions of all kinds. At the same time, there has to be a societal standard that sets limits to what somebody with physical disabilities can demand of fellow citizens in the way of assistance. Thus, it seems to me reasonable to suggest that, even if it would be possible with enough high-tech equipment and logistical support for somebody who lacks the use of arms or legs to go hang-gliding or rock-climbing, there would be no valid claim on the other members of the society to finance it.

The upshot of this discussion is, I suggest, that the concept of real freedom has nothing useful to contribute to the analysis of special needs. It is bad enough that it appears equally plausibly to be open to two opposite interpretations with violently opposed implications. What is worse is that on neither interpretation do we get a remotely plausible basis for a public policy on special needs. To compensate everyone who loses a big toe at a rate that would make a tennis fanatic indifferent between having the injury and not having it would be much too expansive. But Van Parijs's alternative, to compensate people only at a rate that would be adequate for people with the most limited aspirations for the use of their faculties, is equally absurd in its stinginess.

We must conclude that an element of collective judgement is inherent in any sensible policy on compensation for special needs. What we have to have is a norm that defines the kinds of activity that should as far as possible be open to everybody. Whether or not tastes are 'expensive' is not something inherent in them: it depends on whether they fall within the norm or lie outside its scope.

Until now the whole discussion has been premised on the assumption that all the members of the society under consideration have identical developed talents, which of course implies that they have identical earning capacities. Hence they have identical choice sets with regard to income and leisure.

As soon as we allow for the fact of differential earning capacity, all this changes because the choice sets of some people will be subsets of the choice sets of other people. Somebody with a capacity for earning £20 per hour can achieve combinations of income and leisure that are unattainable by somebody who is capable of earning only £10 per hour. This is true whether a basic income is in place or not, and regardless of the structure of income tax, so long as the marginal rate is less than 100 per cent.

As in the case of special needs, there are two ways of putting the concept of real freedom to work. In contrast with the case of special needs, however, one of these seems to me quite attractive theoretically, though of only limited practical applicability. Unfortunately, however, Van Parijs opts for the other one, which seems to me not in the least plausible, and in fact highly obnoxious. The approach that Van Parijs rejects would require lump-sum taxation of earning capacity. Under this arrangement, those with the most earning capacity pay the most tax, and are then constrained to work in the lucrative jobs that they are (*ex hypothesi*) capable of doing. More precisely, that is what they have to do if they want to have an average income after paying the lump-sum tax. Within this approach, somebody who dislikes doing a lucrative job and prefers doing a less-well-paid one may be regarded as having an 'expensive taste'. Such a person is faced with a choice between the combination of a lucrative but distasteful job plus an average income and the alternative combination of a more agreeable but less-well-paid job plus a below-average income.

It is worth noting that in any society talented people may face exactly the same trade-off between income and job-satisfaction. Academics (in Britain, anyway) are clearly people who have opted for a job they like rather than incomes that many of their less-able students are making within a few years of graduation. The only difference in the scenario is that, because there is currently no lump-sum tax on ability, even academics still attain incomes above the average for their society as a whole. They thus face a more benign trade-off than they would under a regime of lump-sum ability taxes. But it remains true that they have an 'expensive taste' in comparison with similarly qualified people who find equal job satisfaction in better-paid occupations.

I do not see any objection of deep principle to the lump-sum tax proposal. Despite this, virtually everybody who has discussed it has dismissed it not for practical reasons (which are strong) but on the ground that it is unfair to the talented. It is said that, under the lump-sum tax proposal, talented people would have to do jobs they dislike in order to attain average post-tax incomes. But so what? Under the existing dispensation, many millions of low-skilled workers have to do jobs they dislike and finish up with post-tax incomes well below the average. Under a lump-sum scheme, the less talented would receive a credit, which would mean that by working at their most lucrative available job they would finish up with an average income. This would put them on a par with the talented in terms of opportunities. Since equal choice sets constitute equal freedom, we would seem to have achieved it by implementing the lump-sum tax proposal.

One might expect Van Parijs to endorse this conclusion. Yet he follows the orthodox line, and rejects lump-sum taxation as a matter of principle. But how can he do this consistently with his treatment of real freedom in the context of special needs?

Suppose somebody says that he is not able to do things he wants to do as a result of a disability. According to Van Parijs, he is to be told that he cannot claim help with the expense of overcoming the disability so long as he *could* adapt his preferences so as to find satisfaction in something that is still open to him. That he does not want to become the sort of person who has those preferences is neither here nor there. It is enough that such preferences are 'accessible' or 'available' to him. And the best evidence (at times Van Parijs writes as if it were conclusive evidence) for the availability of preferences is that at least one person can be found who has them.

Why, then, is not sauce for the disabled sauce for the talented? The talented should surely be told that it is jolly well up to them to cultivate a taste for well-paid jobs. We have only to find a happy banker or accountant somewhere and the resistance to the tax by someone capable of being one who dislikes the prospect must surely be on shaky ground. But instead of accepting this line of reasoning, which seems to me a straightforward application of the analysis developed for disability, Van Parijs says that 'a low earning power does not provide a ground for compensation as long as someone in the society concerned does not mind earning so little' (RFA, 198). All we have to do, then, is find somebody with a low income who agrees with Mother Teresa that 'poverty is a great gift' given to people by God. We can then dismiss all claims from those with low earning capacity. It may be noticed that this makes use of the version of 'availability' according to which the mere existence of somebody with perverse preferences is sufficient to ground the conclusion that if anybody else does not share these preferences it is their own fault. But even if we were to bring the doctrine on low earning capacity into line with the one adopted most of the time with respect to disability, it would still be totally unacceptable.

I do not see how real freedom as a criterion of social justice can survive this interpretation of it. Surely, if the concept is to have any cutting edge at all, it must lead to the conclusion that people with low earning power have less real freedom than those with high earning power. For it is quite clear that somebody who can turn time into money at a high rate has open to him combinations of income and leisure that are not open to somebody whose capacity to turn time into money is lower. Looking at the matter from the point of view of justice, it seems to me axiomatic that low earning power, unless it arises wholly from a deliberate refusal to take up realistically available opportunities to acquire qualifications, is something for which people are not responsible. And on any sort of conception of egalitarian justice, it must follow that those with greater earning power have an unfair advantage over those with less, to the extent that they are permitted to turn a given length and intensity of effort into more final income.

As it happens, the implausibility of Van Parijs's ethical views about differential earning capacity does not translate into equally absurd policy conclusions. The reason for this is that a concern for fairness has to be tempered by a concern for feasibility and also a concern for maintaining incentives to work. The lump-sum tax based on earning capacity is a way of combining fairness with incentives: this is why economists find the idea so attractive.[15] But it is not feasible. We can avoid providing any public subsidy to higher education, thus ensuring that the cost of acquiring the increased earning power bestowed by a degree is paid for by the beneficiaries. But I do not see how much more can be done, and I have yet to see any plausible proposal for implementing a lump-sum tax. Once we start trying to individualize assessment there is no way of proceeding except to invest some official body with enormous discretionary powers. This simply cannot be acceptable in any society that gives a value to the rule of law.

If we (reluctantly) dismiss the lump-sum tax, we are left with income tax. But then we start running into the problem of incentives. Creating equality between those with high earning capacity and those with low earning capacity through income tax would mean that there was no incentive to work. The result would be, unless people were prepared to work for nothing, that there would be no production and everybody would starve. We must therefore settle for marginal rates of tax of less than 100 per cent. But how should we decide what is the optimal rate? The proposal put forward by Van Parijs in *Real Freedom for All* is (as we saw in section 4.1) that all economic arrangements are to be judged by the size of the basic income they make available. It follows from this that the optimum tax rate is one that maximizes the total revenue yield. But this is also, I believe, an answer that somebody who starts from egalitarian premises and accepts a need for incentives will also find attractive.

Notes

[1. Chapter 4 is an abridged version of Brian Barry's response to *Real Freedom for All*, which omits sections 1, 2 and 7 of a paper originally published as 'Real Freedom and Basic Income', *Journal of Political Philosophy* 4 (1996), pp. 242–76. In section 1, the author distinguishes two types of argument for basic income. 'Pragmatic' arguments justify basic income by appeal to its overall effects on the achievement of certain ends which are appropriate objectives for social policy. 'Principled' arguments do not rely merely on such instrumental considerations, but instead claim that the relationship between social justice and basic income is more direct. In the final section of Chapter 5, Robert van der Veen returns to Barry's distinction between pragmatic and principled arguments.]

2. To be precise, the criterion proposed by Van Parijs is not maximin real freedom (maximizing the minimum) but leximin. Leximin is a lexicographic refinement of maximin, which differentiates itself only when two alternatives generate the same minimum level. If there are fewer people at the lowest level in one than in the other, leximin tells us that the first is better. If the numbers are the same, leximin directs us to look at the next level up, and tells us that the one with the higher level is better. The matching process is continued if necessary until the tie is broken. Fortunately, the entire discussion can be carried out without having to invoke the distinctive features of leximin. I shall therefore use the less esoteric concept throughout.

3. Mark Holloway, 'Introduction' to Norman Douglas, *Siren Land* (London: Secker and Warburg, 1982), first page of 'Introduction' (not numbered).

4. 'Keeping our options open is desirable because we do not know in advance what we will rationally desire. A person may change in ways she can't now predict. Furthermore, she may rationally *wish* to change in ways she can't now predict.' Partha Dasgupta, *An Enquiry into Well-Being and Destitution* (Oxford: Clarendon Press, 1994), p. 69.

5. An intermediate position would give an independent value to both the most preferred element in the choice set and the range of choice available. This position has recently been advanced by Ian Carter. See his two recent articles, 'The Independent Value of Freedom', *Ethics* 105 (1995), pp. 819–45, and 'Interpersonal Comparisons of Freedom', *Economics and Philosophy* 11 (1995), pp. 1–23.

6. Julian Le Grand, *Equity and Choice: An Essay in Economics and Applied Philosophy* (London: HarperCollins, 1991), pp. 93–4.
7. If choice sets are identical, this guarantees that another proposed criterion of equity will necessarily be satisfied. This is envy-freeness: the property that nobody would prefer another's allocation to his own. Although Van Parijs takes it seriously (see RFA, 52), this for me simply illustrates the severe limitations of the criterion of envy-freeness.
8. See Kenneth Arrow, 'Little's Critique of Welfare Economics', *Social Choice and Justice: Collected Papers of Kenneth J. Arrow* (Oxford: Basil Blackwell, 1984), vol. 1, pp. 30–44. 'Since individuals have different tastes, equal money incomes cannot always mean equal real incomes. For suppose that in an initial situation the equivalence did hold. Then certainly we can find a shift in relative prices which will make some people better off, keeping money incomes and the general price level constant, so that in the second situation equal money incomes will no longer coincide with equal real incomes' (p. 36).
9. Ronald Dworkin, 'What Is Equality?' I and II, *Philosophy and Public Affairs* 10 (1981), pp. 185–246 and 283–345.
10. G. A. Cohen, 'The Currency of Egalitarian Justice', *Ethics* 99 (1989), pp. 906–44.
11. See Richard J. Arneson, 'Equality and Equal Opportunity for Welfare', *Philosophical Studies* 56 (1989), pp. 77–93, and 'Liberalism, Distributive Subjectivism, and Equal Opportunity for Welfare', *Philosophy and Public Affairs* 19 (1990), pp. 158–94. Cohen's formula is 'equal opportunity for advantage', where 'advantage' is intended to include more than 'welfare' (i.e. want-satisfaction). But for the present purpose the difference is immaterial. The crucial point is that 'advantage' like 'welfare' is personalized: something does not count as an advantage to somebody if it would benefit that specific person, even if it would benefit somebody with different tastes, beliefs, etc.
12. This is adapted (so as to illustrate the opposite point from the one he was making) from p. 36 of Le Grand.
13. To be precise, Van Parijs lists three conditions for a free society, of which only the third is leximin real freedom (RFA, 25). (For leximin see above note 2.) The first is security, which means roughly the implementation of the usual liberal rights ('negative liberty'). The second is self-ownership, a notion that I find opaque except in as far as it is taken to rule out slavery (i.e. being owned by somebody else). Van Parijs thinks that seat-belt laws and regulation of sexual behaviour are violations of self-ownership, but I have no idea what the connection is. The first is said by Van Parijs to have lexicographic priority over the second and the second over the third. Having made leximin real freedom one of the three conditions of a free society, and put it at the bottom of the hierarchy, he then confusingly treats leximin real freedom as constitutive of a (maximally) free society. As I understand it, his intention is to express the idea that a (maximally) free society leximins real freedom subject to the constraint that the requirements of the other two conditions are met. Fortunately, none of this matters much, since the other conditions play very little part in the rest of the book.
14. See Will Kymlicka, *Contemporary Political Theory: an Introduction* (Oxford: Clarendon Press, 1990), pp. 4–5.
15. Van Parijs cites the economist Richard Musgrave as an example (RFA, 96).

5
Real Freedom and Basic Income: Comment on Brian Barry

Robert J. Van der Veen

5.1 Introduction

Brian Barry's discussion of Philippe Van Parijs's *Real Freedom for All* contains many interesting thoughts on an issue which has received increasing attention from economists, political philosophers and social policy analysts.[1] The issue is whether replacing the conditional minimum income benefits of the welfare state by an unconditional basic income is an economically viable and morally attractive proposition. In his highly critical analysis of RFA, Barry mainly concentrates on the moral part of the issue. He is prepared to assume, for the purpose of the discussion, that it is economically feasible to dispense basic incomes to all adult members of society at the welfare state's customary level of subsistence income for a single person. This is a tall assumption indeed, but, in commenting on Barry's contribution, I shall go along with it.[2] To make things as simple as possible in what follows, I also assume that a basic income at subsistence level is the maximum that can be sustained unconditionally.

Before responding to Barry's critique, I must first explain his general point against the project of RFA. His point is that Van Parijs unsuccessfully tries to derive a purely 'principled' case for basic income from social justice. The first central claim of RFA is that social justice in a free society requires us to judge the desirability of alternative social arrangements from a principle of *leximin advantage*, and that we should measure 'advantage' in terms of *real freedom*, where someone's real freedom is captured by her *choice set of attainable income–leisure combinations*. The second central claim of RFA is that leximin real freedom requires a society to distribute the maximum feasible basic income to its members.

In the present context, these central claims entail that it is more just to distribute the subsistence income unconditionally to all (call this the regime of basic income or 'BI') than it is to distribute that same income on conditions of neediness, and of willingness to accept paid work (call this the regime of the welfare state or 'WS'). In order to properly assess the two claims, it is necessary to be clear on what the leximin criterion of justice says generally. It consists of two parts. A regime X is optimally just if *either* (a) those who are worst off in X are better off than those who are worst off in any other relevant regime Y (this part captures the well-known maximin criterion), *or* (b) for cases in which the worst off in X and Y are equally well off, the second worst off under X are better off than the second worst off are under Y. And so forth, for the third... n-th worst off, until one finally breaks the tie between X and Y, if need be, by finding the best off members in X to be better off than the best off in Y. In applying the leximin criterion to the issue at hand, 'worse' or 'better off' is to be measured in real freedom, 'X' is the basic income regime BI, and the relevant alternative 'Y' is the welfare state regime WS.

The bulk of the article is devoted to a demolition of both central claims of RFA. Barry first argues that introduction of the highest feasible basic income cannot be defended on the ground that it brings about leximin real freedom, because 'the concept of real freedom is too weak to do what is required to make the relevant comparisons' between BI and WS (p. 70). And secondly, he argues that if – contrary to what he has just asserted – basic income could be recommended on that ground after all, then the recommendation would still be of doubtful status because Van Parijs has not provided a good defence of his criterion of social justice. In particular, Barry criticizes Van Parijs for wanting to judge the extent of a person's advantage in a given social regime by the extent of her real freedom. It should be noted, however, that Barry does not object against Van Parijs's view on the justice of distributing advantage in a leximin fashion.

Clearly, Barry's two arguments have the structure of an overkill case. If the first argument succeeds, we must accept that basic income cannot be supported by leximin real freedom. But then the second argument becomes superfluous, since there is no need to ask whether the criterion of leximin real freedom can be cogently defended as far as the issue of basic income is concerned. However, I am sure the first argument against Van Parijs rests on a mistake. Leximin real freedom does recommend the dispensation of basic income, as I will show in section 5.2.

One reason why I think it worthwhile to spell this out is that I believe that the value of Barry's present contribution to the basic income debate lies in his second argument, and notably in his main objection against regarding real freedom as a valid 'currency' of justice. He says – and I agree with this – that a valid metric of advantage should take account of the well-being that people can achieve in various situations, given the views of the good *which they actually hold*. And he objects to Van Parijs's defence of real freedom on the ground that it violates this requirement, since the defence implies that what people actually want to achieve, in using their options of choice within their domain of real freedom, is unimportant from the standpoint of justice. What is important about real freedom, from that standpoint, is what the person *might* want to achieve within a plurality of different views of the good that exist in the society he belongs to.

I am not absolutely sure that this is really what Van Parijs wants to claim, but I do agree with Barry that certain passages in RFA can be so interpreted. But whatever the case may be, I think that Barry's objection can be met. For in so far as the well-being of persons depends on having access to income and leisure, the well-being they can achieve in different situations is captured by the comparative extent of real freedom which they enjoy, however they happen to value income relative to leisure, given their actual views of the good. In section 5.3, I then show that the basic income dispensation also comes out on top, as against the welfare state alternative, if the leximin criterion of justice is operated on the satisfaction which people derive from choosing income–leisure options rather than on real freedom.

The upshot of what I hope to have established, in sections 5.2 and 5.3, is that considerations of leximin real freedom have moral weight and that the basic income proposal is supported by these considerations once the case is properly clarified. But I am not claiming that we now have a knockdown argument from social justice speaking in favour of the proposal. In section 5.4, I make a more modest claim. It addresses another side of Barry's contribution. At the start of his article, he explains what he thinks to be the main 'pragmatic' advantages that underlie the program of reforming welfare state transfers in the direction of basic income. What I want to suggest is that some of these advantages constitute an expression of the leximin real freedom view in concrete terms, whereas other ones come along contingently, as part of the package. I end this note by commenting on a remarkable tension between Barry's pragmatic case for basic income and his principled view on the moral virtues of the Swedish Economic Model.

5.2   Why leximin real freedom requires maximum basic income

As I said above, Barry's first argument against Van Parijs is that real freedom is 'too weak' a notion of advantage. It does not allow one to conclude that regime BI is favoured over regime WS by leximin justice. The argument runs as follows. First, in the context of the comparison, a person's real freedom is identified as that person's *choice set* of disposable net income and leisure, given his earning capacity, and given the taxes and transfers in each of the two regimes. Secondly, a person's real freedom is said to improve from one regime to another if and only if his choice set unambiguously expands, which is to say that some combinations of income and leisure are added, and none are deleted in the process. If someone's choice sets in two regimes contain non-overlapping income–leisure combinations, it then follows that the extent of his real freedom in these regimes cannot be compared. Thirdly, for reasons which will appear shortly, Barry assumes that all members of society face *identical choice sets*.

It is easy to see that, on this last assumption, the switch from WS to BI will not improve nor reduce anyone's real freedom. For, on the one hand, 'unconditional basic income provides combinations of income and leisure that would be unobtainable if benefits for able-bodied adults were conditional on willingness to work'. But on the other hand, 'the taxation required to pay for the basic income is virtually certain to foreclose other combinations of income and leisure obtainable in a system under which benefits are conditional on willingness to work' (p. 68).

The point may be put somewhat more precisely as follows. Given that the tax rate to support the unconditional subsistence income exceeds the tax rate needed for financing conditional subsistence, the net income obtainable from full-time work in BI must be less than it would be in WS, when everyone has the same ability to earn. As a result, those who choose to work a lot will lose from the regime change, income-wise, and those who decide to take it easy will gain. Somewhere in between, there must be a break-even amount of work for which the change does not affect net income. At that particular amount, the basic income received just equals the additional tax on income which is needed to finance it, so that net income remains constant. The break-even amount of work is the one at which the post-tax/transfer 'budget lines' of BI and WS intersect, as shown in Barry's Figure 4.3 (p. 69). These budget lines show how leisure is transformed into net income in each of the two regimes. Thus, the change from WS to BI modifies everyone's identical choice set by adding options at the leisure-intensive end and deleting options at the work-intensive end. It follows that the real freedom enjoyed by any person in the two regimes cannot be compared. Hence maximum basic income cannot be justified on the ground that it brings about leximin real freedom.

The validity of this conclusion, however, rests entirely on the assumption of identical choice sets. In the context of the problem at hand, this is a rather strange assumption to make. For with identical choice sets (at maximum earning capacity well in excess of subsistence) everyone is equally well off in terms of real freedom before the change to a basic income occurs, and no one has to depend on the conditional subsistence transfers which the welfare state has on offer. Hence there is no need for even considering whether a basic income would improve matters for the least-advantaged.

Barry's motive for assuming equal choice sets is that Van Parijs himself derives the case in favour of a maximum sustainable basic income on the assumption that everyone is equally talented. Barry then infers from equal talents to equal ability to transform leisure into income, hence to equal income–leisure choice sets, which is to say equal real freedom (p. 66). But this inference is too quick, for two reasons. First, according to Van Parijs, equal talent actually generates unequal capacity to earn from doing paid work, when labour markets are imperfect. Despite equal talent, some will then be out of work, others will be able to work only at low wage rates and/or part-time, and still others will monopolize full-time and highly wellpaid jobs.[3]

Secondly, in making the real freedom case for basic income, there is not really a compelling motive to stick to equal talent in the first place, even though this is what Van Parijs actually does.[4] On the contrary, a natural way of treating the case would be to suppose that, in general, people's earning capacities (that is, the maximum incomes they are able to earn before taxes and transfers) vary as a result of both inequality of talent, labour market imperfections of various kinds and inequality of non-work income from unequal holdings of wealth and the like. Under these more realistic conditions, Barry's conclusion is no longer valid. The change from WS to BI now produces the following result: those who are absolutely worst-off in real freedom are not affected by the change, those who are second worst-off benefit, and those who are best off in real freedom either lose from the change or end up with incomparable extents of real freedom in WS and BI. Thus the right conclusion is that the replacement of WS by BI is recommended, if one accepts the criterion of leximin real freedom.

To derive this conclusion it must be possible to rank the real freedom of different persons in both regimes and place them into non-arbitrary categories whose real freedom is compared before and after the change. Barry thinks that this is impossible, 'barring some sort of catastrophic decline, or almost miraculous improvement, between the two situations' (p. 58).

I will show, however, that the specific comparisons which are required in order to operate the leximin criterion can be made under perfectly normal circumstances.

In what follows next, I take it that earning capacities vary between persons from zero upwards, for the reasons stated above. As a consequence, two people with the same earning capacity may then have entirely different abilities to transform leisure into net income, depending both on how much work they can perform at their highest achievable wage rates, and on the income they obtain from non-work sources, such as invested wealth. This means that their choice sets may also be different. Like Barry, I also suppose income taxes to be proportional, with a high tax rate in BI and a lower one in WS. But, unlike Barry, I shall assume the transfer rule of the WS regime to be of the following form: those who are unable to work are granted the subsistence income. Those who are able to work but cannot earn the subsistence income after the WS-tax deduction are entitled to the difference between the subsistence income and whatever they can earn.[5]

5.2.1 Step one

The derivation of the leximin conclusion now proceeds in two stages. In the first stage, persons with different earning capacities are assembled in three groups. The object is to study how the choice sets of members in each group are affected by the change from WS to BI.

Group 1: Zero earning capacity

The choice sets of all members of this group are identical in WS and BI. Both the conditional and the unconditional transfers are paid out at subsistence level to persons who are necessarily forced into full-time leisure. This may be due to disability or involuntary unemployment. Such persons are therefore equally placed in both regimes. As far as their real freedom is concerned, the change of regime produces no effects. It should be noted, however, that the basic income regime may well increase the likelihood that involuntarily unemployed persons move out of Group 1. This point is mentioned by Barry and I shall return to it in section 5.4.

The two other groups each consist of persons with positive earning capacities. These are distinguished from one another relative to a *threshold level of earning capacity*, denoted by 'T'. At T, a person's maximum net income (at her highest obtainable wage rate, and at the maximum amount of work she can perform) is *equal in BI and WS*. As noted above, the BI tax rate is higher than the WS tax rate. Then, at the level T, the additional tax to be paid by someone on pre-tax income from maximum work, and from non-work income (if any), will just cancel out the receipt of basic income. This explains why total maximum net incomes in WS and BI are the same. At any level of earning capacity below T, however, maximum net income in BI will exceed that in WS, since the additional tax paid in BI will then be less than the amount of basic income dispensed. And at any level of earning capacity above T, maximum net income in BI will fall short of that in WS. For now the additional tax paid in BI must surpass the amount of basic income dispensed. Thus,

Group 2: Positive earning capacity at, or below, the threshold value T

There is one single case in this Group for which the change from WS to BI makes no difference in real freedom. In this case, the person's earning capacity just equals T, and his earnings consist only of non-work income, on account of disability or involuntary unemployment. In all other cases, however, members of Group 2 will gain income–leisure opportunities from the change, and lose none. This can be seen as follows. Persons who are likewise unable to work, but whose pre-tax non-work income is below T, will pay less additional tax on that income than the basic income is worth, as a result of the move from WS to BI. Hence their net income at full leisure in BI must always exceed their net income in WS, so that their real freedom increases.

The remaining members of Group 2 are able to earn by working. Then at full leisure they must always have a pre-tax income below T. Therefore their net income at full leisure in BI exceeds their net income in WS. But their net incomes at maximum work in BI will be as large as, or larger than, those in WS (depending on whether their earning capacity is at or below T). Taken together, these conditions ensure that all such persons obtain additional income–leisure opportunities in BI, while losing none of the opportunities they had in WS, which is to say that they gain in real freedom from the regime change.

Group 3: Positive earning capacity above the threshold value T

Members of this group who are unable to work lose out in real freedom from the BI–WS change. For at full leisure their net income in BI falls short of that in WS. Some able-bodied and affluent members of Group 3 also suffer a loss of real freedom. These are persons whose pre-tax, non-work income is at least T. Then, at most, their net income at full leisure in BI equals that in WS. Also, maximum net income in BI is below that of WS for anyone in Group 3. For these affluent persons, then, the change will destroy opportunities to earn by hard work and offer no additional income at any amount of leisure.

Those remaining in Group 3 have pre-tax, non-work incomes below T. At full leisure, their net income in BI is now larger than it is in WS. But their net income at maximum work in BI falls short of that in WS. For them, the regime change eliminates opportunities to earn at high-work effort, while adding opportunities to spend income at high leisure. Therefore the extent of their real freedom in BI and WS cannot be compared. Notice that these last cases correspond to the ones analyzed by Barry on the equal choice set assumption, in his Figure 4.3.

5.2.2 Step two

The second step of the derivation consists in comparing the real freedom of persons who belong to different groups within both of the two regimes, BI and WS. The rule of interpersonal comparison is the one put forward by Barry: the real freedom of person X is larger than that of person Y if and only if X's choice set contains all income–leisure opportunities of Y's choice set, and more besides. This demanding rule may be called the 'inclusion rule' on choice sets.[6] The inclusion rule generates incomparability of real freedom in many cases, as Barry has pointed out. As a result it will not be possible to say, for instance, that everyone in Group 1 is worse off in real freedom than anyone who belongs to the other two groups.

The following example illustrates the difficulty. We are in WS. Now we compare a member of Group 1 to a member of Group 3. The former is an unemployed person who is involuntarily confined to subsisting at full leisure. The latter is someone without non-work income, who is able to earn a very high salary. His net income at full leisure in WS will then be nil on the austere transfer rule of the welfare state adopted here. Clearly, the choice sets of the two are incomparable. We cannot say that the unemployed person enjoys less real freedom than the well-to-do salaryman because the salaryman cannot subsist without working. This example illustrates what Barry means by calling real freedom a 'weak' metric when it comes to interpersonal comparisons. It is not difficult to think of other examples of incomparable choice sets, even between two able-bodied persons with the same earning capacity. At first sight, then, it seems that Barry is right after all: we cannot rank all members of our three groups. However, for the purposes of the leximin regime comparison it is not necessary to be able to rank the real freedom of *any* two persons on the inclusion rule. But it is necessary that partial rankings of the following types exist.

(a) Some in Groups 2 and 3 are better off in real freedom in both regimes than anyone in Group 1, whereas no one in Group 1 is better off in real freedom than someone in Group 2 or 3, whatever the transfer regime may be.

This type of partial ranking is obtained between persons who are unable to work and whose real freedom therefore depends on their net incomes from wealth and transfers. Of these persons, those who belong to Groups 2 or 3 will invariably enjoy more real freedom than anyone in Group 1. As the above example shows, the real freedom of those in Group 2 or 3 who are able to work, but have no income from wealth, will always be incomparable to that of anyone in Group 1, within the WS-regime.

(b) For anyone in Group 2, one can always find some in Group 3 who have more real freedom in both regimes, whereas no one in Group 2 has more real freedom than anyone in Group 3.

This type of partial ranking is exemplified by comparing two people who are able to work the same amount of time at the same maximum wage rate, but have unequal amounts of non-work income. One belongs in Group 2, the other in Group 3. Then the latter's total net income will be higher than the former's at any amount of work performed, so that his real freedom is superior in each of the regimes. The impossibility of finding anyone in Group 2 with more real freedom than anyone in Group 3 is due to the fact that at maximum work the latter always have higher net incomes than the former.

The existence of these partial rankings completes the second stage of our derivation. To the extent that the inclusion rule allows real freedom comparisons between persons with given earning capacities, the worst-off are located in Group 1, the best-off are located in Group 3, with the second worst-off placed in between, in Group 2. Given how the real freedom of members in each group changes from WS to BI, it now follows that BI is recommended by the criterion of leximin real freedom: for equal real freedom of the worst-off in both regimes, those who are second worst-off in BI are better off than those who are second worst-off in WS.

5.3   Real freedom and achievable well-being

As mentioned in section 5.1, Barry raises important critical questions about the relevance of real freedom in a conception of social justice. I do not think Barry anywhere denies that justice at least mandates that we pay close attention to the fate of the least-advantaged members of society. But he is concerned to inquire why it is that a person's advantage should be represented by the extent of that person's real freedom in income–leisure space in assessing the justice of social arrangements. So the issue is: given that justice can be presumed to move us towards some conception of leximin advantage, why select real freedom as the metric of advantage? In his comments on RFA, Barry takes a close look at Van Parijs's general definition of real freedom, which he cites as 'the opportunity ... to do whatever one might want to do' (p. 54).[7]

Now Barry holds that if real freedom is to be a metric of any significance in a moral theory of distributive shares, then one reason why it is significant must be surely that it makes you able 'to do the things you actually want to do, and some other things besides', in case you happen to change your mind about what it is you actually want. And the problem he sees with Van Parijs's own interpretation of real freedom is precisely that it drives us to place *'no value at all'* on getting what you actually want (p. 54). Barry does not see a valid rationale for such a view. I prefer to leave it to Van Parijs to judge whether Barry correctly attributes this particular view to him. But speaking for myself, I agree that the main point of including real freedom in a calculus of justice is that it promotes the well-being that people can achieve from choosing among the options in their choice set, given what they want from life in actual fact rather than given what they might want, or could want, but in fact do not want to achieve.

Nevertheless there remain reasons for placing value on the non-chosen options of the choice set. As Barry mentions, people tend to change their minds as to the options they currently prefer because of independent developments in their lives. Moreover, one's current preferences may be heavily influenced by the regime to which one is subject. And one might not be able to assess what one would most likely prefer in the circumstances of a different regime. The presence of 'endogeneous preferences' can make it questionable to compare the desirability of alternative social arrangements exclusively in terms of people's current preferences. With all these caveats in mind, I now examine the validity of using real freedom in the leximin comparison from this admittedly restricted viewpoint.

The notion of real freedom has been specified in terms of a choice set whose elements are the primary goods of income and leisure. But then there should exist a close link indeed between this choice set and the well-being that its holder can achieve, given her actual plans in life, in so far as 'well-being' depends on those goods. If someone's choice set expands from one situation to another, thereby giving access to more income at any level of leisure, then, other things equal, that person's achievable well-being must increase, whichever way he actually happens to value income relative to leisure.[8] Also, if person A can enjoy more income at any level of leisure than B, and both value income relative to leisure in the same way, then A can achieve a higher level of well-being than B.[9] So what we are able to say, on the basis of section 5.2, is that in so far as the choice sets of persons in our three different groups are comparable on the inclusion rule, the change from WS to BI is recommended not merely by leximin real freedom. It is also recommended by the leximin distribution of preference satisfaction for all subsets of persons with common income–leisure preferences.

On this last criterion, however, one should also attend to the satisfaction of persons whose preferences are the same but whose choice sets cannot be compared on the inclusion rule. And it is then possible to identify cases in which some person X (whose earning capacity puts him into Group 2) can satisfy his preferences to a larger extent than some person Y (who belongs to Group 3), while X gains from the regime change and Y loses, in terms of their common preferences.[10] These cases are in conflict with what the leximin rule of preference satisfaction prescribes.

However, such offending cases are bound to be rare in reality for the following reason. A person's earning capacity is determined by her maximum attainable wage rate, maximum ability to perform work and her income from non-work sources. In general, those who can earn at high wage rates during their working lives will be much more likely to work in full-time jobs and to gain access to sources of non-work income, in comparison with low wage earners. Thus, the income–leisure choice sets of the former will generally tend to dominate the choice sets of the latter on all three determinants of earning capacity. It follows that replacing the conditional WS-regime by the unconditional BI-regime produces a far better approximation of 'leximin achievable preference satisfaction' than the reverse change could ever produce. Thus there is a strong pragmatic reason to favour BI from the leximin point of view even if one decides to focus exclusively on the levels of utility which people can derive from their income–leisure choice sets rather than on the real freedom conferred by the choice sets themselves.

5.4 Pragmatic and principled defences of basic income

I have tried to show that the political program of basic income can be defended by appealing to an abstract principle of justice, leximin real freedom. It holds that a reform of the welfare state should be judged by how it affects the fate of members of society with low earning capacities, who are at a disadvantage in respect of the income and leisure they can command in pursuit of their well-being. For the reasons explained above, I believe that Barry has dismissed this theoretical position too quickly, in the course of his searching review of RFA. At the same time, Barry's own reasons for supporting basic income are much more closely linked to the leximin defence than he seems prepared to recognize. In his introduction, Barry holds that the basic income program is desirable because of its 'pragmatic' advantages in better serving certain ends of social policy than the usual welfare state regime is able to do under present circumstances. At the end of the article, he specifies some of these policy ends by reference to the dignity and freedom of the poor, that is to say those who belong to the large group of persons with insufficient opportunity to secure an adequate income. Basic income is conducive to the dignity of the poor by relieving them from the unsolicited 'advice, monitoring and control by social workers', and basic income contributes to their freedom 'by making it possible...to drop out of the world of paid employment to pursue an education, look for a new job, start a business, raise children or care for relatives, or to work for some good cause'. Clearly, a major reason why these policy ends would be intuitively seen as desirable is because they contribute to social justice. But among the different views on social justice, the principle of leximin real freedom explicates those intuitions particularly well.

As I mentioned in section 5.1, however, I do not think that one can regard the case for basic income to be simply summed up by appealing to the justice of its distributive effects on the real freedom of poor people. For the change from WS to BI also produces effects relevant to other aspects of social justice. These come along with the change as part of the reform package. One such effect, mentioned briefly in section 5.2, is the improvement of incentives for low-productivity work. Unconditional access to subsistence makes it possible to remove constraints on the labour market which now prevent employers from hiring people with meagre skills at low wage rates. Basic income, then, helps many of those who would remain involuntarily unemployed, under WS, to find such jobs, and making it worthwhile to take them without loss of transfer income. As Barry says, [b] 'basic income enables people to price themselves into a job'.

Referring back once more to the groups of section 5.2, the regime change helps to transform unemployed people in Group 1, whose earning capacity is nil in WS, into wage-earning members of Group 2 in BI. This can be seen as a desirable end of policy, which certainly contributes to social justice in a wider sense of 'equal opportunity'. However, this particular aspect of the regime change is not covered by the leximin real freedom principle. It rather flows from the fact that BI simply creates more options for the poor to do gainful work than does WS under conditions of mass unemployment.

There is one other morally salient aspect of the change, which receives due attention in Barry's discussion. Unlike the work incentive effect, it comes along as the inevitable consequence of promoting the real freedom of poor people by means of unconditional subsistence incomes, independently of whether there is mass unemployment or full employment. As Barry phrases it: 'A subsistence-level basic income would enable able-bodied people of working age to live lives of self-indulgence (admittedly at a modest material level) even if there were socially useful things for them to do'. It is interesting to note that Barry cites this as an 'objection that immediately arises whenever basic income is proposed', and explains it in terms of an 'ethic of social responsibility'. Barry refrains from taking an explicit moral stand on the validity of the objection. But he does appear to take its underlying ethic seriously to the point of regarding the social responsibility inherent in the (now largely defunct) Swedish Economic Model's 'active labour market policy' as a morally superior alternative to the basic income regime. According to Barry, the institutional and cultural preconditions of the Swedish Economic Model are far from being met in the other countries of the European Union, where basic income is on the agenda. So he concludes that if 'basic income is second best to an unattainable alternative, that makes it the best feasible option'.

It would seem to follow from this that Barry attaches a huge moral importance to the objection of social irresponsibility in a first-best world, given that basic income would be a possibility there too. If so, his judgement of feasibility leaves wide open the question as to whether the manifold policy advantages he cites in favour of introducing basic income in the second-best world of contemporary Europe are sufficiently weighty, in the face of the possibility that poor people will use their basic incomes to take it easy at the expense of their fellow citizens. As Barry explains, one could try to exclude irresponsible 'surfers' by making the receipt of basic income contingent on the performance of items on some list of 'socially useful activities', in a system of 'participation income'. But he is not really in favour of such a modification of basic income because, among other things, it would engender enormous bureaucratic cost and require discretionary powers for lowlevel administrators to intrude in people's personal circumstances. Now obviously, the problem with this assessment is that it is open to challenge by egalitarian reformers of the present welfare state who insist on the ethic of social responsibility even in the second-best world. They can (and many of them do) say that the conditionalities of a participation income will contribute to the formation of the 'institutional and cultural preconditions' for implementing that ethic, and accept the bureaucratic intervention into people's lives accordingly.

So I think there is a marked tension between what Barry morally regards to be the ideal type of social policy regime, on the one hand, and what he thinks to be the 'pragmatically' next best regime of basic income, on the other. I would not want to be so presumptuous as to try and resolve the tension for him. But I suggest that in reflecting on the matter, it would help to be less dismissive of the principled view on real freedom advanced in Philippe Van Parijs's book. At any rate, I myself believe that the pragmatic arguments for basic income advanced by Barry can be better accounted for by invoking that view, at least in the (hopefully not too rare) instances where political philosophy matters in politics.[11]

Notes

1. Brian Barry, 'Real Freedom and Basic Income', *Journal of Political Philosophy* 4 (September 1996), 242–77; page numbers in parentheses in the text refer to this article. Philippe Van Parijs, *Real Freedom for All* (Oxford: Oxford University Press, 1995), henceforth abbreviated RFA.
2. In the Netherlands, where basic income is considered by the current government to be one of the (perhaps more far-fetched) proposals for a future social security reform, there is wide agreement that it is infeasible to sustain the tax cost of a subsistence-level basic income. In so far as the proposal is politically relevant in other European countries at all, the same holds.
3. RFA, chapter 4.4.
4. The reason for this is that Van Parijs considers inequality of talent to be a separate problem which cannot be properly addressed by the basic income dispensation. His proposal to compensate for inequality of talent is discussed by Barry in section 4.4 of his article. I shall not comment on the issues raised there.
5. The conditionality of welfare state subsistence transfers presents something of a problem. One may distinguish two extreme versions of transfer rules. The most austere of these is the one specified in the text above. The other extreme is an extremely generous transfer rule, which is in effect assumed by Barry. It allows people to cash in on the subsistence income without working. But once they do work, at whatever wage they happen to choose, the transfer is diminished pound by pound until earnings reach the subsistence income, when the transfer ceases. This rule explains the horizontal segment in the welfare state budget line of Fig. 4.3 (p. 69). The austere rule would imply a straight budget line running upwards from the full-leisure point 'l' on the horizontal axis of

Fig. 4.3. If the austere transfer rule could be fully enforced, it would offer no incentives to remain dependent on a transfer. By contrast, the generous transfer rule amounts to a basic income with a 100 per cent withdrawal rate. It induces all who are unable to earn well above subsistence to remain in voluntary unemployment. As a consequence, the tax rate needed to support the generous rule will be much higher than it would need to be if the austere rule were in force. In reality, the transfer rules of various welfare states lie in between these two extremes. But it is fair to say that most welfare states nowadays try to approximate the austere rule in administering welfare benefits, and strenuously try to avoid the generous one. However, the reason why I here adopt the austere transfer rule is not only because it is more realistic, but also because it makes the leximin case for basic income harder to sustain than the generous one does, as will become apparent in section 5.2 below.

6. See Robert J. van der Veen, *Between Exploitation and Communism* (Groningen: Wolters-Noordhoff, 1991), chap. 3, which includes a version of the present argument.

7. RFA, p. 23.

8. Of course it is true that the all-purpose means of income and leisure are not the only important ingredients of well-being. People also differ quite substantially in their 'internal' capacities to convert all-purpose means, such as income and leisure, into well-being. Any proposal to use the notion of real freedom as the preferred metric of advantage in a theory of distributive justice must therefore be further defended in the face of implausibilities which may derive from ignoring these factors. But in Barry's critique this point does not play any role, so far as I have been able to see. So I am going to suppose that it is not a point of contention at present.

9. This ranking judgement can be made because the 'well-being' that A and B can achieve is here supposed to depend exclusively on the primary goods of income and leisure. What A and B can achieve when all other determinants of their well-being are taken into account is another matter, which would need to be carefully considered in a fuller account of 'advantage'.

10. An example of such a case: person Y (Group 3) faces a high wage rate and has no income from wealth. He maximizes utility in his WS-choice set at a high amount of work because he is keen on earning high income and does not care much about leisure. He then loses utility from the change to BI. Person X (Group 2), who gains in utility from the change, is just as keen on earning income. But in contrast to Y, he faces a low wage rate and enjoys some income from wealth. Thus the choice sets of the two are incomparable on the inclusion rule. Now because leisure is much cheaper for X than it is for Y in terms of foregone wage income, X is able to maximize utility at a higher indifference curve than Y, not only in BI but also in WS. Another example would be one where both X (Group 2) and Y (Group 3), with the same type of 'income-loving' preferences, have no non-work income. X faces a much higher wage rate than Y, but Y can work a full-time week, and X is only able to work two days a week. Then it is possible that X can achieve higher utility than Y in both BI and WS, while Y loses and X gains utility from the change.

11. I wish to thank Jeroen Knijff for valuable comments on a draft of this note.

6

Should Surfers Be Fed?

Richard J. Arneson

The cover tells the story perfectly. The photo shows a bronzed surfer riding an enormous, beautiful wave. The caption beneath the photo is the title of Philippe van Parijs's book: *Real Freedom for All* in large type and in smaller letters *What (if anything) can justify capitalism?*[1] Van Parijs espouses the ideal of a just society as one which, subject to constraints of security and self-ownership, leximins real freedom or the opportunity to do whatever one might choose to do. A leximin distribution maximizes the position of the worst off member of society, then as a second priority maximizes the position of the second worst off, then the third worst off, and so on through the best off. Van Parijs argues that leximinning real freedom requires a tax and transfer system that provides an unconditional basic income grant for all at the highest sustainable per capita level. In an affluent society, instituting Van-Parijs-style justice would be good news for the would-be surfer, who can use the basic income grant to reduce or eliminate hours spent working for pay so as to have more time available for glorious days at the beach. The towering wave in the picture is an attractive image of the possibilities of freedom, a value that Van Parijs tells us is of 'paramount importance'. The depiction of the surfer also serves to remind readers of the opposed position (on the basic income grant issue) of John Rawls, who has stipulated an interpretation of his Difference Principle yielding the policy implication that 'those who surf all day off Malibu must find a way to support themselves and would not be entitled to public funds'.[2] Finally, the larger type for the words 'Real Freedom for All' signals the importance of the proposed marriage of left libertarianism and egalitarianism in Van Parijs's position and the decreased salience of capitalism versus socialism debates (smaller type for the query about what might justify capitalism).

Van Parijs's book is an exciting and stimulating discussion that succeeds very well at two different levels of inquiry. On one level the book addresses abstract issues in the philosophy of distributive justice; at another level the book contains shrewd insights into the practical advantages of the basic income grant proposal, construed as a policy recommendation for affluent Western democracies. (Yet his ultimate principle is that we should maximize the real freedom of the least free on a global scale, not merely in this or that or even each country. I agree that the scope of egalitarianism should be global, but the irony is that on this scale a basic income grant would not be desirable even on his own theory.) For all I know Van Parijs may care more about the basic income grant policy proposal than about the nuances of distributive justice. Certainly he has been an ardent and eloquent defender of the basic income grant idea for several years. Nevertheless, this review addresses the book's contribution to the philosophy of distributive justice.

The image of the surfer on the cover of the book triggers my own two main objections to the line of thought that Van Parijs pursues. He envisages real freedom for all in the form of basic income for all at the highest sustainable level. This is a tax-and-transfer scheme whereby those who earn income support those who have no income at all or a small income. But those with small income are a heterogeneous class. Nothing guarantees that all will be truly needy or disadvantaged. Some of Van Parijs's surfers may be among those who enjoy far above average real freedom – they are talented individuals who happen to have a pronounced taste for leisure over remunerative activity. Some of Van Parijs's surfers will indeed be among the group that he should count as truly needy, those with the least real freedom. Whether people are truly needy or not depends on their potential income (the income they could earn if they chose to seek it), not their actual income, but the basic income grant proposal varies its treatment of individuals according to their actual income. From a distributive-justice standpoint, the ideal of maximizing basic income is flawed.

My second objection is that surfing is an excellent sport played in beautiful oceanic settings. The problem is that the fact that this activity is admirable is strictly irrelevant to an assessment of Van Parijs's ideal of maximizing the real opportunity to do whatever one might choose for those with least opportunities. Justice according to Van Parijs is done when people are fairly treated according to the metric of freedom. What individuals do with their freedom is no part of the proper business of society in its role as agency of distributive justice. Justice would be done equally if people used their opportunities wisely or utterly squandered them. If we think that the merits of Van Parijs's basic income scheme hinge on the quality of the lives that people would actually lead under it, we are thereby registering fundamental dissent from his freedom-oriented conception of distributive justice. Neutrality on the good is one of his central axioms. I suggest that to eliminate the halo that the excellence and beauty of surfing place round his position, a halo that is irrelevant to its actual merits, a more apt cover illustration for this book would depict individuals sitting on a couch eating potato chips and watching surfing on TV.

Van Parijs would quite reasonably ask on what basis I claim to know that surfing is a better activity than eating potato chips and watching mindless TV. Better by whose standard? But the confident pressing of this question reveals an unargued asymmetry between the status of the good and the right in the 'resourcist' family of liberal theories of justice. Van Parijs supposes that we can obtain objective knowledge of what is right and just fit to serve as a basis of social cooperation among reasonable persons. But no such agreement about what is intrinsically good or worthwhile in human life can be forthcoming. Reasonable people will find themselves forever in disagreement about the nature of the good life. Hence the theory of justice must adopt an austere posture of neutrality on the good: we should not enact policies that aim to favor any one conception of the good over rival alternatives, nor should we base any policy decision on a judgment that any one conception of the good is better than others. But all of this is just assertion. If we appeal to our considered judgment after ideally extended reflection as the arbiter of what counts as reasonable and unreasonable in matters of the right, why cannot we appeal to the same standard to arbitrate conflicts about the good? No doubt there will be considerable uncertainty, unresolved judgment and partial commensurability with respect to both claims about what is just and claims about what is good. We see through a glass darkly. But so far as I can tell, we see the good and the right through the same glass. However Van Parijs claims to know that, for example, the libertarian ideal of formal freedom is inferior to his view that justice is concerned with the distribution of real freedom, I would claim that by similar 'reflective equilibrium' methods I can show that eating potato chips and channel surfing on the TV is less valuable than surfing.

Indeed, there is a deep tension between the egalitarianism of Van Parijs's do-the-best-one-can-for-the-least-advantaged conception of distributive justice and his insistence on strict neutrality on the good in the style of John Rawls and Ronald Dworkin.[3] Contemporary egalitarians such as Rawls hold that it is morally arbitrary that some people should have far better life prospects than others simply because they are lucky enough to have been given an initial stock of wealth, and that if such wealth inequalities are tolerable this can only be to the extent that they are made to operate to the benefit of the worst off. In the same spirit, contemporary egalitarians hold that it is morally arbitrary that some people should have far better life prospects than others simply because they are lucky enough to start life with a generous endowment of talent, and that if talent-generated inequalities are morally tolerable this can only be to the extent that they are made to operate to the benefit of the worst off.

But the abilities to choose and follow sensible values and fundamental life aims that could withstand rational critical reflection are distributed unequally across persons. The differences in people's life prospects that stem from this unchosen initial inequality are ignored on principle by 'resourcist' or opportunity-oriented conceptions of distributive justice that counsel neutrality of response to variations in individuals' conceptions of the good. Thus Rawls writes that justice properly conceived 'does not look behind the use which persons make of the rights and opportunities available to them in order to measure, much less to maximize, the satisfactions they achieve. Nor does it try to evaluate the relative merits of different conceptions of the good'.[4] On this theory, which Van Parijs espouses, if one person is born into extreme poverty and in consequence cannot obtain decent meals, justice offers remedies, and if another person is born with a low level of marketable ability and in consequence cannot obtain decent meals, justice again offers remedies, but if a third person is born with poor values selection skills and in consequence chooses a disastrous way of life that blocks him from obtaining decent meals, justice regards it as a matter of principle to offer no remedy whatsoever. To put my misgivings somewhat aggressively, I would say that theories of distributive justice that on principle do not allow the treatment of individuals to be responsive to assessments of their conceptions of the good are ideologies that favor the good choosers over the bad choosers even when the bad choosing is beyond one's power to control.

Suppose that in the role of theorists of justice we have a limited ability to distinguish better from worse conceptions of the good. For many goals that individuals seek for their own sake, we have no basis for saying one is better than another: the enjoyment of jazz may be neither superior nor inferior to the enjoyment of classical music, participation in sports, or the development of relations of friendship or love. But other goals sought for their own sake, such as the enjoyment of titillating gossip, we believe to be good, but less good than those just mentioned. And given the basic values and goals and individual prizes, there will be a fact of the matter as to whether one or another life plan is more efficient as a means to maximizing the satisfaction of basic goals and values. Now suppose for the moment that we accept Van Parijs's notion that justice accords lexical priority to the achievement of advantages for the least advantaged when we must choose between helping the least advantaged and the second-least advantaged or those even better off. (This priority rule counterintuitively holds it to be morally better to get a tiny benefit for a single worst-off individual than to secure a huge windfall for many people who are just slightly better off, but let that pass.) Van Parijs identifies the worst off with those who have least real freedom and holds that the basic imperative of justice is to maximize the real freedom of those who are worst off in this respect. Under this vision of the just society, it doesn't matter what the worst off do with their maximal freedom: what you do with your own life is your business, not the business of society.

But if the class of the worst off includes good choosers and bad choosers, then some individuals in the ideal Van Parijs society will be leading avoidably miserable lives. If we had arranged institutions and policies differently, as we might have done, these individuals, call them the truly needy, would have had richer, better lives. For example, society might channel benefits to the worst off in the form of in-kind benefits that encourage some ways of life rather than others. Aid might be offered in the form of employment opportunities rather than cash income if it is known that on the average the worst off will be better off with jobs than with other benefits they might get instead. Society might also enforce certain nonstigmatizing forms of paternalism, for example, by declaring illegal the sale and use of recreational drugs that provide very unfavorable short-term pleasure to long-term pain ratios. In my view, freedom, even 'real freedom', is a very important means to what is intrinsically worthwhile in human life and also for many individuals one intrinsic good, worthwhile for its own sake. (The scare quotes signal that this review does not treat the important question whether Van Parijs's interpretation of the ideal of freedom is cogent.)[5] Theories of justice should no more make a fetish of freedom than of any other means to the good life or part of it. In elevating freedom to the status of paramount value Van Parijs incorrectly privileges a means over ends, a part over the whole. The ultimate concern of distributive justice should be the quality of people's lives, and no single component of the good life should displace that concern.

Van Parijs takes a hard line on the alleged obligation of the state to be neutral on issues about the nature of the good or choiceworthy life. He tends to focus on a single worry: if the metric of distributive justice were preference satisfaction, then we would regard the worst off as those with least preference satisfaction, and a leximin principle of justice would aim to maximize the preference satisfaction level of the person who is worst off in this respect. But consider two persons, one with expensive tastes for plover's eggs and pre-phylloxera claret, another with cheap tastes for popcorn and beer. Van Parijs supposes that a theory of distributive justice that takes utility or preference satisfaction to be the measure of people's condition will systematically favor those with expensive over those with cheap tastes. But people are responsible for their tastes and preferences and values, hence we should assess people's condition by the extent to which each has the opportunity to do whatever she might choose to do. People's actual preferences and preference-satisfaction levels are neither here nor there so far as distributive justice is concerned. Call this the Responsibility Argument.

But the Responsibility Argument deployed by Van Parijs does not succeed. First, it's wildly implausible to suppose that anybody can choose any preferences at will. Suppose that each individual could choose or cultivate any one set among an array of sets of preferences, a different array being available to each individual. For simplicity, suppose that this choice of preferences is costless for each individual. We might then respond to Van Parijs's Responsibility Argument without retreating to neutrality on the good by supposing that justice should be concerned to leximin the opportunities for preference satisfaction of the least advantaged. An individual's opportunity for preference satisfaction is the level of it she would reach if she made the best choice of preferences and lived her life prudently with the aim of satisfying these preferences. So the Responsibility Argument does not push us toward resourcist views of distributive justice that altogether ignore the kinds of lives that resources enable individuals to achieve. Moreover, according to a leximin opportunity for preference-satisfaction account, it will sometimes be right in theory to compensate an individual for her expensive preferences, for the expensive preference might have been inculcated in her in ways that are beyond her power to control (so that the expensive preference is included in every set of preferences among which she could choose). Where an individual myopically or lazily selects inappropriate preferences, the leximin opportunity for preference-satisfaction principle does not recommend compensation for expensive preferences.

A second flaw in Van Parijs's Responsibility Argument is that its line on responsibility is too unforgiving. Responsibility for one's fundamental aims and values is more diffuse than the unrealistic picture of choice of preferences suggests. To an extent the quality of an individual's aims and values may depend on the individual's exercise of critical reflection and avoidance of bad choice-forming environments (what religious moralists sometimes call the 'near occasions of sin'). But the individual's abilities to reflect and avoid are themselves talents that are in the first instance bestowed by genetic endowment and early socialization. Very roughly, we may hold individuals responsible for doing as well as could reasonably be expected, with respect to their values formation and selection and pursuit of life plans, given their initial endowments of pertinent talents. And even when an individual clearly behaves in a seriously imprudent manner for which she is to blame even on a fine-grained account of responsibility, the actual outcome suffered by the individual will typically depend on luck as well as her choice of conduct and may be far worse than was reasonably expectable in the circumstances. To the degree that individual responsibility is understood to be problematic and difficult to gauge, and in any event very imperfectly correlated with the good or bad outcomes reached by variously deserving individuals, a theory of justice like the Van Parijs model that limits the job of justice to the provision of a fair share of opportunities for individuals will be too harsh. Individuals vary in their ability to make good use of opportunities, and these variations cannot in any remotely plausible fashion be held to be matters that are within each individual's power to control.

Another misleading feature of the Van Parijs way of disposing of the issue of neutrality on the good is that actual preference satisfaction is a poor measure of the quality of an individual's life. Hence the notion that distributive justice principles should ultimately be concerned with securing improvements in the value of the lives that people lead is not given a fair hearing if the value or quality of someone's life is identified with the satisfaction of any sort of preferences she happens to have. Preferences do not closely track what ultimately matters to us about our own lives. What we want is to lead a really choiceworthy life, not merely a life that satisfies our preferences, however ill-informed, silly, or selfish these might be. Of course Van Parijs is deeply skeptical concerning the possibility that any knowledge of what is truly choiceworthy could be available to social planners arranging institutions to bring them into conformity with justice. I have raised principled doubts about his variety of skepticism already in this review, but I would wish to emphasize that, on the practical level of actual policy formation, the differences between Van Parijs and me might lessen, because information that is in principle available may be unavailable in practice.

Setting worries about neutrality on the good to the side, I also deny that establishing an unconditional basic income for all at the highest sustainable per capita level is an adequate means to the implementation of the principle that real freedom should be leximinned. My main objection at this point was that making the basic income grant as high as is feasible, at least in an affluent society, would include among the net beneficiaries of tax and transfer redistribution some individuals who are above average in the real freedom they enjoy, but who happen to have a strong preference for leisure over income-generating activity. The redistribution policies that society establishes could do more to advance the real freedom of the least advantaged if they were better targeted at the least-advantaged class than a basic income grant ever is.

This objection needs to be stated more carefully or it will be vulnerable to swift rebuttal. Van Parijs's view develops in stages. He first argues that in a world in which everyone has identical talents, leximinning real freedom would require instituting the highest feasible sustainable basic income. He then argues that in a world in which there is variation in the endowment of talents broadly construed that individuals get from their genes and early socialization, justice requires compensation to those with a poor endowment of talents to satisfy a norm of undominated diversity. So we need to examine the undominated diversity condition in order to determine if my objection against the basic income grant scheme is decisive.

'Undominated diversity' obtains in a society in which individuals have heterogeneous internal endowments of talents just in case for any two individuals' comprehensive sets of endowments, including their external endowments (wealth) and their internal endowments (talents), it is not the case that every individual in society prefers one individual's comprehensive endowment over the other's. If this ideal is not met, there is some individual whose comprehensive endowment is so poor that it is deemed worse than another individual's comprehensive endowment according to everyone's tastes. Van Parijs holds that the arrangement of society so that undominated diversity obtains is the appropriate response required by justice to the variation in talents and traits across persons. Van Parijs adds that the preferences that judge your endowment to be at least as good as anyone else's must be well considered and also genuinely available to you.

The undominated diversity norm seems to me far less than justice requires by way of compensation for people's bad luck in the natural lottery that determines one's talents. If Smith is blind and legless, but there is a single individual in society who genuinely judges that inability to move about freely and enjoy normal vision promotes the avoidance of worldly distractions and is a boon to one's spiritual growth, then, provided that

Smith could choose these spiritual growth preferences, distributive justice according to Van Parijs requires no transfer to offset Smith's very grim disabilities. This seems to me nonsense. At least, it makes the egalitarian credentials of his position highly dubious. But it is instructive to examine what has gone wrong. From my own standpoint, I would be inclined to rate people's endowments according to the degree that they help the individual to achieve one or another choiceworthy life. One problem with Van Parijs's undominated diversity construal of the requirement of compensation for lack of talent is that it does not require that the set of preferences that deems Smith's endowment acceptable be a reasonable set of preferences that would withstand rational scrutiny. Another problem is that the bare fact that a set of preferences could be chosen by Smith does not render those preferences an appropriate guide to the value of his talent endowment. The question is rather what sort of life Smith could lead given the aims and values he has (been given in early socialization) and the variations in these aims and values that it would make sense for him to choose or that it would be reasonable to expect him to reach in the course of his efforts to improve his aims and values. These difficulties seem to me to be knockdown objections against undominated diversity. But Van Parijs must resist them, because his insistence on neutrality on the good sharply constrains the distributive justice norms of compensation for talent deficit that he is willing to consider. The inadequacy of the undominated-diversity component of his theory is one of the theoretical costs of Van Parijs's rigid insistence on neutrality on the good.

My initial objection against the fairness of a basic income scheme thus stands. Even in a society that satisfies undominated diversity (because this norm is too little responsive to talent deficits), the maintenance of an unconditional basic income grant at the highest sustainable per capita level predictably leads to transfers of unconditional income supplements to a heterogeneous class of individuals that includes individuals who have above average real freedom prior to this transfer and should be net givers not takers in a just tax and transfer scheme.

A further interesting wrinkle in Van Parijs's analysis of distributive justice deserves mention. He expresses the worry that maximizing an unconditional basic income grant with undominated diversity prevailing is an inadequate implementation of the norm of leximinning real freedom, because under the basic income scheme two identically talented persons with opposed preferences for leisure as against income-generating activity will receive very different treatment. One may well be taxed to support the other. Why is this fair? Van Parijs interprets this as a worry that the basic income grant scheme arbitrarily favors those with pro-leisure rather than pro-paid work preferences. He allays the worry to his own satisfaction by noting that if external endowments (wealth) are from a moral standpoint owned by all of us, then an individual who foregoes the use of her per capita share of wealth for productive activity is owed compensation at market rates for her abstinence from the use of society's capital. He extends this account by appealing to efficiency wage and insider–outsider theories of the labor market to support the claim that since labor markets do not clear in equilibrium in actual economies, the holder of a job commands a wage that includes a large component of rent, which should be taxed away to increase the legitimate basic income grant. The idea, roughly, is that jobs may be considered external assets, abstinence from which entitles individuals to compensation. In this way we are led back to something close to the idea of maximizing the sustainable level of the basic income grant as the means to secure real freedom for all.

To my mind the inadequacy of undominated diversity as a distributive justice response to talent inequalities among persons haunts this entire complex discussion. To begin with, if an individual is extraordinarily talented, I would say that ideally the individual should be taxed on her ability to the point that a fair division of reasonable opportunities for a good life, a fair distribution of life prospects, is achieved. Fair division in this context requires maximizing a function of life prospects that gives substantial extra weight to securing improvements in the life prospects of those whose life prospects are below average. The worse off one is, the more it is a matter of moral urgency to alleviate one's plight. If one is measuring advantage levels in terms of real freedom rather than life prospects, it remains the case that with undominated diversity in place, giving a basic income grant to talented persons to the degree that they do not use in their work activity a per capita share of society's capital will predictably generate transfers to some advantaged persons who should not be beneficiaries of distributive justice transfers. Imagine that labor markets happen to perform in simple textbook fashion, so that markets clear at equilibrium (no one who is competent to perform a given task and wishes to do so at less than prevailing rates is unable to obtain such a job by underbidding current jobholders). In this world, with undominated diversity prevailing, distributive justice according to Van Parijs would recommend transfers only by way of a basic income grant that compensates those who use less than a per capita share of society's capital for their forbearance. Under plausible factual assumptions, this would be a morally topsy-turvy world in which distributive justice transfers would incorrectly require some of the disadvantaged to subsidize the incomes of some of the advantaged. Some surfers should not be fed.

Van Parijs associates the ideal of leximinning real freedom with two further resourcist norms of social justice, the notion of an envy-free distribution of resources and the notion that the appropriate measure of an individual's bundle of resources in a theory of distributive justice is the price the bundle would command at a competitive exchange equilibrium. The latter idea is further qualified: the value of an individual's resources so far as distributive justice is concerned is what others would be willing to pay for them at a competitive equilibrium that is determined by an initial fair distribution of purchasing power. In a large economy with a continuum of tastes, the envy-free condition can be met only by a distribution of resources such that the competitive exchange value of each person's bundle of resources is the same. These resourcist notions are worth examination independently of their purported links with the real freedom ideal.

The envy-free condition is met when no one prefers anyone else's bundle of resources to his own. The test can be applied without relying on any interpersonal comparisons of welfare and is on this ground attractive to those who are skeptical of the project of finding a nonarbitrary standard of interpersonal comparison. However, at the very least it does not appear to be suited to be the sole test of distributive fairness. Consider that if resources consist entirely of beef, a distribution of resources across a population of Moslems and Hindus in which Moslems have all the beef and Hindus have none will qualify as envy-free (at least if resources are to be used only for consumption and not for further trade). The studied indifference of the envy test to the utility that people get from resources is starkly illustrated here. Moreover, at the very least one should want distributive justice to include a standard for appraising the fairness of the processes that produce stocks of resources to be distributed.

Consider a world in which there are a number of goods that some people do not want at all. To address the point that even if one does not like X, one might still want to have some X, other things being equal, in order to sell this good to those who like it, suppose there are some goods that some people do not want at all – even to trade to others. (I am so repelled by guano, say, that I do not wish even to talk about the stuff to an agent who would trade it on my behalf.) Now consider a distribution in which all goods are distributed in identical lots to all members of society, followed by trade to equilibrium, and compare that distribution of resources to several others in which some good that some do not want is distributed among those who want it, and the remaining goods are distributed equally to all members of society, and trade to equilibrium then occurs. Call the distributions in which some goods that no one wants are treated specially in this way *targeted distributions*. The envy test does not distinguish among these distributions. All of them will equally pass the no-envy test. But there might well be fairness grounds for preferring some of these distributions over others, despite the fact that the envy test ranks them all equivalent. If so, the envy test is not a sufficient test for the justice of distributions.

Another worry about the envy test is that people's reasons for not envying the resources bundles of others might be ill-considered or otherwise problematic. Suppose that an oppressed housewife does not envy the resource allocations of men even though men have more of every resource than she does, because she is deferential, thinks men inherently deserve more than women and does not covet what she thinks for no very good reason she does not deserve. This objection is closely linked to an objection that has been lodged against simple desire satisfaction or life plan fulfillment conceptions of what individuals are owed according to justice. Unfair social conditions might crimp the desires and life plans of the disadvantaged, so their unfair treatment would not register if justice rates a society according to the extent to which individuals' desires are satisfied or life plans fulfilled. The unfair social conditions that crimp desire and distort the formation of life plans might also inhibit envy.

This point might be pushed further. Thomas Nagel has urged that the mere fact that another person has a preference for something does not in itself generate a reason for you to help the person get what he wants. After all, a preference could be a mere whim. The object of the preference might be bizarre. Even a persistent and heartfelt preference might strike a reasonable observer as lacking links to the person's well-being and to anything else that has any importance in human life. So a mere preference does not generate obligations on the part of others to bring about its satisfaction. Nagel's claim makes sense.

But under a regime in which the envy test is enforced as a fundamental justice norm, the mere fact that a great many people happen to have a particular preference partially determines the fair allocation of resources. Suppose I need a certain plastic for eyeglasses, but a whim of fashion dictates that many people want this same plastic for hula hoops, so its price is high. Why does justice require me to accept lesser satisfaction of my need for eyeglasses just because the preferences of other people happen to take an odd configuration? This line of thought suggests the desirability of shifting to a more idealized version of the hypothetical market that determines the just distribution of resources under the equal-division, trade-to-equilibrium formula. One might hold that the hypothetical market that determines the ideally just distribution of resources should be driven by ideally well-considered preferences – preferences that people would have if they engaged in ideal reflective deliberation about their values and aims. Under these conditions, the value of allocating a particular resource to one individual is determined by the cost of withholding it from others, with cost here measured not in terms of people's actual and perhaps whimsical or otherwise ill-considered preferences but in terms of their hypothetical ideally well-considered preferences.

Even with this idealization in place, we might still be beset by qualms about the fairness of the market procedure that is implementing the no-envy condition. Your idealized preferences for a certain scarce resource might be strong, while my idealized preferences for that resource are very weak, but the configuration of idealized preferences across persons brings it about that I can form a coalition with many persons with like-minded idealized preferences and bid up the cost of the resource. In this scenario your need (strong preference that would withstand critical scrutiny) is frustrated or made difficult to satisfy so that others can satisfy a very slight preference. It remains the case that mere preferences are ruling the roost.

Against this entire line of thought it might be protested that I am just assuming what the advocate of a resource-oriented conception of distributive justice denies and doing so without supporting argument, hence begging the question at issue. I am supposing that we can distinguish needs from mere preferences and true needs from false needs and what really contributes to someone's well-being from what does not, or contributes to a lesser extent. The moral basis of resourcism is the denial that these interpersonal comparisons of well-being can be made on a nonarbitrary basis. In a diverse democracy there is intractable disagreement among reasonable persons on the nature of the good, so reasonable persons must agree to disagree about these matters and agree on fair terms of social cooperation that are established on some noncontentious basis.

I have already indicated some reasons for being skeptical about the epistemic asymmetry claim that underlies this epistemic argument for resourcism. Leaving that issue to the side, I would hold that the moral appeal of the no-envy condition relies upon some implicit interpersonal comparisons of people's opportunities for well-being. My hunch is that we find attractive the ideal of a state of affairs in which no individual envies anyone else's bundle of resources because we vaguely suppose that such an allocation fairly divides opportunities for well-being.

But suppose we take seriously the idea that for purposes of distributive justice theory we have no basis whatsoever for looking behind people's resource shares to estimate what those resources might enable them to achieve by way of a good life. From the fact that Smith envies Jones's bundle of resources, nothing whatsoever follows about the goodness of the life that lies within Smith's reach as compared to what Jones can get. For all we know, the good life might be the attainment of a state of grace and the amount and character of the resources one possesses, regardless of one's preferences on these matters, are strictly irrelevant to one's prospects for a good life. Smith's envying Jones's resource bundle is equally compatible with Smith now having greater or smaller opportunity for a good life than Jones has. Shifting resources so that the direction of envy is reversed would leave it possible that Smith then would have greater or lesser opportunity for a good life than Jones would then have. We have no way at all to estimate which of these possibilities obtains. In these circumstances, I challenge that we have any reason for caring whether or not some agents envy the resource bundles of other agents. If we really have no idea whether the poor peasant with few resources has lesser prospects for a life of decent quality than the rich landlord with ample resources, then there is no fairness reason for transferring resources from one to the other. A strict agnosticism about human good should lead not to affirmation of a resource-oriented conception of justice but to euthanasia of distributive justice.

Neutrality on the good is the driving force that shapes the contours of Van Parijs's theory of distributive justice. Van Parijs holds that neutrality on the good requires that distribution be insensitive to ambition. That is to say, according to Van Parijs, the just society does not vary its treatment of individuals depending on their preferences and values. In a just society, the compensation for disadvantageous circumstances that distributive justice mandates will not be different for two individuals because their preferences are different. Ambition-insensitivity is Van Parijs's reason for disallowing compensation for inequalities in people's native talent endowments beyond what is dictated by the undominated diversity requirement. In particular, Dworkin's hypothetical insurance market against the risk that one's talents should turn out to have low-market value is rejected on the ground that it violates ambition-insensitivity.

It is worth pointing out that ambition-insensitivity also gives Van Parijs a response to my claim that the imperative of compensating individuals for their bad brute luck in their initial resource endowments requires compensating individuals for their defective ambitions when the domain of resources is extended to include internal resources such as personal talents. The argument was that among the talents that differ across persons are ambition and value selection talents. If one person has a low ability in this respect, it may afflict his life by leading him to embrace bad ambitions and values, and the logic of compensation for bad brute luck now requires compensation for bad brute luck that takes the form of coming to have such ambitions and values. A simple response not so far considered is available to Van Parijs. He can stipulate that the Dworkinian imperative of compensating for bad brute luck is attractive but must be subordinated to ambition-insensitivity, the more compelling justice requirement. When compensation for bad brute luck would conflict with ambition-insensitivity, the latter must trump, hence no compensation should be forthcoming for defective preferences even if the norm of compensation for bad brute luck taken on its own would support such compensation.

The obvious next question is why the fundamental value in the theory of justice is supposed to be ambition-insensitivity combined with neutrality on the good. One person values the cultivation of great art; a second values political achievement; a third values the cultivation of fine vegetables. Why should it be thought an imperative of justice that the treatment of persons mandated by justice should not vary with variations in values espoused? If we assumed that values were entirely imposed on each individual by early childhood socialization, it would seem puzzling that we would think we should hold the individual responsible for the consequences that befall her as a result of the particular values she espouses. It makes sense to hold individuals responsible for their ends in the sense of expecting them to bear the consequences of espousing them only if we think individuals really are responsible for their ends, that is, the best explanation of why an individual holds the values she does is that she has chosen or ratified them freely after critical reflection.

Notes

1. Philippe Van Parijs, *Real Freedom for All: What (if anything) can justify capitalism?* (Oxford: Clarendon Press, 1995).
2. John Rawls, 'The Priority of Right and Ideas of the Good', *Philosophy and Public Affairs* 17 (1988), pp. 251–76.
3. For Rawls, see his *A Theory of Justice* (Cambridge: Harvard University Press, 1971); also Rawls, *Political Liberalism* (New York: Columbia University Press, 1993). For Dworkin, see his 'What Is Equality? Part 1: Equality of Welfare', *Philosophy and Public Affairs* 10 (1981), pp. 185–246; his 'What Is Equality? Part 2: Equality of Resources', *Philosophy and Public Affairs* 10 (1981),

pp. 283–345, both of which are reprinted in *Sovereign Virtue* (Cambridge: Harvard University Press, 2000).

4. Rawls, *Theory of Justice*, p. 94.

5. I have argued that Van Parijs fails to show that the ideal of real freedom as he conceives it is sufficiently determinate to support the claim that leximinning real freedom requires instituting an unconditional basic income at the highest sustainable level. See my 'Is Socialism Dead? A Comment on Market Socialism and Basic Income Capitalism', *Ethics* 102 (1992), pp. 485–511; see esp. pp. 501–6. In *Real Freedom for All* Van Parijs concedes this point. The argument for basic income now hinges not on a claim about real freedom but on claims concerning the implications of neutrality on the good and the no-envy test.

7
Resource Egalitarianism and the Limits to Basic Income[1]

Andrew Williams

In his widely-discussed book, *Real Freedom for All*, Philippe Van Parijs argues that justice requires the provision of a universal, unconditional basic income.[2] Some critics reject that conclusion on the grounds that it violates requirements of reciprocity or prohibitions on exploitation, freeriding and parasitism.[3] This paper explores a less familiar critique, which operates within the same resource egalitarian parameters as Van Parijs's argument, and leaves unchallenged his conviction that justice requires a basic income. Instead, the paper suggests two reasons to doubt his ambitious claims about its magnitude. First, the paper argues that if envy elimination is the fundamental egalitarian aim then Van Parijs's argument for boosting basic income by including jobs within the class of external assets to be equalized is unsuccessful. Second, it argues that Van Parijs fails to show that the provision of basic income should not be constrained by a more restrictive principle for correcting inequalities in personal resources than his favored compensatory norm. Before defending these criticisms, two preliminary sections describe Van Parijs's distributive principles and his central argument for basic income.

7.1 Real libertarianism and resource egalitarianism

Van Parijs's conception of justice combines two elements. The *real libertarian* element claims that a society is just only if it satisfies principles of *security*, *self-ownership* and *leximin opportunity* (p. 25).[4] Despite their rhetorical prominence, it is important to understand that Van Parijs relies on far more than real libertarian principles. In fact, security and self-ownership are not reasons for, but constraints upon, the provision of a basic income, whilst leximin opportunity is never claimed to require such provision.[5] In order to show that basic income is the uniquely fair way of leximinimizing opportunity, Van Parijs relies upon a second resource egalitarian element. Since that element plays a major role in my later criticisms, it requires further description.

Van Parijs initially appeals to resource egalitarian considerations to defend his presumption that basic income should be provided in cash rather than kind. He concedes that because of the difficulties in ranking non-inclusive opportunity sets by means of leximin opportunity such a presumption cannot be established on real libertarian grounds alone (pp. 48–9). Discussing the case of Funny and Sunny, who have identical basic incomes but quite different preferences regarding the rental of cliff and beach space, he presents an alternative solution. The prices for beach and cliff rental should not be influenced by transfers in kind, but should instead be *'perfectly competitive equilibrium prices*, that is … the set of prices that would equalize supply and demand as a result of the atomistic, perfectly informed, and unhindered interaction of Funny and Sunny, and all their fellow citizens, each endowed with an equal basic income' (p. 49). Defending that solution, he invokes two related resource egalitarian conceptions of what constitutes a fair distribution of opportunities, which I shall term *value equalization* and *efficient envy elimination*, or *envy elimination* for short.

Describing value equalization, Van Parijs points out that his proposal requires that 'the heterogeneous bundles of goods … different people are endowed with should all have the same competitive value. In other words the proposal amounts to choosing competitive values as the appropriate metric for judging whether external-resource-based freedom is fairly distributed' (p. 49). According to the appeal to value equalization, distributions of opportunities which are non-comparable in terms of leximin opportunity can still be ranked by focusing on only one of the factors which the extent of individuals' opportunity-sets depends upon, namely their external endowments. The appeal requires that each individual's external endowment should have the price it would command in a competitive market with equal purchasing power. Therefore, according to Van Parijs, fairness in the distribution of real freedom requires an *equal-endowment competitive equilibrium*, in which each individual's assets possess the same market value.

Van Parijs assumes that such a requirement has some immediate appeal, but provides further support for it 'by pointing out its close link to the notion of *equity*, as characterized by a number of economists in terms of the conjunction of efficiency and envy-freeness' (p. 52). According to this second conception of fairness, as envy elimination, if a distribution of assets is fair then (1) there is no alternative feasible distribution preferred by at least one individual, which makes no other individual worse off, and (2) there is no individual who prefers some other individual's endowmènt to her own. Since they possess those properties, Van Parijs suggests that equal-endowment competitive equilibria are morally attractive for two reasons. First, such equilibria, because they arise via free-exchange between identically-situated individuals, achieve an efficient and envy-free distribution of endowments. Second, and more importantly, where preferences take a particular form – to be discussed in section 7.5 – *only* such equilibria do so.[6]

7.2   From resource egalitarianism to basic income

Van Parijs's resource egalitarian argument for basic income is developed at greatest length in his treatment of a second example, the case of Crazy and Lazy, who are identical in their personal endowments but attach varying priorities to income and leisure. Faced with the radical proposal to maximize basic income, which Lazy prefers, Van Parijs imagines Crazy to respond with the following challenge: 'You and I have identical talents. So why on Earth do we need a basic income at all?' (p. 93). He then presents two diametrically opposed Rawlsian responses to the challenge, one of which provides reasons to maximize basic income whilst the other prohibits its existence (pp. 95–6). Having criticized the latter because of what he asserts is its 'discriminatory' and 'perfectionist' bias, Van Parijs suggests that a principled argument exists to solve the dispute between Crazy and Lazy.

To do so, Van Parijs returns to the resource egalitarian strategy he adopted to identify a fair distribution of non-inclusive opportunity sets between Funny and Sunny. He describes its relevance to the present parable in a passage worth quoting at length:

> [T]o generate the level of income she wants to reach, it is safe to assume and crucial to notice, Crazy needs certain assets external to her talents, say a plot of land. Endowing (identically talented) Crazy and Lazy with equal plots of land certainly constitutes one non-discriminatory allocation of real freedom between them. But if this allocation is not tradable, if they are both stuck with it, this allocation cannot be optimal from a real libertarian standpoint. It will not give either Crazy or Lazy the highest attainable level of real freedom. Crazy may be desperate to use more than her plot of land, while Lazy would not mind being deprived of some or even all of his in exchange for part of what Crazy would produce with it. This directly

yields the following suggestion. *There is a non-arbitrary and generally positive legitimate level of basic income that is determined by the per capita value of society's external assets and must be entirely financed by those who appropriate these assets.*

(p. 99, emphasis added)

Van Parijs's solution is to suggest that individuals such as Lazy, in virtue of their equal entitlement to external assets, can rightfully claim an unconditional income set at the price which the assets they relinquish would command in an auction arising through trade from an initial position in which those entitlements were respected (p. 100). Generalizing from his treatment of land to other assets, Van Parijs adds that 'the whole set of external means that affect people's capacity to pursue their conceptions of the good life, irrespective of whether they are natural or produced' (p. 101) should be treated similarly. The value of gifts and bequests of those assets should be taxed at a yield-maximizing rate, which takes into account incentive effects on their depletion and production, and the proceeds distributed via basic income.

Though Van Parijs emphasizes that 'a work-independent income is unambiguously justified' (p. 100) by his proposal, it is also worth noting that, in setting the level of that income, the proposal steers a middle course between the pro-Lazy and pro-Crazy Rawlsian responses. Unlike the former, it does not recommend maximizing basic income as such. For example, as Van Parijs himself notes, it cannot support basic income in 'a world where Crazies need no land (or any other scarce asset)' (p. 262, n. 18). Rather it requires maximizing the level of basic income which can be financed from taxes on unequally distributed scarce external assets. Thus, Van Parijs concedes that the

> difference between the criterion involved here – which could be called the Dworkinian criterion – and our initial [pro-Lazy] criterion … is then not more nor less than the restriction on the tax base. Subtracting from Crazy's income more than the value of the external endowment she has somehow received, as allowed by our initial criterion but not by the Dworkinian one, would amount to giving her a smaller endowment than to Lazy, and is therefore inconsistent with our real-libertarian perspective, duly specified so as to rule out discrimination.

(p. 102)

Whilst rejecting the pro-Lazy scheme, which maximizes basic income, Van Parijs's proposal is still ambitious. For although he grants that the level of basic income financed from gifts and bequests might be low – amounting to only 0.25 per cent of GNP in France (p. 102) – he advances the following intriguing argument to boost the level of basic income. It claims that the legitimate tax base is sufficiently extensive to warrant 'under contemporary conditions in the advanced capitalist world, a very substantial basic income' (p. 106). Such is the case since we live in *job societies*, where production is mostly organized through the employment relation, which have *non-Walrasian economies,* insofar as their labor markets do not tend to clear. Under such conditions, employment opportunities are one highly important though scarce means to pursue a conception of the good. Thus, Van Parijs concludes that, along with wealth and personal endowment, 'holding...a job constitutes a third type of asset' (p. 108).

Such an asset, Van Parijs maintains, should be treated in an equivalent manner to other external assets:

> In the case of scarce land, we gave each member of the society concerned a tradable entitlement to an equal share of that land, and the endowment-equalizing level of the basic income was given by the per capita competitive value of the available land ... Similarly, in the case of scarce jobs, let us give each member of the society concerned a tradable entitlement to an equal share of those jobs. The endowment-equalizing level of the (additional) basic income will then similarly be given by the per capita competitive value of the available jobs.
>
> (p. 108)

Fully implementing this proposal under ideal conditions, he explains, requires identifying the *employment rent* associated with each job type, which is given by subtracting its counterfactual competitive price from the actual income and other advantages associated with it, and then redistributing all such rents via basic income. But, because of strategic considerations which might render such a high tax rate self-defeating, Van Parijs recognizes – as in the case of external assets – the need to limit redistribution to preserve the level of basic income (pp. 114–15). And, because of epistemic difficulties in identifying rents, given that some jobs have non-pecuniary advantages, he finally concludes the 'generalized Dworkinian criterion recommends that *wages* should be taxed up to the point at which the tax yield, and hence the basic income financed by it, is maximized' (p. 116, emphasis added).

7.3   The restriction objection

My initial criticism of Van Parijs's argument claims the possibility of eliminating envy without equalizing value undermines his attempt to boost basic income by treating jobs similarly to other external assets. The criticism assumes that value equalization is not of ultimate moral value, but possesses only derivative importance because of its contribution to envy elimination. That assumption, though debatable, is plausible. As noted previously, the only support which Van Parijs provides for value equalization appeals to envy elimination (p. 52). Furthermore, he provides no reason to demand more than the efficient elimination of envy where that principle can be satisfied without equalizing value. I now argue that, granted my assumption about the relative importance of value equalization and envy elimination, justice does not require that all share in the full value of job assets.

To understand the *restriction objection*, as I shall term it, consider again a world of Crazies and Lazies, each with an equal entitlement to the external assets of land and jobs. Note that an important dissimilarity exists between these two assets. No liabilities are standardly involved in possessing land assets. Individuals may toil on their land, as Crazy prefers, but need not do so in order to qualify as owners and beneficiaries. Instead, like Lazy, they can relax and wait for their rents to roll in. However, a job asset – at least on one not unnatural construal, to be scrutinized in section 7.5 – is liability-involving since an individual possesses it only if she fulfills certain duties. One does not reap the full benefit of the asset unless one discharges the liabilities, which generally involve forgoing leisure. This, we suppose, is an implication of Van Parijs's remark that jobs are 'packages of tasks and benefits' (p. 90). Evidently those tasks are burdensome to many individuals. Furthermore, they may be sufficiently burdensome that some individuals would, all things considered, prefer not to possess a job asset due to the liabilities associated with doing so.

Suppose now that the return from Lazy's share of land is sufficiently high that he prefers to be free of all the liabilities involved in possessing job assets. Thus, even when holding no job, and no further external asset to take its place, he does not prefer the circumstances of job-holding Crazy. Assuming equality requires only the elimination of envy, Lazy's equal entitlement to external assets can be satisfied despite the fact that he does not hold any job assets but remains unemployed. If so, individuals' equal claims on external assets do not require that the market value of *all* such assets is redistributed by means of a basic income which is both *universal* and *unconditional*.[7]

It appears then that, unless Van Parijs can show that equality requires more than the elimination of envy, he must choose between the following two options. First, he can tax the full set of external endowments, including all job assets, and restrict receipt of the proceeds to individuals with an interest in those assets. Second, he can restrict taxation to a reduced set of external endowments, excluding at least some job assets, and maintain his commitment to universal, unconditional redistribution. Thus, Van Parijs's dilemma involves either abandoning basic income, by relinquishing universality and unconditionality, or reducing the level of basic income by limiting its tax base. I conclude from the restriction objection that if Van Parijs is to maintain his fundamental conviction that justice requires a universal unconditional basic income, then he must concede that he has overestimated its magnitude.

7.4   Is restriction illiberal or unfair?

How might Van Parijs reply to the restriction objection? His most immediate defense occurs in his response to those who suggest that one should 'restrict the benefits of rent sharing to the involuntarily unemployed, those who are really affected by the scarcity of jobs' (p. 109). One should not do so, he argues,

> as long as one wishes to stick to the *liberal ban on discrimination between conceptions of the good life*, for adopting a policy that focuses on the involuntarily unemployed amounts to *awarding a privilege to people with an expensive taste for a scarce asset*. Those who, for whatever reason, give up their share of that asset and thereby leave more of it for others, should not therefore be deprived of a fair share of its value.
>
> (p. 109, emphasis added)

To evaluate this defense, note first that it elides two distinct criticisms of the restriction objection.

The *liberal criticism* claims that such restriction is objectionably illiberal because guided by the conviction that the voluntarily unemployed have a conception of well-being unworthy of desire. Endorsing restriction is therefore comparable to refusing public funds to Christian or gay groups on the grounds that they peddle superstition and sin. Like those refusals, restriction should be rejected because it is animated by considerations which are illegitimate reasons for political action. Construed as such, however, the liberal criticism is inapplicable to my argument since it does not deny that voluntary unemployment is a worthwhile way of life.

In contrast, Van Parijs's second *expensive taste criticism* is more forceful and exposes an interesting aspect of the deceptively simple charge that it is unjust to reward expensive tastes. The criticism alleges that the proposed restriction is objectionable because it is unfair rather than illiberal. Endorsing restriction – Van Parijs implies but does not explicitly claim – is comparable to recommending redistribution in Dworkin's well-known example of Louis. In order to evaluate that charge, and explore the issues it raises, I now describe the example and the lesson Dworkin draws from it.[8]

Dworkin argues against welfare egalitarianism by, amongst other things, constructing the following counter-example. We are to assume equality of welfare has been achieved with an equal distribution of resources, and one individual, Louis, acquires a new-found taste for the high-life. Louis's later ambitions are expensive relative to his earlier ones, since his welfare will now decrease unless he acquires more resources than he currently possesses. Most importantly, they are also expensive relative to others' ambitions, which have remained unchanged. Louis will now enjoy the same welfare as them only if he has a larger share of resources than they possess. Under such conditions, Dworkin suggests, equality of welfare may well recommend redistributing resources to Louis. But, he supposes, we find such a recommendation unjust. Since our conviction that it is so depends on the fact that Louis requests more than an equal share of resources, resource egalitarianism best explains our opposition to Louis's demand. Thus, it is a superior conception of justice to welfare egalitarianism.

Suppose we share Dworkin's opposition to Louis's request for redistribution. Does it follow that we should also accept that there is reason not to restrict receipt of employment rents to the involuntarily unemployed since it 'amounts to awarding a privilege to people with an expensive taste for a scarce asset' (p. 109)? In answering this question, I shall argue that Van Parijs's critical use of the notion of expensive tastes assumes rather than provides independent support for his conviction that all should benefit from job assets. Furthermore, endorsing Dworkin's response to Louis is consistent with advocating restriction.

Let me begin by conceding that there is one sense in which the involuntarily unemployed do possess an expensive taste when compared with the voluntarily unemployed. Given their occupational ambitions, *ceteris paribus*, the former require more scarce resources than the latter to obtain the same level of welfare. The question is, however, whether their receiving those resources as a result of them possessing that taste is inequality-generating in a morally objectionable respect. Van Parijs's description of them as being awarded a 'privilege' implies that it does possess this objectionable feature, as does his description of the voluntarily unemployed being 'deprived of their fair share' (p. 109). It is important, nevertheless, to note that these claims require defense, and are not entailed by the mere fact that the involuntarily unemployed receive more of some asset.

To see why, consider a distribution of pork chops between those who love and loathe them. Suppose we assume that the latter's aversion is so great that they would not even wish to trade let alone consume them. Given such preferences, a distribution in which the former receive all the pork whilst the latter receive none would still be envy-free. Suppose, like Dworkin, we endorse the envy-test as our fundamental criterion for an equal distribution of non-arbitrarily constructed bundles of resources. If so, then we would regard such a distribution as equal. We would deny that those averse to pork had been the victims of inequality, or deprived of their fair share, though it would still be true of each pork lover that they possessed a relatively expensive taste, and that they had received more of a resource than others in part because of their taste for it. We can draw the intermediate conclusion that if Van Parjis's insinuation that the involuntarily unemployed are comparable to Louis is defensible, he cannot merely claim they have more than others as a result of their tastes. He must appeal to some specific conception of equality which explains why their having more should be objectionable to egalitarians. Only then can he explain why restriction is unjust.

It would be wrong to suggest that Van Parijs does not appeal to such an explanation; indeed, his later reference to the voluntarily unemployed being entitled to a fair share of the *value* of job assets does so. It is possible then for Van Parijs to elaborate his second objection by claiming that subsidizing Louis and restricting rent redistribution are morally comparable because both violate the principle of value equalization. However, once we appreciate the need to elaborate the second objection, and the most likely means of elaboration, its failure to provide independent support for Van Parijs's position becomes apparent. For in order to explain why allocating more resources to individuals with expensive tastes is objectionable in this case, Van Parijs needs to invoke a conception of equal entitlement which itself requires that rents be distributed uniformly between the voluntarily and involuntarily unemployed. But if that conception is sound, reference to expensive tastes can be eliminated. The offensive against restriction can be conducted by showing how it flouts the equal entitlement to benefit from employment rents. There is then a sense in which the second objection is circular: Van

Parijs's expensive taste criticism assumes, rather than provides independent support for, his conviction that all should benefit from job assets.

Reflecting on the distinction between value equalization and envy elimination also indicates how we can consistently share Dworkin's opposition to Louis whilst advocating restriction. We can do so by claiming that Louis's request for more resources is objectionable since it asks that more than an equal share of resources be devoted to his life in the sense identified by the envy test. Distributing more job assets, or the rent from those assets, to those who are involuntarily rather than voluntarily unemployed is not inequality-generating in the same respect. Therefore, since we can forbear appeal to value equalization, we can reject Louis's demand whilst consistently advocating restriction. The restriction objection, I conclude, withstands both the liberal and the expensive taste criticisms.

7.5   Further replies

At least two further replies to the restriction objection are implicit in *Real Freedom for All*. They provide both formal and informal reasons to doubt that envy elimination and value equalization will diverge significantly when the class of external assets is expanded to include jobs. Van Parijs mentions the relevant formal reason when explaining how the gap between the two resource egalitarian principles can be bridged under certain conditions. Proof exists that, given assumptions about population size and preference variation, all envy-free distributions are value equalizing.[9] Van Parijs sketches the proof's conclusion, and its relevance to the problem of showing why equal-endowment competitive equilibria are uniquely attractive, as follows:

> In a large economy with tastes widely scattered, it is no longer true that there are many allocations which are not equal-endowment competitive equilibria and yet are both efficient and envy-free. In the extreme case in which there is a continuum of smooth preferences, it can be shown that only a competitive equilibrium allocation with identically endowed traders at the start can both be efficient and satisfy the no-envy test. To the extent that the real world resembles this continuous world rather than the polarized Funny/Sunny one, our problem [of further justifying value equalization] is solved.
>
> (pp. 53–4, and cf. p. 100)

It appears then that where each individual has a neighboring individual, whose preferences only barely differ, any inequality in the value of assets must generate envy. Such is the case because those advantaged by the inequality will make choices unavailable to their neighbors, who because of their similar ambitions would wish to change places.[10]

It would be interesting to know if our world, which Van Parijs's case for basic income addresses, exhibits the relevant conditions. However, because Van Parijs makes the following two further claims, it seems unlikely that he would rely on this type of contingency. First, he claims that his case succeeds in the possible worlds inhabited by Crazy and Lazy, yet these do not exhibit the requisite continuity in preference. Second, such reliance implies that an individual's entitlement to basic income depends upon her having preferences relevantly similar to some other individuals, thereby jeopardizing the unconditionality upon individual preference which Van Parijs claims is characteristic of basic income.

The second informal reason to doubt that envy elimination and value equalization will diverge concerns the specific case of job assets. It challenges the construal of those assets employed by the restriction objection when it claims that envy elimination might be achieved even if the voluntarily unemployed lack some share of the value of job assets. In so doing, it highlights an important aspect of the equity approach to distributive justice by reminding us that the implications of a conception of equity depend upon how the items to be distributed equally are characterized. Such dependence applies both to the value equalization and the envy elimination variants. We can calculate the price of some asset only if we can estimate how much individuals, given their preferences, would be willing to pay for it in an equal endowment competitive equilibrium. Yet this depends upon the rights and duties involved in its possession. Similarly we can judge whether one individual prefers another's assets to her own only if we have an accurate specification of the rights and duties attached to each set of assets.

The informal reason forces us to examine more carefully the characterization of job assets presupposed by the restriction objection. It thereby calls into question the suggestion that whether Lazy would react with envy to the news that Crazy possessed more scarce external assets than him depends on which assets are involved. For, recall, I did not challenge the claim that Lazy would envy Crazy's larger share of land, even though he had no desire to use it productively. It was granted that, because land is an alienable asset, Lazy could value it as a means to gain the product of others' labor. Instead I challenged the claim that Lazy would react similarly to Crazy's larger share of job assets. In so doing I assumed that job assets were liability involving, and that possession of the asset required, for example, relinquishing a certain quantity of leisure. Given Lazy's preference for leisure, I inferred that he would not envy Crazy's assets. And I employed this as a premise to argue that he, and those in our society who are voluntarily unemployed, should not share fully in the redistribution of employment rents. The informal reply claims my premise rests upon a mischaracterization of job assets: even if liability involving, their possession, and thus the right to benefit from them, does not require forgoing leisure.

To appreciate the reply more fully consider this analogy. Suppose car-ownership is encumbered with liabilities; for example, performing repairs at regular intervals. If an individual retains possession of her car, then she must eventually forgo some leisure. Even so, such encumbrance does not preclude her possessing the power to alienate the property, via market exchange. Thus, it is consistent with her possessing a right which enables her to benefit from the asset without fulfilling the liabilities. The liability then will merely reduce the extent to which she benefits, assuming potential buyers are liability averse. The restriction objection then appears flawed because it overlooks one crucial aspect of Van Parijs's recommendation that, in the case of scarce jobs, we assume each individual has a '*tradable* entitlement to an equal share of those jobs' (p. 108, emphasis added). The marketability of job assets renders them enviable items even for leisure lovers like Lazy, or the willingly unemployed.

These considerations suggest that the restriction objection needs to be buttressed. Let the objection now also claim that Van Parijs has not justified characterizing job assets as tradable. But, unless they are so characterized, the willingly unemployed will not envy those who possess job assets, and hence can be legitimately excluded from the redistribution of employment rents. Thus, a conclusive refutation of the strengthened objection depends on showing that the characterization of job assets as tradable can be justified. I shall suggest that the argument Van Parijs provides to justify this characterization of other external assets fails. The most obvious alternative method of characterizing assets, however, warrants treating jobs differently from external assets. I therefore conclude that, at best, Van Parijs's argument for boosting basic income is incomplete.

Despite the centrality of asset tradability to Van Parijs's case for basic income, it is notable that the assumption receives relatively little defense. However, as mentioned earlier, Van Parijs does suggest that the market inalienability of entitlements to land would produce a sub-optimal distribution of real freedom (p. 99). The suggestion appeals to the fact that tradability may enhance both Crazy's and Lazy's real freedom to produce more, or to enjoy more leisure, than they otherwise could. For, given tradability and others' willingness to trade, they consequently have the opportunity of buying or selling land in order, respectively, to expand production or to diminish the need to produce. Unfortunately, however, it neglects to consider whether leximin opportunity might be too indeterminate to warrant so substantial a conclusion. That suspicion seems well founded, since it is not true that market alienability always renders opportunities more extensive, all things considered. Instead, creating some real freedoms may come at the price of destroying others.[11] For example, if assets are tradable, Lazy no longer has the opportunity to bestow gifts on the land-hungry which they otherwise could not buy. It appears then that since Van Parijs's explicit defense of tradability fails even in the case of standard external assets, it is unlikely to succeed for job assets. How then should those assets be characterized?

One natural answer is that they should be characterized realistically, in the following sense. If we are attempting to identify an equitable distribution of assets in some particular society, and we include jobs with the class of assets, then we should characterize jobs by means of the rights and liabilities actually associated with being a job-holder in that society. Suppose, plausibly, that in the societies Van Parijs is addressing, possession of a job depends on the performance of certain tasks and is inalienable via exchange or donation. Our answer then implies that, when applying the envy test to job assets in those societies, they should be characterized as liability involving in the sense assumed by the restriction objection. We can, therefore, persist in claiming that the willingly unemployed are not forced to endure less than their equal share of assets even if they do not benefit from employment rents. We should conclude that Van Parijs's case for boosting basic income depends on an assumption of tradability which has not been successfully defended, and is open to criticism.

7.6   Undominated diversity

Thus far I have abstracted from one urgent problem which exercises many egalitarians. I have assumed that individuals do not differ in their internal resources in any respect which warrants redistribution. It has therefore been unnecessary to ask how inequalities in such resources should be conceived, and what treatment they should receive.

Like other egalitarians, Van Parijs recognizes the need to deal with these questions, but he responds in a highly distinctive manner. He accepts that justice requires more than the enforcement of real libertarian principles and implementation of the resource egalitarian case for basic income. In addition, he claims that individuals should be compensated for deficits in personal endowment until a condition termed *undominated diversity* has been achieved (p. 73). That condition requires that no individual's *comprehensive endowment*, comprising her internal and external resources, is dominated, in the sense that there exists some other individual whose endowment is unanimously preferred to hers. Because self-ownership prohibits compensation via the redistribution of internal resources, undominated diversity is to be pursued, where necessary, by redistributing external assets until no individuals remain dominated.

Since the achievement of undominated diversity has weighty though non-absolute priority in determining how the tax yield is to be redistributed (pp. 83–4), it constitutes an important moral limit on the provision of basic income.[12] My second *constraint objection* suggests that Van Parijs underestimates the extent to which the level of basic income should be reduced to make amends for personal endowment inequalities. I shall argue that his own compensatory proposal cries out for defense, yet the grounds Van Parijs supplies for it are vulnerable to criticism. Assuming alternative proposals would require greater redistribution, the constraint objection provides a second reason to doubt Van Parijs's optimism about the magnitude of a legitimate basic income.

Before evaluating Van Parijs's position, note one reason, internal to *Real Freedom for All*, why undominated diversity requires considerable defense. The unanimity requirement, central to Van Parijs's conception of inequality in internal assets, renders undominated diversity significantly different from the various other principles he employs in conceiving inequality in external assets. As noted earlier, according to undominated diversity, A's internal resources are worse than B's only if *everyone* prefers the latter to the former. The form of this claim contrasts with leximin opportunity, envy elimination and value equalization. The unanimity requirement could, in at least some cases, be met when even the weakest of these principles, leximin opportunity, is not satisfied. Despite the fact that, given their respective endowments, A's opportunities are a proper subset of B's, A's endowment still might not be dominated since some individual might not value, or might be averse to, B's additional opportunities. Furthermore, both conceptions of equity are clearly more difficult to satisfy than undominated diversity.

Van Parijs himself expresses the former difference when he notes that,

> What is required by … envy-freeness over external endowments is that there be no pair of people such that one prefers the other person's endowment to her own. What undominated diversity requires

is only that there be no pair of people such that *all* prefer one person's endowment to the other's.

(p. 76)

Furthermore, in order for one comprehensive endowment to possess a higher competitive price than another requires only that some and not all prefer it and so are willing to pay more for it.

Given such contrasts, it is pressing to ask how Van Parijs defends undominated diversity. Without an adequate explanation, critics might assume his adoption of that principle is merely a marriage of convenience, contrived to preserve a high basic income. That assumption, however, is unwarranted. Van Parijs does provide a complex and original case for undominated diversity. Much of that case appears to have the form of argument by elimination, and proceeds via a series of objections against three rival resource egalitarian approaches to personal resource variation. The former pair involve generalizing envy elimination and value equalization to internal assets, whilst Dworkin's hypothetical insurance scheme is the third alternative. Insofar as he pursues this strategy alone, Van Parijs risks the predictable rejoinder that his own proposal is itself flawed.[13] He therefore also attempts to rebut that rejoinder. I shall now argue that two of Van Parijs's major eliminative arguments are unsuccessful, and that his rebuttal is unconvincing.

7.7   The slavery of the talented

Suppose that we require that comprehensive endowments possess equal competitive value, as measured by a hypothetical auction in which identically situated individuals bid not only for external resources but also for internal resources, taking into account only their effects on earning power. Against this *extended auction*, Van Parijs urges us to consider the case of Lonely and her sibling Lovely, which he describes as follows: 'Regarding taste, both siblings are identical. In particular, they both care comparatively little for a high income, while attaching great importance to the enjoyment of free time. Regarding talent, they are identically mediocre in all respects except one: unlike Lonely, Lovely is truly ravishing' (p. 64). Both characters, he claims, can justifiably complain that the extended auction treats them unjustly. I shall concentrate on Lovely's objection, since, unlike Lonely's (pp. 64–5), it does not depend on the unnecessarily restrictive assumption that personal endowment differences are relevant only insofar as they affect earning power.[14]

Van Parijs argues that assuming that 'Lovely's gorgeous looks enable her to earn a handsome income by displaying them in a peep-show' and that 'she hates that job – as would her sibling if she were given it' (p. 64), Lovely can reject the proposal. Such is the case since her remunerative abilities would command a high price in the extended auction. The proposal therefore demands that she pay a much higher lump-sum ability tax than Lonely, which she may be able to meet only by working in the peep-show. Van Parijs defends Lovely's complaint against the demand as follows:

> Far from being able to indulge in the same leisurely life pattern as her sibling, she is forced to devote a large chunk of her time – not all of it, but enough to pay the tax and subsist – doing a job she thoroughly hates. Is this not frightfully *unfair to Lovely*, indeed *a form of slavery that violates self-ownership* and constitutes an obvious insult to the ideal of real-freedom-for-all?
>
> (p. 64, emphasis added)

As his question suggests, Van Parijs's defense of Lovely draws upon two distinct types of consideration. It implies both that Lovely is unfairly treated compared with her sibling, and that she is unjustly enslaved in a manner which need involve no comparison with how others are treated.

To appreciate the complexity involved in Van Parijs's opposition to what has become known as 'the slavery of the talented', it is useful to distinguish two senses in which the talented might be considered enslaved, or forced to work, by the extended auction.[15] *Comparative slavery* obtains if there exist non-enslaved individuals, and their circumstances are preferred by the enslaved. Though this is the most familiar form of slavery, it is not the only conceivable variety. It contrasts with *non-comparative slavery*, which obtains when individuals are enslaved but there exist no non-enslaved individuals, whose circumstances are preferred by the enslaved. For illustration, suppose that as a war intensifies the states involved move from a regime of non-universal to universal conscription of labor. In so doing, they replace comparative with non-comparative slavery.

Our distinction is important since comparative slavery is vulnerable to an egalitarian objection to which non-comparative slavery is immune. In the former regime an enslaved individual will be able to complain that she envies the lot of some other individual. That may not suffice to render the regime unjust – perhaps the elimination of envy is a futile or counterproductive aim – but it does possess some prima-facie force. However, that complaint is unavailable in the latter regime, objections to which must be expressed in some other form.

To evaluate Van Parijs's objection to the extended auction we need to ask if it assumes Lovely is a victim of the comparative or non-comparative slavery of the talented. Answering this question, however, is difficult since Van Parijs's example is under-described, in at least one important respect. We are told that Lovely has the same income–leisure trade-off as her sibling, and prefers the latter's leisure prospects. But we are unaware of what could be termed her beauty–leisure trade-off. It is, therefore, an open question whether Lovely does, or does not, prefer Lonely's leisure prospects when combined with the personal endowment on which they depend, namely 'her spotty face and funny nose' (p. 64). I shall now argue that in either case Van Parijs's critique of the extended auction is less persuasive than it first appears.

Suppose Lovely does think her liability to the lump-sum tax is too high a price to pay for her gorgeous looks, and prefers Lonely's combined leisure and beauty resources. She can then object to the extended auction on the egalitarian ground that it treats her unfairly, by making her a victim of comparative slavery. However, if that is her complaint, it can be accommodated by a natural revision of the extended auction. It recommends that individuals who are unfortunate in their personal endowment should be compensated via lump-sum taxes on those who are more fortunate *provided the level of the tax does not reverse the direction of envy*. We must not over-compensate those who lose in the natural lottery by taxing the winners at such a high rate that they prefer the endowments and tax exemptions of the losers. But that concession does not prohibit all taxes upon personal endowments.

Suppose instead that Lovely does not envy Lonely's combined leisure and beauty resources. If so, then she cannot employ the egalitarian objection we described in order to sustain the claim she is unfairly treated. She could, however, still object that she is a victim of non-comparative slavery for a reason suggested by Van Parijs's references to self-ownership. According to that objection any ability-tax, payment of which requires extensive and costly sacrifices of leisure, violates individual rights (pp. 64, 21). Pursuing this argument, Lovely might claim that even if each individual is required to make similar sacrifices of leisure as herself, they might still all have the same legitimate complaint against the regime which enforced such requirements. For, in so doing, the regime fails to respect their self-ownership.

As a criticism of the extended auction proposal, the appeal to self-ownership has the merit that it cannot be by-passed by modifying the proposal in a way which does not deprive it of substance. I shall not, therefore, respond by claiming that self-ownership merely diminishes the rate, rather than eliminates the possibility, of legitimate ability taxes. However, the appeal has the demerit that, despite being recognized as controversial (p. 9), the principle of self-ownership receives virtually no defense in *Real Freedom for All*, and sits uneasily with other elements of real libertarianism, such as the concern to leximinimize opportunities.[16] Furthermore, whilst the appeal opposes lump-sum taxes forcing individuals to devote large chunks of their time to jobs they hate, it does not condemn them having – like many actual individuals in societies lacking ability-taxes – to make similar choices because of the combined effects of the property structure, their lack of marketable skills, and need to subsist. Van Parijs's employment of the principle of self-ownership assumes that, but does not explain why, these two types of situation are not morally comparable.

I conclude then that, once the two types of objection to the slavery of the talented are distinguished, Van Parijs's case against the extended auction faces a dilemma. Its egalitarian opposition to the unfairness of ability taxes can be accommodated by an extended auction which is suitably constrained by the envy test. Its libertarian opposition to the injustice of those taxes is implacable. But, when clearly distinguished from the former objection, it appears dogmatic and incomplete.

7.8   Fair insurance

Suppose instead of the extended auction, we endorse Dworkin's suggestion that individuals should be compensated for bad brute luck in their personal endowment, at a level to be calculated by the operation of a fair insurance market. Van Parijs alleges the following decisive objection applies to all variants of that suggestion, when applied in an individualized fashion:[17]

> Suppose you and I have identical internal endowments, including a pathetic disposition for playing the oboe. I am stubbornly sticking to the ambition of becoming a brilliant oboe player, whether for its own sake or because of the fortune I believe I could earn that way. You instead have wisely shifted your aspirations to table football, which we are both far more gifted for.
>
> (p. 70)

Under such conditions, Dworkin's general approach allegedly requires that two identically endowed individuals receive different levels of transfer in virtue of their different ambitions. Van Parijs objects to the apparent horizontal inequity involved in such a differential transfer by claiming that it is 'vulnerable to the expensive-taste objection, since it gives more or less compensation...depending on people's tastes' (p. 70). To do so is objectionable since by 'giving more resources to those with expensive tastes, it depresses the real freedom of those with cheaper tastes to do whatever they might want to do' (p. 70). I shall now argue that, even if Dworkin's proposal is defective for other reasons, this objection fails.[18]

The objection is flawed in part because it neglects to emphasize the fact that, if Dworkin's proposal is to apply, further individuals must possess the talent for oboe playing which Van Parijs's two characters lack. Such is the case, since Dworkin recommends compensation in order to ameliorate luck in the distribution of personal resources which is *bad* as well as *brute*. An individual's entitlement to compensatory transfers therefore depends on two conditions being satisfied. First, it is necessary that her luck, relative to others' luck, has been bad in the sense that she envies some other individual's personal endowment. Second, it is also necessary that her luck has been brute, in the sense that her circumstances were neither chosen nor due to her acceptance of, or refusal to accept, estimable risks. Because of the first of these conditions, Dworkin does not recommend transfers merely on the ground that an individual's ambitions are costly, or impossible, to fulfill due to circumstances she has not chosen. Individuals who appeal solely to that consideration will be treated similarly to immigrants who wish that fate had cast them ashore either on a desert island more hospitable to their ambitions, or with fellow survivors whose preferences made theirs easier to satisfy.[19] Resource egalitarianism will deny their request since they are unable to satisfy the former bad luck condition, and point to some individual whose circumstances they prefer. Thus, if Dworkin's proposal recommends redistribution in Van Parijs's example, we must assume that the stubborn individual prefers the musical talents of some other individual. The presence of that individual, perhaps a virtuoso, is important for the following reason.

Because of the envy which the presence of the virtuoso induces, we must accept that there is an inequality between her and the stubborn player. We need not, however, accept that there is any inequality between the virtuoso and the less stubborn individual; *ex hypothesi*, the latter has no passion for the oboe.[20] Given these conditions, and the uncontested principle that inequalities in personal endowment due to brute luck support redistributive claims, there is at least a *pro tanto* reason to transfer resources from the virtuoso to the stubborn player in order to diminish the presence of envy between them. Van Parijs's objection is flawed in part because it overlooks this consideration by focusing only upon the relationship between those with equivalent endowments.

Nevertheless, Van Parijs might have identified a countervailing consideration, which defeats the reason to redistribute we have identified. Perhaps such redistribution involves a sufficiently objectionable form of horizontal inequity that we should, all things considered, reject it. Van Parijs suggests as much when he claims it is unjust that the stubborn player, due to his expensive taste, has more resources than the identically-endowed adaptive ex-player. This suggestion, however, is inconclusive for at least two reasons.

First, as the earlier case involving those who either love or loathe pork suggested, the mere fact that an individual has more of a resource than another because of their ambitions does not establish that they have an unequally large share in a morally objectionable sense.[21] Van Parijs has not even established that the adaptive individual envies the stubborn individual. Furthermore, there is no reason to believe that the fair insurance market would necessarily produce envy. Such a possibility might be taken into account when devising the market, and employed to justify in kind rather than cash insurance pay-offs. Thus, just as the market might compensate the sick with medical treatment, the stubborn individual could be allocated intensive oboe tuition, for which the adaptive individual had no remaining desire. Second, even if Dworkin's proposal does create some envy between identically endowed individuals, that horizontal inequity might be a price worth paying to reduce vertical inequity. After all, as Dworkin himself concedes, even his own proposal need not succeed in fully eliminating envy in worlds with variation in internal resources. Van Parijs might merely have drawn our attention to one more example of this general phenomenon. I conclude then that Dworkin's proposal withstands his central objection.

7.9   Against undominated diversity

Van Parijs's eliminative arguments exaggerate the need for resource egalitarians to embrace undominated diversity. But perhaps his positive defense of undominated diversity has more success. That defense is a response to the objection that its unanimity requirement is implausibly restrictive. It emphasizes that when evaluating whether an individual's comprehensive endowment is inferior, the preferences involved 'must be both genuine and available' (p. 79). By this, Van Parijs means that they not only must be informed by knowledge and understanding of the consequences of possessing the endowment, but also must be ones which the relevant individual involved could, in some sense, acquire; for example, their possession must not depend upon a socialization process which she cannot, perhaps any longer, undergo (p. 77). Stressing the latter consideration, he writes,

> What matters [in judging whether people have an inferior comprehensive endowment] ... is whether people could feasibly adopt – and hence could fairly be held responsible for failing to adopt – a view by reference to which their endowment would be no worse than the one to which it is being compared. This is what availability (in any number) in the person's community is meant to provide a (roughly) sufficient condition for.
>
> (p. 80)

Van Parijs's defense of undominated diversty reminds us that envy may be eliminated in two ways. Circumstances can be modified by redistribution, whilst personalities remain unchanged. Instead personalities can change, whilst circumstances are constant. He recommends the former method for eliminating envy over external resources, but switches to the latter when dealing with comprehensive endowments. Thus, the legitimate division of labor between collective and individual varies depending upon which resources are under consideration. Where internal resources do not vary, the collective bears responsibility for achieving equality by redistributing external resources. Yet where variation exists, individuals may legitimately be left to pursue the task themselves by adapting their personalities to their circumstances.

Even if one does not immediately reject this asymmetry between the treatment of external and internal resources, the following question still requires an answer: namely, is it justifiable to leave an individual to bear the full cost of an endowment she would choose to exchange because she could instead have preferred not to exchange?

To focus attention on this question, consider the case of Eva, who wants to bear children but is found to be infertile, and so prefers the internal resources of fertile women. She presses for compensatory redistribution, but some individuals deny that her endowment is inferior. Perhaps they welcome the liberation from involuntary pregnancy infertility brings, or think it morally preferable to adopt needy children rather than reproduce. Let us grant that their preferences are available in whatever sense Van Parijs regards relevant. If so, undominated diversity rejects her request.

Now compare Eva's treatment with that of a second infertile woman, Eve, who is dissimilar in only one respect: the preferences of those who accept infertility are unavailable to her. For example, she may have been socialized in a community in which infertility was universally regarded as a personal catastrophe. Thus, undominated diversity does not reject Eve's request for compensation despite her endowment and ambitions both being identical to those of Eva. Furthermore, it treats Eve more generously than Eva regardless of the two individuals' attitudes to each others' circumstances. For example, it does so even if Eva values Eve's socialization, and consequent inability to adapt, far more than her own socialization and accompanying ability.

Faced with this case, it seems unjust to deny Eva's request whilst granting Eve's request. Conferring different levels of compensation on two individuals identical in endowments and actual ambitions merely because they differ in potential ambition is an indefensible form of horizontal inequity. Because undominated diversity demands such inequity, there is a weighty reason to reject it.

7.10   Conclusion

I conclude that *Real Freedom for All* violates two moral limits on the provision of a basic income defensible on resource egalitarian grounds. The restriction objection shows that it exaggerates the tax base appropriate to fund universal, unconditional transfers, whilst the constraint objection shows it underestimates the need to compensate for differences in internal resources. Advocates of basic income, however, should not be dispirited by my conclusions. As stressed initially, neither objection implies that their proposal is inherently unjust. Furthermore, defenses of basic income other than Van Parijs's resource egalitarian case remain open. Thanks to his work, those investigating such possibilities have a brilliant example of how to proceed.

Notes

1. I am indebted to an anonymous referee and T. M. Wilkinson for their excellent written comments. I am also grateful to J. Burley, P. Casal, M. G. Clayton, M. Otsuka, W. Rabinowicz, P. Van Parijs, R. van der Veen, G. van Donselaar, S. White and the Nuffield Political Theory Group.
2. More specifically, he claims that economic institutions should be evaluated by their sustainable capacity to generate an allowance 'paid by the government to each full member of society (1) even if she is not willing to work, (2) irrespective of her being rich or poor, (3) whoever she lives with, and (4) no matter

which part of the country she lives in'. See *Real Freedom for All: What (if Anything) Can Justify Capitalism?* (Oxford: Oxford University Press, 1995, p. 35). Unless specified, page numbers refer to this book.

3. For an example of this type of criticism, see S. White, 'Liberal Equality, Exploitation, and the Case for an Unconditional Basic Income', *Political Studies* 45 (1997), pp. 312–26.

4. Note that an individual's *real freedom* depends upon her opportunities to satisfy *potential* rather than *actual* preferences, and that, within a society satisfying leximin opportunity, 'the person with least opportunities has opportunities that are no smaller than those enjoyed by the person with least opportunities under any other feasible arrangement; in case there exists another feasible arrangement that is just as good for the person with least opportunities, the next person up the scale … must have opportunities no smaller than the second person up the scale of opportunities under this arrangement; and so on' (p. 25).

5. Nevertheless some critics proceed as if Van Parijs's case for basic income rests solely upon leximin opportunity. See, for example, B. Barry, 'Real Freedom and Basic Income', *Journal of Political Philosophy* 4 (1996), pp. 264–6. The assumption is mistaken since, as Van Parijs clearly explains, 'It is not really the size or extent of their real freedom that real-freedom-for-all requires just institutions to maximize for the worst off' (p. 32).

6. Since my first objection relies on them diverging, it is important to note that value equalization and envy elimination are logically distinct principles which only contingently converge. As Van Parijs explains, 'Whereas equality of resource bundles as measured by their competitive prices entails equality of opportunity-sets in the weak sense of envy-freeness, the reverse is not true' (p. 53). For further illustration see the example of Funny and Very Funny (p. 250, n. 43).

7. It would be unwarranted, however, to conclude that it is not possible to increase legitimate transfer payments to some voluntarily unemployed individuals by expanding the category of external assets to include jobs. To appreciate why that inference is invalid, note there may be two types of individuals who can obtain employment but prefer to remain unemployed. The *reluctantly unemployed*, whilst refusing those jobs which are available to them, prefer the job assets of at least some individuals, but are unable to obtain them. The *willingly unemployed* have no such frustrated desires, and would remain unemployed no matter what their employment prospects. The latter clearly can take no solace in the above criticism. But nothing in that criticism implies that the former class of individuals are not entitled to share in the employment rent enjoyed by consultants and company bosses. What they cannot claim, if those less desirable positions are available to them, is further redistribution at the expense of office-cleaners and burger-flippers.

8. See 'What Is Equality? Part 1: Equality of Welfare', *Philosophy and Public Affairs* 10 (1981), section viii, and especially the comparison with Jude on p. 239.

9. Van Parijs (p. 250, n. 43) cites H. Varian, 'Two Problems in the Theory of Fairness', *Journal of Public Economics* 5 (1976), pp. 249–60, and the generalization in P. Champsaur and G. Laroque, 'Fair Allocations in Large Economies', *Journal of Economic Theory* 25 (1981), pp. 269–82.

10. Compare Varian's intuitive explanation in 'Dworkin on Equality of Resources', *Economics and Philosophy* 1 (1985), p. 114, cited in *Real Freedom for All*, p. 250, n. 45.

11. For classic illustration, see P. Singer, 'Altruism and Commerce: a Defence of Titmuss against Arrow', *Philosophy and Public Affairs* 2 (1972), pp. 312–20, especially p. 316.

12. Van Parijs, however, is sanguine about the constraint's impact: 'under the conditions that now prevail in advanced industrial societies, the highest sustainable basic income consistent with both formal freedom and undominated diversity can confidently be expected to be quite substantial, indeed to exceed what is there unanimously considered as belonging to the bare necessities. In a society that is not only sufficiently diverse (which makes dominance less frequent for "subjective" reasons), but also sufficiently healthy (which makes dominance less frequent for "objective" reasons) and sufficiently wealthy (which drives up the average external endowment), a small minority of "handicapped" people will be entitled to differential transfers, but the majority consisting of "normal" people will remain entitled to a substantial basic income' (p. 84).

13. Richard Arneson, discussing an earlier presentation of undominated diversity, pursues the latter strategy with considerable force, in 'Property Rights in Persons', *Social Philosophy and Policy* 9 (1992), section v. But see *Real Freedom for All*, section 3.6 and 3.8, for some replies.

14. Lonely objects that the extended auction is unfair since it compensates for ugliness only insofar as it affects earning potential, yet, she urges, 'Good looks may matter a great deal even if they do not add a penny to one's earning power' (p. 64). As will become apparent, I exploit that thought in criticizing Lovely's objection.

15. Dworkin uses the phrase in his own critique of the extended auction in 'What Is Equality? Part 2: Equality of Resources', *Philosophy and Public Affairs* 10 (1981), p. 312.

16. Suppose A's opportunities for income and leisure are a proper subset of B's, yet could be improved by a lump-sum ability tax on B, which still leaves B able to do all that A can do and more. Self-ownership might condemn even this modest proposal in favor of those with least opportunities. Therefore – unless his remark risks triviality since 'liberty' means self-ownership – it appears strange that Van Parijs claims 'If one wishes to attack it [self-ownership] ... one has to do so on grounds other than liberty' (p. 9).

17. For convincing arguments concerning why the application of Dworkin's suggestion should be individualized, see E. Rakowski, *Equal Justice* (Oxford: Oxford University Press, 1991), p. 136, n. 11.

18. For further criticism of the proposal, see Rakowski's thorough discussion in *Equal Justice*, section 6.2, which contains a related horizontal equity objection at pp. 135–7, and is mentioned by Van Parijs on p. 225, n. 9.

19. See 'What Is Equality? Part 2: Equality of Resources', pp. 287–8.

20. Furthermore, recall that the less stubborn player 'wisely' revised his ambitions. Unlike the 'battered slave' and 'tamed housewife', effectively employed by Sen to criticize welfare egalitarianism, he is not the victim of adaptive preference formation. Thus, Sen's criticism cannot be extended to my use of the envy test in Van Parijs's example. For relevant discussion, see A. Sen, *The*

Standard of Living (Cambridge: Cambridge University Press, 1987), p. 11, and J. Elster, 'Utilitarianism and the Genesis of Wants', in A. Sen and B. Williams (eds), *Utilitarianism and Beyond* (Cambridge: Cambridge University Press, 1982), pp. 219–38.

21. For that reason, I am unconvinced by Fleurbaey's 'Equal Resource for Equal Handicap' axiom. For a description of the axiom, which might be employed to object to my differential treatment of the two oboe players, see M. Fleurbaey, 'On Fair Compensation', *Theory and Decision* 36 (1994), pp. 277–307 (283).

8
Fair Reciprocity and Basic Income
Stuart White

8.1 Introduction: basic income and the exploitation objection

Philippe Van Parijs's *Real Freedom for All* is, amongst other things, a determined defence of the proposal to introduce an unconditional basic income (UBI): an income grant paid to each citizen as an individual without any test of financial means or any corresponding test of work or willingness to work. UBI is, for Van Parijs, the economic basis of universal 'real freedom'. However, critics claim that UBI is a recipe for injustice on the grounds that payment of a substantial income grant, on the relevantly unconditional terms, would allow citizens to share in the social product without contributing to its generation thereby 'free-riding' on the productive efforts of, and so exploiting, their fellow citizens who do contribute to its generation.[1] Thus, a central question in the philosophical debate over UBI, a debate that Van Parijs's work has done much to stimulate and frame, is whether and how this exploitation objection can be met. In this chapter I set out a version of the objection and a response to the objection that I believe is more compelling than that offered by Van Parijs in *Real Freedom for All*. This response is admittedly somewhat concessionary in that it accepts that, across a wide range of circumstances, the original UBI proposal may have to be modified to defuse the objection. But the suggested modifications do not, I think, detract very much from the attractive features of the 'pure' UBI proposal. The pure UBI proposal needs to be seen as just one member of a family of proposals, I argue, other members of which may sometimes offer a more appropriate means of advancing the full range of justice-related concerns than a pure UBI.

Intuitively, the exploitation objection would seem to appeal to a principle of reciprocity: a principle which insists, very roughly, that citizens who share in the social product make a productive contribution of their own to the community in return. Section 8.2 clarifies the principle of reciprocity and offers an account of its ethical motivation. I defend a particular version of the reciprocity principle as one expression of a deeper and broader ethic of solidarity. In section 8.3, I indicate in more detail how the reciprocity principle can be integrated with other solidaristic commitments into a more complete conception of distributive justice that I term *fair reciprocity*. I review Van Parijs's arguments against the exploitation objection as presented in *Real Freedom for All* and explain why I think these arguments fail to defuse the objection when the objection is understood as coming from the standpoint of fair reciprocity.

This is not to say, however, that the conception of distributive justice as fair reciprocity does not contain resources that might be used to defend UBI or closely related policy proposals against the exploitation objection. Section 8.4 sets out one argument for UBI which appeals to considerations internal to the conception of justice as fair reciprocity (including the reciprocity principle). This is not a rights-based argument, as is Van Parijs's main argument for the proposal, but a consequence-based argument that appeals to the way in which a sizeable UBI can be expected to help prevent various 'bads' that the solidaristic ethic underpinning fair reciprocity commits us to prevent. I believe something like this is the most promising line of defence for supporters of the UBI proposal. There is, however, a weakness with this type of argument. Various modifications of the original UBI proposal are imaginable which qualify eligibility for the UBI along some dimension. If these modified versions of UBI can produce the same desirable effects as the original UBI proposal while creating less risk of exploitation (violation of the reciprocity principle) then these modified proposals must be preferred to the original. Section 8.5 outlines and briefly evaluates three such variants of UBI: (1) republican basic income (variants of UBI qualified by a broad work requirement); (2) selective basic income (non-universal variants of UBI targeted specifically at disadvantaged groups); and (3) time-limited basic income (a variant of UBI under which eligibility for a sizeable UBI is limited to a fixed number of years over the course of a working life). All three policy proposals appear to offer ways of advancing the solidaristic concerns which underpin fair reciprocity without offending the reciprocity principle. They illustrate how a concern for reciprocity and commitment to basic income might be reconciled. Section 8.6 concludes.

8.2   The reciprocity principle

There is a widespread intuition that a just distribution of the social product must satisfy a principle of reciprocity according to which those who willingly enjoy a share of the social product have a corresponding obligation to make a productive contribution to the community in return for this share. In some theories of distributive justice, this obligation is derived from a more basic idea that citizens ought to share in the social product in strict proportion to the value product they individually create (where value might be understood in Marxian or neo-classical terms). Given background inequalities in citizens' capacities to contribute product to a given value, this version of the reciprocity principle has clear anti-egalitarian implications. But many egalitarian theorists have also apparently endorsed a version of the reciprocity principle. They have endorsed the idea that citizens who enjoy a sufficiently generous share of the social product (generous enough to give them a sufficiently high absolute and relative level of 'life-chances'[2]) have a corresponding obligation to 'do their bit' productively, within the bounds of their respective abilities, in return for this share of the social product.[3]

Assuming that I am right in this historical claim, why have egalitarian thinkers tended to incorporate such a principle of reciprocity into their conceptions of distributive justice? One answer to this question is suggested by Eduard Bernstein's essay, 'What Is Socialism?' In this essay, Bernstein tells us how he asked 'five workers what they understood socialism to mean'. He 'handed them some paper on which to write their response. Silently an old laborer returned his sheet, on which only one word was written: *solidarity*.'[4] At the heart of egalitarianism is an ethic of solidarity. The obligation to assist the disadvantaged is one side of this solidarity ethic. The obligation to make a reasonable productive contribution to the community in return for a sufficiently generous share of the social product – to do one's bit in this sense – can be seen as another expression of this same solidarity ethic. One somehow fails to stand in a sufficiently solidaristic relationship with other citizens when one shares willingly in the social product that they have made without making a reasonable contribution back to the community in return (or being willing to do so as/when the opportunity arises).

Let me try to elaborate this raw intuitive account of the importance of reciprocity. We may picture individual citizens as members of a cooperative community: a community in which various benefits are intentionally created through the industry of members, and distributed amongst them, in accordance with shared rules of production and transfer. I contend that a suitably solidaristic (and therefore just) scheme of cooperation necessarily respects a norm of weak mutual advantage. According to the norm of weak mutual advantage: anyone who is a willing beneficiary of a cooperative economic scheme (a willing claimant on the social product) must make a reasonable effort, appropriate to his/her capacities, to ensure that other members of the scheme also benefit from and (the flip-side of this) are not burdened by his/her membership of this scheme. Other citizens have the *right* to expect you to make this effort. There is no claim here that one must necessarily match the benefit one creates to the benefit that others provide for you. But you must make a reasonable effort to make good the contribution of other citizens to your material well-being and/or opportunity through their creation of a social product in which you share, and, as the flip-side of this, make a reasonable effort to avoid imposing a material burden upon them. What a reasonable effort is for you will depend partly on the degree of benefit one takes from others (the size of the share of the social product that you claim) and partly on one's relative capacity to produce reciprocal benefits.[5] At the limit, your capacity in this respect may be non-existent, in which case we shall here assume that the obligation to make such an effort does not apply.

Now the reciprocity principle, understood in the more egalitarian sense, would seem to be a natural expression of this norm of weak mutual advantage. For how does one make a reasonable effort to ensure that others benefit/are not burdened by one's membership of the same cooperative community if not by making a reasonable productive contribution in return for the share of the social product that others provide?[6] The obligation to do one's bit productively in return for a sufficiently generous share of the social product (the obligation asserted by the reciprocity principle in its broadly egalitarian form) would seem to follow from the supposed obligation that one make a reasonable effort to see that others benefit from/are not burdened by your membership of the same cooperative community (the obligation asserted by the norm of weak mutual advantage).

Let us consider some of the ways in which economic relationships might violate the norm of weak mutual advantage (and the ethic of solidarity of which the norm is a partial expression). A first candidate for violation of the norm is the relationship of *economic free-riding*. Members of a community may perceive a shared need for a specific good. They may try to organize its production. The good is eventually produced and maintained by a subset of the community. The free-rider, in this context, can be understood as someone who shares, willingly, in the consumption of the good without contributing to its production even though he/she is capable of doing so. Such an individual benefits from the efforts of others in the community, but, by virtue of his/her free-riding, he/she also refrains strategically from making a reasonable effort to benefit these others. By refusing to make a reasonable contribution to cover the cost of the benefits that he/she willingly enjoys, he/she thereby off-loads these costs onto others. Though the concept of free-riding finds its classic application in relation to 'public goods', the scope of the concept can be readily extended to cover other goods that are collectively provided and which are then made available for general consumption. Imagine, for example, that we institute a 'social right' assuring all citizens of a decent minimum of income. If, as a citizen, I accept that there is such a right – and that it is an equal right held by all citizens, not merely a privilege peculiar to me – then I must also accept that each citizen, myself included, has a correlative obligation to help sustain the scheme that will assure citizens of this level of income. I cannot in all consistency will the one without willing the other. If assuring citizens of this level of (real) income requires that work be done, then, as part of my obligation to help sustain the scheme for assuring citizens of this income, I surely have a prima facie obligation to share in this work. I free-ride if I continue to claim the benefits of this scheme without accepting and acting upon this obligation.

Closely related to the concern with free-riding is a concern over what we may term *economic parasitism*. Following David Gauthier and Gijs van Donselaar, we may begin by defining a distributional arrangement as parasitic if/when it allows one party to the arrangement, Smith, to make him/herself better off than he would be in the absence of a second party, Jones, while Jones, by virtue of this arrangement, is at the same time made worse off than he would be in the absence of Smith.[7] Now this notion of parasitism is certainly one that we have to handle with care. Some might argue, for example, that we should minimize redistribution from the able-bodied to the handicapped because forcible redistribution of this sort may well be parasitic in the foregoing sense – the less talented may end up better off than they would be in the absence of the talented, while the talented may end up worse off than they would be in the absence of the less talented. As I will make clear below, I do not think that redistribution of this sort is in fact necessarily morally objectionable – indeed, I think that, on any plausible elaboration of the ethic of solidarity with which I began this discussion, significant redistribution of this kind will be morally required. At the same time, some transfers that fit the foregoing criterion of parasitism do seem to me to be morally objectionable. In particular, parasitism arguably violates the norm of weak mutual advantage, and is therefore morally objectionable, when the party that is the putative parasite imposes a net cost on the consumption possibilities of his/her fellow citizens (making them worse off than they would be if he/she were absent from the scene) and this net cost is one that the putative parasite could with reasonable effort avoid imposing. Once again, what counts as a reasonably avoidable burden will depend on individuals' respective capacities and opportunities to avoid claims on the social product and/or to produce off-setting benefits, and thus on their respective endowments of handicaps, talents and so on.[8]

In view of its link to the norm of weak mutual advantage, and to the prevention of economic free-riding and parasitism, the reciprocity principle may be regarded as a distributive principle of intrinsic ethical importance. But recent work in the political economy of redistribution and the welfare state suggests, in addition, that there are strong instrumental reasons for incorporating such a principle into a public conception of justice. This point is perhaps especially significant for egalitarians. If egalitarian objectives are pursued in a way that is inattentive to concerns about free-riding and parasitism, then there is a clear risk that the egalitarian institutions in question will provoke feelings of alienation and resentment and so undercut the very spirit of solidarity on which they depend.

This point is emphasized by Samuel Bowles and Herbert Gintis in a recent analysis of the prospects for egalitarian reform in contemporary capitalist societies. Bowles and Gintis argue that popular resistance to the American welfare state derives not from an opposition to egalitarian redistribution per se, but to redistribution that enables citizens to evade the contributive responsibilities that derive from a widely shared norm of 'strong reciprocity'.[9] Bowles and Gintis start with the observation, confirmed in a variety of experimental settings, that individuals tend not to conform to the standard model of 'homo economicus' who rationally pursues his/her self-interest without regard to any norms of fairness. The evidence rather supports an alternative model of 'homo reciprocans'. People tend not to be rational egotists, but conditional cooperators, willing to do their bit in cooperative ventures to which they belong so long as they can be assured that others will also make a reasonable contribution. Their commitment to the implied norm of reciprocity is such that they are often willing to accept costs to themselves rather than see this norm violated with impunity. Widespread adherence to the norm may be explicable in evolutionary terms: communities in which homo reciprocans predominates may find it easier to solve important problems of trust and collective action, and so survive and expand, than communities in which homo economicus predominates. If, however, commitment to the norm is so deep-rooted, then egalitarians must frame their reform proposals in a way that explicitly acknowledges and upholds the norm rather than being indifferent to it. A similar argument concerning the necessary conditions under which citizens will grant their 'contingent consent' to egalitarian social policy is made by Bo Rothstein in relation to European universalistic welfare states. According to Rothstein, citizens will support programmes that are quite strongly redistributive, even if they are not (or not clearly) net beneficiaries, if they are assured that all other beneficiaries will also make a reasonable contribution to the costs of the programme. Where social policies are universalistic in the sense that there is an inclusive share-out of both benefits and contributions, these policies will consequently have greater perceived legitimacy and, Rothstein argues, will thus be relatively resistant to the politics of welfare state retrenchment.[10]

8.3   Fair reciprocity and the exploitation objection

So reciprocity appears to matter, both intrinsically and instrumentally in building and maintaining legitimacy for policies and institutions that pursue (other) egalitarian values. From an egalitarian point of view, however, the reciprocity principle must be elaborated and implemented in such a way as to respect other considerations of justice which capture other important demands of the solidarity ethic with which we began. Different egalitarian theorists will elaborate these demands in different ways, but we can identify at least some range of agreement as to the content of these demands. First, citizens must be protected to some substantial degree from certain kinds of significant, brute luck disadvantage: that is, there are certain respects in which it is unjust for one citizen to be substantially worse off than another through no fault of their own and the ground-rules of economic cooperation should be so designed as to prevent, correct, or compensate for this kind of disadvantage. Secondly, citizens must be protected from vulnerability in the market-place that might otherwise lead them to engage in various types of 'desperate trade'.[11] Thirdly, it is important that citizens regard themselves and each other as equals and that the ground-rules of economic cooperation accordingly work to maintain this egalitarian ethos rather than to undermine it. When the reciprocity principle is elaborated and implemented in a manner that respects these other independent commitments, we move from mere reciprocity to a conception of justice as egalitarian, or, as I shall call it, *fair* reciprocity.[12]

I have, of course, only begun to sketch out this conception of justice here, but it is not difficult to see how such a conception might provide a way of making sense of the exploitation objection to UBI. According to this conception of justice, citizens who are guaranteed access to a sufficiently generous share of the social product have a corresponding obligation under the reciprocity principle to make an appropriate personal productive contribution to the community in return (where the level of personal contribution appropriate for a given citizen will depend on the precise amount of social product enjoyed and his/her capacity and opportunity to make a valuable contribution). The community can define a 'reasonable work expectation' which citizens are expected to meet in order to satisfy this obligation: a specified number of hours of employment (employment, moreover, which does not squander one's earnings potential).[13] The general level of this expectation is something that can be settled by local democratic decision-making, guided by consideration of the society's level of productive development and the standard of living the community aspires to put within reasonable reach of all citizens. The expectation can and should be adjusted to accommodate other forms of work that are reasonably seen as contributive, such as certain forms of care work that are frequently unpaid in contemporary capitalist societies;[14] and in the case of the unemployed we can imagine a parallel obligation to make a good faith effort to find the work necessary to satisfy this expectation. Payment of an UBI, however, would allow citizens to enjoy a non-trivial share of the social product without meeting, or doing enough to meet, this reasonable work expectation. It would allow citizens to share in the social product without 'doing their bit' productively in this sense, so violating the reciprocity principle. Given the radical unconditionality of UBI on productive activity of any kind or level for any citizen, one can adjust the definition of what counts as a reasonable work expectation or productive contribution in numerous ways and UBI will still look vulnerable to this objection.

What arguments does Van Parijs present that might defuse the exploitation objection? Van Parijs's main argument for UBI in *Real Freedom for All* proceeds as follows. He starts from the premise that, abstracting from inequalities in talents and handicaps (internal endowments), individuals have rights to equal shares of certain external assets; he then argues that the best way to implement these rights in practice is to give each citizen a uniform basic income equal to a per capita share of the current market value of the relevant assets; that the relevant assets include so-called job assets (scarce employment opportunities); and that once we include job assets in the pool for financing the basic income it will in general be possible in advanced capitalist countries to finance a basic income at or close to a level sufficient to meet a standard set of basic needs (if not above this level). Putting possible internal problems with the argument to one side for present purposes,[15] and focusing on the argument's merits as a way of anticipating the exploitation objection, the argument's starting point, the assertion of an unconditional right to an equal (and tradeable) share of certain external assets, seems to beg the question. In the case of some external assets, in particular natural resources, one can certainly see how a citizen who lays claim to a share of the relevant assets is not thereby necessarily pressing a claim to a share of his/her society's social product. He/she could conceivably be a would-be hermit, uninterested in the supposed benefits of cooperative industry, who merely wishes to be granted a fair share of the community's natural patrimony with which he/she will then withdraw to contemplate, in quiet isolation, the idiocy of the rat race. But in the case of other external assets, a citizen's claim to a share of the relevant assets does seem to me to be closely linked to, if not to derive from, the citizen's right to fair treatment as a member of a community engaged in the creation and distribution of a social product. The claim to be given a fair share of society's available supply of 'job assets', for example, only makes sense against a background of at least moderately sophisticated productive endeavour, and as a claim to be included in that endeavour and the benefits that issue from it. But if this is so, then surely the distribution of rights to such assets ought to fall within the scope of the reciprocity principle – as a principle which, according to the argument of section 8.2, properly regulates citizens' claims to share in the social product. In which case, the posited right to a share of such assets ought to carry with it (and perhaps be made conditional upon satisfying) a corresponding obligation to make a productive contribution to the community in return for the access to and enjoyment of the social product which the suggested asset rights will confer on the holder. It is not, one should note, that the fair reciprocity perspective cannot accommodate the idea of citizens having claim-rights to things like job assets. Rather, an approach to property rights grounded in the fair reciprocity perspective would interpret such a right not as a right to appropriate a share of available jobs as a tradeable asset, but as a right of access to, to press into service, some share of available jobs.[16] The gates of the 'social factory' should be closed to no citizen who wishes to enter the factory and work. But those uninterested in making a productive contribution ought not, as it were, to be given an allocation of tickets to the factory which they can then use to extract a share of the factory's product from those who do wish to enter and work.[17]

If Van Parijs's main argument for UBI does not anticipate and defuse the exploitation objection, Van Parijs also presents, in chapter 5 of *Real Freedom for All*, a more direct argument against the objection. Van Parijs's strategy here is to try to identify various distributive principles that might underpin the objection and then to indicate various problems with the candidate principles he identifies. A recurring criticism of the principles he identifies is that their application would sanction significant brute luck inequalities. This makes the principles objectionable on familiar egalitarian grounds, and this in turn casts a shadow of illegitimacy over the exploitation objection which supposedly derives from one of these in/anti-egalitarian principles.[18] However, this line of argument runs into obvious trouble when it is confronted with a version of the exploitation objection that is grounded in a conception of distributive justice like fair reciprocity, a conception of distributive justice which combines a substantive principle of economic reciprocity with a commitment to the prevention of significant brute luck disadvantage. In effect, Van Parijs seems to be saying that we can have reciprocity *or* egalitarianism; he does not give much (if any) consideration to a conception of distributive justice which, by integrating the two concerns, would at one and the same time support an exploitation objection to UBI *and* condemn the inequalities sanctioned by the distributive principles which Van Parijs identifies as possible grounds for the exploitation objection.

Even if I am right, however, and Van Parijs's arguments are insufficient to defuse the exploitation objection to UBI, we must distinguish between the *validity* of an objection to a particular policy proposal and the *decisiveness* of this objection. I think that the exploitation objection is a valid objection to the UBI proposal. But I am not at all sure that, if it is valid, it is also a decisive objection – at least *if the objection is pressed from a standpoint akin to that of fair reciprocity*. Fair reciprocity is defined by a cluster of independent commitments which, though all rooted in an underlying ethic of solidarity, may nevertheless be difficult to reconcile in practice; for example, while it may be possible, as suggested in the previous paragraph, to integrate the demands of the reciprocity principle and egalitarian concern for the prevention of brute luck disadvantage at the conceptual level, it may be much more difficult to integrate them at the practical, policy level. If such conflicts do arise, then a proponent of the UBI proposal might argue that UBI is, from the standpoint of fair reciprocity, the most (or at least a) legitimate policy since it achieves the most (or at least a) reasonable balance between the conflicting commitments that enter into this conception of distributive justice.[19] It is this thought that I shall try to elaborate and then critically assess in the next two sections.

8.4   Basic income as an instrument of fair reciprocity?

The introduction of a UBI, and perhaps especially one set at the generous level that Van Parijs envisages, can be expected to have a number of effects that must be regarded as highly desirable from the standpoint of fair reciprocity. Some of the more important possible effects are as follows:

(1) *Employment opportunity*. Fair reciprocity surely requires that citizens have adequate opportunity to work so as to satisfy their contributive obligations under the reciprocity principle in a psychologically fulfilling way.[20] It is sometimes suggested that UBI will affect the level and/or flexibility of wage rates in a way that conduces to higher and more stable levels of employment. One version of this argument focuses on the complementarity between UBI and revenue-sharing within productive enterprises. Under revenue-sharing arrangements, workers are paid at least part of their pay as a share in the firm's profits or net revenues rather than as a fixed wage. Some economists argue that this mode of labour remuneration, if adopted by enough firms, will make for a higher and more stable level of employment than would arise under an otherwise equivalent fixed-wage economy.[21] From the worker's point of view, however, the diminished risk of unemployment comes at the price of greater variability of income while in employment. In order to offset the increased variability in employment income, it is argued that workers in such an economy must receive a sizeable slice of income that is independent of their employment status. This is precisely what a UBI would provide.[22] A UBI, in other words, might be the precondition of an institution, revenue-sharing, that might itself be essential for a high and stable level of employment which is in turn, as said, a precondition for citizens being able to meet their obligations under the reciprocity principle in a psychologically fulfilling way.

(2) *A guaranteed social wage*. It is arguable that productive contributions in satisfaction of the reciprocity principle need not take only the form of paid employment but that certain forms of care work, which are not typically paid, ought also to be seen as providing services to the community worthy of a 'social wage'. But how can we ensure that those whose contribution largely takes the form of care work receive the decent minimum of income to which they are correspondingly

entitled? In addition, how can we supplement the pay of low wage workers, who have satisfied their contributive obligation, so as to bring their final incomes up to a decent level? One possible answer is: UBI. Payment of a UBI, set at an appropriate level, will help to ensure that productive contributions which do not get adequately acknowledged with monetary reward in the market place are nevertheless properly reciprocated with income. This represents one way in which a UBI can be expected to bring the overall distribution of rewards closer into line with that required by the reciprocity principle.

(3) *Reduced domestic exploitation and abuse.* Where one party within a household bears a disproportionate share of the household's total labour, relative to the cash or in-kind income she consumes, then free-riding and/or parasitism may have emerged at the domestic level. Now while it would arguably be improper for the state to require households to conform internally to a principle of reciprocity in the distributions of work and benefits, it should at least take care to ensure that individuals are not pressured into exploitative domestic relations because of financial dependency.[23] Such dependency is additionally worrying because it may lead to physical and psychological abuse. By reducing the costs of exiting the household, a UBI could serve to empower otherwise vulnerable partners, enabling them to press for non-exploitative and non-abusive domestic relations.

(4) *Job quality.* By disconnecting income from employment, UBI obviously enhances the citizen's ability to refuse unpleasant jobs. In consequence, as Philippe Van Parijs and Robert van der Veen have argued,[24] it puts employers under pressure to improve job quality. As wages for unpleasant (typically low-skilled) jobs are bid up in the effort to attract people to them, technological development should become geared towards the creation of labour processes and workplaces that offer greater intrinsic job satisfaction. A UBI can thus help ensure that the burdens of productive contribution do not fall with inequitable heaviness on the shoulders of some (typically low-skilled) citizens.

(5) *Residual safeguard against significant brute luck disadvantage and market vulnerability.* Fair reciprocity requires that we enforce citizens' reciprocity-based obligations in a manner that does not expose individuals to significant brute luck disadvantage or to pressure to make a 'desperate trade'. Where access to income support is subject to a work-test, it may be difficult to calibrate the work-test so as to ensure this. Work-tests can have the unintended effect of consolidating market vulnerability, or of disadvantaging someone who is, contrary

to appearances, unemployed through no fault of his own.[25] There are a number of ways we can grapple with these problems. But UBI can make a contribution here. Even a modest ('partial') UBI would provide a critically important residual safeguard against market vulnerability and brute luck disadvantage that might unintentionally creep through the net of an income support system that ties every penny of support to work or willingness to work.

Acknowledging these various possible effects of a UBI, one might now advance the following argument in defence of the UBI proposal:

> While UBI has one effect that is a bad from the standpoint of fair reciprocity – the exploitation it permits – it nevertheless has other effects that are good from the standpoint of fair reciprocity; thus, on balance, a contemporary capitalist society might get closer to satisfying the overall demands of fair reciprocity with a substantial UBI than without one.

We try to defuse the exploitation objection by showing how it points only to the debit side of the moral ledger, ignoring the sizeable credits which must be entered on the other side of the ledger's page.

There is, I think, a great deal of force to this argument. I think it certainly shows that, from the standpoint of fair reciprocity, the exploitation objection need not always be a decisive objection to UBI. It suggests that UBI can have a legitimate place in the policy toolkit which citizens look to in trying to engineer their economic arrangements to satisfy the demands of fair reciprocity. In contrast, the argument need not always be a decisive rejoinder to the exploitation objection. There are two main worries with the argument.

The first is the uncertainty of the effects to which it appeals, and the possibility that UBI may in fact have a negative impact in (some of) the areas covered above. For example, while we can tell one plausible story about how UBI will expand employment opportunity, we can tell another about how it will increase equilibrium unemployment (and so make it harder for some citizens to meet their contributive obligations in a psychologically fulfilling way): with a UBI in place workers will look less hard for jobs and due to this fall in 'search intensity' it will take more involuntary unemployment to keep a lid on inflationary pressures.[26] In addition, some argue that the introduction of a sizeable UBI would lead many people to participate much less actively in the labour force and to invest less in human capital.[27] The results of this may be to exacerbate financial dependencies in the household context, particularly if the impact on participation and human capital is stronger for women. Low participation and limited human capital investment may also create the very 'poor quality job trap' that UBI was supposed to spring. It is not just that each individual who chooses not to work much or to train may be diminishing their own options. The aggregate effect of a lot of people doing this might well be to drag job quality down in general as employers, constrained by a dearth of skilled and committed labour, adopt low cost-based product market strategies.

8.5 Variants of basic income

The second problem with the foregoing argument for UBI is that there may be other feasible policy instruments that (in isolation or combination) could have the same desirable effects as a UBI but which are not so vulnerable to the exploitation objection. The proponent of UBI cannot appeal to these effects to justify the moral cost of a UBI, however, if these effects can be produced in other ways that do not involve this (or an equivalent) moral cost. It is particularly interesting at this juncture to note some policy instruments that share many of the features of a UBI, and so can be expected to have certain of its effects, but which carry certain modifications that make these instruments less vulnerable to the exploitation objection. I shall consider three sets of such proposals here: republican basic income; selective basic income; and time-limited basic income.

8.5.1 Republican basic income

A first set of proposals link the UBI proposal with a commitment to public service thereby addressing the reciprocity-based concerns that underpin the exploitation objection. In view of the animating public service ethos, we may refer to these as proposals for republican basic income.

One such proposal is the *participation income* outlined by Anthony Atkinson.[28] A participation income is identical to a pure UBI except that eligibility for the income grant is conditional on satisfying a broadly defined participation requirement in the case of all working-age, productively capable adults. Atkinson defines participation to include paid employment or self-employment; certain forms of care work; participation in education and training; job search; and various approved forms of voluntary work. A participation income could have similar empowerment effects as a pure UBI, but is less vulnerable to the exploitation objection precisely because of the participation condition.

A second form of republican basic income would be what one might term a *citizens' service dividend*. There has been some interest in recent years, in Britain and in the USA, in the establishment of so-called citizens' service schemes. On leaving school, individuals would be eligible to participate in a national community service programme. Work assignments might include environmental task-forces, help with urban renovation, school assistance and refurbishment, and help with delivery of health-care or personal social services. Aside from the concrete goods that participants would produce, Mickey Kaus argues that the shared experience of participating in a nation-wide citizens' service scheme will help break down class and racial barriers and so contribute to the creation of an egalitarian public culture.[29] Interestingly, Philippe Van Parijs also suggests such a scheme as a possible way of cultivating the spirit of 'solidaristic patriotism' without which it will be impossible to build and maintain political support for any significantly redistributive reforms.[30]

Citizens' service might be introduced as a complement to UBI.[31] One possibility, suggested by Ronald Dore, is to run a compulsory system of citizens' service alongside a UBI. An unconditional income right in one domain would be matched by an enforceable (though time-limited) obligation to perform productive service for the community in another. Van Parijs also expresses his sympathy for this idea. Alternatively, participation in citizens' service might be strictly voluntary, but life-time eligibility for a UBI-style income grant would be tied to participation in the citizens' service scheme: all those who choose to participate in such a scheme would be eligible for the rest of their lives, after completing their period of citizens' service, to a UBI-style grant. One could perhaps vary the level of the subsequent grant according to length of citizens' service. A particularly radical version of this proposal was advanced by the eco-socialist Andre Gorz in the 1980s. Gorz proposed guaranteeing each citizen a minimum income for life in return for an agreement to perform 20,000 hours of socially necessary public labour.[32] Finally, the UBI proposal might be left in its original form, but complemented by a concerted programme of civic education, from primary schools on up, to emphasize the importance of productive service to the community, some of the funds that would otherwise be used to finance a UBI being used instead to finance this educational programme.

8.5.2   Selective basic income

Another variant on UBI that may produce many of its desirable effects without being as vulnerable to the exploitation objection is *selective basic income.* In the case of the selective basic income, we do not retreat one iota from the unconditionality of the UBI on work; instead, as Andrew Williams has suggested,[33] we retreat from its universality. Instead of paying an income grant out to all citizens we might instead try to identify those citizens who are relatively disadvantaged in the labour market, in particular those who are likely to have the least attractive work opportunities, and pay unconditional income grants specifically to them. Even if this income grant is set below subsistence level, entitlement to this grant will make it easier for those who are labour market disadvantaged to achieve a decent standard of living without having to bear an inequitably heavy (unpleasant) productive burden. The main problems with the proposal concern how we might identify the group of disadvantaged workers, and whether an income grant can be paid selectively to the disadvantaged without stigmatizing those who receive it. I shall here consider two concrete policy proposals which perhaps indicate how a non-stigmatizing selective basic income might be put into effect: a *tax credit/income grant based on degree of childhood underprivilege* and an *occupationally differentiated state pension age.*[34]

The first is a development of Bruce Ackerman's and Anne Alstott's recent proposal for a childhood privilege tax.[35] Ackerman and Alstott argue that individuals enter the market place (indeed, adult life in general) on unequal terms in part because of unequal degrees of 'childhood privilege'. As a partial corrective for this they propose to phase in, over a number of years, a tax which varies according to an individual's estimated degree of childhood privilege. The suggested measure of childhood privilege is the level and consistency of parental income in one's childhood years. The precise details of Ackerman's and Alstott's proposal matter less for our immediate purposes, however, than the idea of using such a measure of childhood underprivilege as a criterion for a selective basic income. To the extent that childhood underprivilege and life-time labour market disadvantage do correlate (and there is evidence, cited by Ackerman and Alstott, which indicates that they do), this tax credit scheme would then be very similar to the selective basic income described above. Moreover, it is arguable that receipt of a basic income of this kind would not be stigmatizing to the recipients.[36]

An obvious objection to the proposal is that it would give parents an incentive to limit their earnings so that their children qualify for the selective basic income. Ackerman and Alstott provide two main responses to this objection. First, they respond that, *at the privilege tax levels they propose*, the present value of the costs incurred by relegating oneself to a lower earnings tranche for the required number of years to enable one's children to qualify for a lower privilege tax (or a subsidy) will in general offset the present value of the benefits to one's child from qualifying for this lower tax (receiving the subsidy). But what if a parent is capable of only just getting over the income threshold defining childhood underprivilege? For a parent in this position the cost of keeping his/her earnings under this threshold, which he/she can anyway only barely surpass, may be much less than the present value of the benefits to his/her child, in the form of lower taxes or future subsidies, from having a parent under this threshold. This worry is addressed by Ackerman's and Alstott's proposal continually to review the relevant income thresholds defining privilege/underprivilege for successive cohorts of children. The income thresholds used to define degree of childhood privilege for a given cohort of children might be announced only when this cohort of children reaches maturity, and the thresholds applicable to this specific cohort adjusted from the previous cohort's thresholds to reflect the particular circumstances of the newly matured cohort. Thus, if a lot of parents reduced their labour supply and depressed their earnings, the thresholds defining privilege/underprivilege for their cohort of children would be correspondingly adjusted down. This method of setting the thresholds makes it more risky for parents to try to game the system: they have to trade-off definite reductions in income and in their children's welfare now against future benefits to their children that are highly uncertain. I think these responses to the parental incentives objection do bolster the case for a childhood privilege tax/subsidy scheme. But, as Ackerman and Alstott would admit, their overall response to the parental incentives objection is concessionary: it is acknowledged that incentive considerations will set an upper limit on the level at which the relevant taxes or subsidies are set. And, as regards our present concerns, this will in turn affect the level of basic income the childhood underprivileged can receive and the additional power it gives them in the labour market.[37]

A second way in which we could conceivably introduce a selective basic income targeted at disadvantaged workers would be to link eligibility for such a benefit to individuals' own employment records. Imagine, for example, that the community uses citizens' juries or some similar institution to determine a set of jobs that will be publicly acknowledged as particularly unpleasant or otherwise burdensome. We could perhaps then create an early retirement/semi-retirement system for those who have spent many years doing what citizens in general regard as particularly unpleasant jobs by assuring all those who have done these jobs, for a sufficient portion of their working lives, a basic state pension at a lower age than for the working population in general. Those who have little choice but to do poor quality jobs during their working life would in this way be compensated with the option of a shorter working life. While the burdens of meeting the reciprocity principle will then fall more heavily on their shoulders in the earlier years of their lives, these burdens will not necessarily be heavier over the full course of their adult lives. There are, once again, obvious objections to the proposal. Could society reach a stable consensus as to which jobs are most unpleasant? Is there also not a risk that citizens might try to abuse such a system? I am unsure how significant the first problem is likely to be, and, as regards the second, I would only add that if the jobs in question really are as unpleasant as we are assuming then this will act as some disincentive to those who have a realistic option to do other forms of work.[38]

8.5.3   Time-limited basic income

One idea that came to dominate debates over welfare reform in the USA in the 1990s, and which was eventually enacted in the 1996 Personal Responsibility and Work Opportunity Reconciliation Act, is that of time-limited welfare. Individuals should only be able to claim welfare, it was argued, up to some fixed period of years over the entire course of their adult lives and only for limited durations over smaller periods. From the standpoint of fair reciprocity, time-limiting income support in this way is almost certainly indefensible. It is perfectly conceivable that citizens may make a good faith effort to find work and yet still find themselves unemployed at the end of the specified time period. Cutting them off at this point, with no further support, violates the commitment to protect citizens from significant brute luck disadvantage.

However, now imagine that we have a system of income support in place that is not time-limited, but which is work-tested: recipients of income support who are work-capable must pass a 'work-test' indicating their willingness to work. A proposal is now made to introduce a nonwork-tested basic income as a complement to this system of work-tested income support. This basic income is to be set at or close to a level sufficient to meet a standard set of basic needs; it is, however, to be time-limited. By this I mean that citizens will not be able to claim this income grant indefinitely, as is the case in the standard UBI proposal,[39] but will only be able to claim it for a maximum number of years over the course of their whole working-age lives and for limited durations over smaller periods. Subject to these time limitations, however, citizens may claim it whenever they want. We would then in effect have a two-tier system of income support: a first tier of conventional income support that is work-tested (for the working-age and work-capable unemployed) but not time-limited; and a second tier of universal basic income that is not work-tested, but that is time-limited. We might set the system up, for example, so that people have a life-cycle eligibility for basic income for a total of, say, four years. Is there much to be said for such a proposal?

I think so. A time-limited basic income of this kind would provide a substantial residual safeguard against the brute luck disadvantage and market vulnerability that could quite conceivably slip through the cracks of a single-tier work-tested system of income support. If people get into difficulty, and the first, work-tested tier of the income support system somehow fails to pick this up, then they can activate this second tier of protection as an emergency measure, giving themselves time to sort their position out.[40] At the same time, because this basic income is time-limited it does not allow citizens who wish to maintain a decent standard of living to withdraw from productive participation in their community over the long-term. The obligations that citizens have under the reciprocity principle should be satisfied, more or less, over the course of the individual's entire adult life. Thus, from the standpoint of fair reciprocity, the proposal for time-limited basic income looks like an especially good bet. We would seem to get an important additional safeguard against brute luck disadvantage and market vulnerability with relatively little cost in terms of undue opportunities for economic free-riding and/or parasitism.

In policy terms, it would be very easy to integrate a time-limited basic income into the provision of a *universal capital grant*. Under this type of proposal, any citizen reaching maturity would receive a substantial initial capital endowment as a social inheritance from the community.[41] For a combination of reciprocity-related and frankly paternalistic reasons use of this endowment might to some extent be linked to specific activities, such as further and higher education, training, job search and so on, that serve productive participation in the community. But some portion of the grant might also be available to citizens as an unconditional but time-limited basic income which they can choose to activate as they wish, and which they can choose to set to one side as a fund for handling emergency situations that the conventional work-tested system of income support fails to pick up.

8.6   Conclusion: on the need to widen the scope of the basic income debate

I have attempted in this chapter to offer an interpretation of the exploitation objection to the UBI proposal, an evaluation of Van Parijs's response to the objection, and, at more length, an independent evaluation of the objection, based on the interpretation offered. The objection can be understood, I have argued, as deriving from a principle of reciprocity; though our understanding of this principle, and of how it is fairly implemented, needs to be informed by other solidaristic values and commitments (such as the commitments to protect citizens from significant brute luck disadvantage and from risk of desperate trades). I do not think that Van Parijs's arguments, as set out in *Real Freedom for All*, succeed in defusing the objection when understood in these terms. However, even if the objection is valid – if the introduction of a UBI would result in (or at least make possible) a morally objectionable form of free-riding or parasitism – it does not follow that, from the standpoint of fair reciprocity, the objection is decisive. For the introduction of a UBI could conceivably have a wide range of effects which are positive and highly desirable from this standpoint, and, if these are strong enough, they can plausibly be said morally to outweigh the free-riding or parasitism a UBI would seem to permit. In addition, however, I have argued that the original UBI proposal can be modified in various ways so as to diminish further the force of the exploitation objection. Variants of the original proposal such as republican basic income, selective basic income and time-limited basic income all offer ways of reaping some of the benefits of the original UBI proposal without creating the same risk of free-riding or parasitism. Of course, more work needs to be done to show that proposals of these types are practicable (particularly, perhaps, in the case of the selective basic income proposal). But policy proposals such as these would seem to offer promising possibilities for a contemporary social reformer concerned to respect and advance all the major solidaristic commitments of fair reciprocity: to give weight both to the demand for universal real freedom *and* the demand that all citizens make a fair contribution to the production of the material conditions necessary for the enjoyment of this freedom.

Notes

1. For sympathetic efforts to understand and state the objection, see also Gijs van Donselaar, *The Benefit of Another's Pains: Parasitism, Scarcity, Basic Income* (Amsterdam: University of Amsterdam, 1997), and Stuart White, 'Liberal Equality, Exploitation, and the Case for an Unconditional Basic Income', *Political Studies* 45 (1997), pp. 312–26.
2. I set to one side for the moment the various ways in which the notion of 'life-chances' might be elaborated, for example, as access to welfare, resources, or some other form(s) of advantage.
3. Here is just one representative statement of the egalitarian reciprocity ethic from a major Marxist thinker and activist: 'in order that everyone in society

can enjoy prosperity, everybody must work. Only somebody who performs some useful work for the public at large, whether by hand or by brain, can be entitled to receive from society the means for satisfying his needs. A life of leisure like most of the rich exploiters currently lead must come to an end. A general requirement to work for all who are able to do so, from which small children, the aged and sick are exempted, is a matter of course in a socialist economy.' This passage is from Rosa Luxemburg, 'The Socialisation of Society', trans., Dave Hollis, www.marxists.org, 1999 (1918).

4. See Eduard Bernstein, 'What Is Socialism?', in Manfred Stegler, ed. and trans., *Selected Writings of Eduard Bernstein, 1900–1921* (Atlantic Highlands, NJ: Humanities Press, 1996), pp. 149–59, specifically, p. 152.

5. And, one should add, on one's capacity to contribute *without unreasonable cost to oneself* (for one might be strictly capable of working, say, and yet afflicted so that one is filled with acute pain the moment one goes to work).

6. This move is not uncontroversial. In particular, some might argue that one makes a sufficient effort to benefit others – sufficient to establish a legitimate claim to a share of the social product – simply by respecting the system of rights which makes it possible for others to go about their productive business. However, if we say that a voluntarily non-working member of the community is entitled to a given quantity of the resources created by a productive member simply because he/she respects the rights of the latter, must we not, in all fairness, also acknowledge that the working member has an equal claim to resources from the non-working individual given that he/she, the working member of the community, also respected the former's rights (he/she did not, for example, try to force the non-worker to work against his/her will)? If so, then no *net* transfer of resources from the worker to the non-worker is justified by such an argument (and we would only impose a pointless administrative cost on society to effect all the transfers for which the argument apparently calls).

7. See Van Donselaar, *Benefit of Another's Pains*, pp. 1–5, 136–9.

8. By way of intuitive illustration, consider the case of Alf. Alf is unemployed and receiving unemployment benefit from the state. Alf is capable of working, however, and in fact there are a number of good jobs available to him. Alf refuses to take a job but continues to draw unemployment benefit. On the face of it, this looks like a case of economic parasitism. For Alf imposes a clear cost on the consumption possibilities of his fellow citizens. But it is reasonably within his power to avoid imposing this cost since he is capable of work and, by assumption, he has good jobs available to him.

9. See Samuel Bowles and Herbert Gintis, 'Is Egalitarianism Passe? Homo Reciprocans and the Future of Egalitarian Politics', *Boston Review* 23 (December/January 1998/1999), pp. 4–10.

10. See Bo Rothstein, *Just Institutions Matter: the Moral and Political Logic of the Universal Welfare State* (Cambridge: Cambridge University Press, 1998), pp. 136–43 and 163–70.

11. I take the notion of 'desperate trade' from Arthur M. Okun, *Equality and Efficiency: the Big Tradeoff* (Washington DC: The Brookings Institution, 1975).

12. I take the term *fair reciprocity* from Alan Gibbard, who suggests that it captures the essence of John Rawls's conception of distributive justice. The conception of justice as fair reciprocity sketched here shares with Gibbard's

conception the attempt to integrate the intuitions that justice is centrally about both mutual advantageous cooperation and egalitarian impartiality. See Alan Gibbard, 'Constructing Justice', *Philosophy and Public Affairs* 20 (1991), pp. 264–79.

13. To the extent that one's contribution takes the form of paid work, and wage rates are a good indication of the value to the community of an individual's contribution (perhaps a large assumption given the extent of market distortions in real world market economies), then the obligation one has under the reciprocity principle is properly understood, I think, as an obligation to realize one's respective earnings/contribution capacity to at least some minimum extent in return for a corresponding minimum share of the social product. A highly skilled worker would fail to satisfy this obligation if he/she chose to work in a low-skilled job that only realized a small fraction of his contributive capacity (assuming more suitable jobs were available). It may be difficult to enforce this aspect of the reciprocity principle directly, but employment agencies, unions and employers may be able to cooperate to prevent widespread underemployment of more skilled workers to the extent that this threatens to become a problem.

14. My intuition here is that our society has two basic systems for meeting needs, a system of market-based work and a system of domestic or family-based work, and that a plausible public conception of what counts in satisfaction of the reciprocity principle must give some recognition to work of the latter kind as well as to the former in view of the public/external goods that work of the former kind can provide. It does not necessarily follow from this that all forms of domestic or intrafamilial labour should count as contributive in this way.

15. One possible internal problem arises when we relax the initial assumption of equal internal endowments. Will not the funds earmarked for a UBI then have to be redirected into compensatory transfers to those with poor internal endowments, so exhausting what is left for financing a uniform basic income? For Van Parijs's effort to anticipate and defuse this possible problem, see *Real Freedom for All*, pp. 58–88.

16. The conception of property rights in job assets supported by the fair reciprocity perspective is akin (if not identical) to the 'social republican' conception of property rights recently elaborated and defended by William Simon. See William Simon, 'Social-Republican Property', *UCLA Law Review* 38 (1991), pp. 1,335–413.

17. The ticket metaphor is suggested by Van Donselaar's discussion of parasitism, equal division of resources, and UBI in *Benefit of Another's Pains*, pp. 104–65. In Van Donselaar's illuminating analysis, the fundamental source of the problem is that Van Parijs insists on distributing resources to individuals without any regard to their 'independent interests' in using them, so allowing those with weak independent interests to extract 'parasitic' rents from those with stronger interests. Van Donselaar offers the following example to illustrate the problem. There are two people, Lazy and Crazy, and 4 identical units of land. In Crazy's absence, Lazy would appropriate and work 1 unit of land. In Lazy's absence, Crazy would appropriate and work 3 units of land. In van Donselaar's terms, Lazy thus has an independent interest in 1 unit, and Crazy an independent interest in 3 units, of land. Say that we now give Lazy

and Crazy each 2 units of the land and allow trade. Lazy will likely lease some of his land to Crazy in return for a share of what Crazy produces on the land; and Lazy thereby ends up better off, and Crazy worse off, than each would respectively be in the absence of the other. The fair division, van Donselaar argues, is to apportion land in accordance with the underlying pattern of independent interests (adjusting the apportionment if/when these interests change). By insisting on strictly equal division regardless of the underlying pattern of independent interests we merely create a scarcity which is not inherent in the situation, a scarcity that Lazy can then exploit to enjoy 'the benefit of another's pains'. What applies to land in this case, applies no less to job assets and to the parasitic rents that an equal division of tradeable job assets would allow a citizen-surfer (or an opportunistic citizen-hermit) to extract from harder working citizens.

18. See Van Parijs, *Real Freedom for All*, pp. 133–69. I discuss this attempt to defuse the exploitation objection in more depth in 'Liberal Equality, Exploitation, and the Case for an Unconditional Basic Income', pp. 323–5.
19. This approach to the defence of UBI can be seen as a variant of the 'pragmatic' approach to the justification of UBI outlined by Brian Barry in contrast to what he terms Van Parijs's 'principled' approach. See Brian Barry, 'Real Freedom and Basic Income', *Journal of Political Philosophy* 4 (1996), pp. 242–76.
20. Citizens who are unable to meet their obligations in this way will suffer frustration and loss of self-respect as a result which seems intuitively to conflict with the concern to protect citizens from significant brute luck disadvantage.
21. Probably the most widely discussed revenue-sharing proposals are Martin Weitzman's proposal for profit-sharing enterprises, and James Meade's proposals for 'discriminating labour–capital partnerships'. On the former, see Martin Weitzman, *The Share Economy: Conquering Stagflation* (Cambridge: Harvard University Press, 1985), and on the latter, see James Meade, *Agathotopia: the Economics of Partnership* (Aberdeen: University of Aberdeen, 1989).
22. See Meade, *Agathotopia*, pp. 29–30 and 34–8.
23. The limited earnings potential of one partner may make that partner financially dependent on the other, and this other can then take advantage of the dependency relationship to pressure for an exploitative household division of labour. See Susan Moller Okin, *Justice, Gender, and the Family* (New York: Basic Books, 1989), pp. 134–69.
24. See Philippe Van Parijs and Robert van der Veen, 'A Capitalist Road to Communism', in Philippe Van Parijs, *Marxism Recycled* (Cambridge: Cambridge University Press, 1993), pp. 155–75.
25. There is also a problem of preventing harm to innocent third parties: if we discipline adult non-workers by cutting their income, this is likely to harm any third parties who are dependants of these adults (such as their children).
26. For an elaboration of the theory of unemployment I am drawing on here, see Richard Layard, Steve Nickell and Richard Jackman, *The Unemployment Crisis* (Oxford: Oxford University Press, 1994).
27. See Rick van der Ploeg and A. Lans Bovenberg, 'Against the Basic Instinct: Why Basic Income Proposals Will Not Do the Job', *New Economy* 3 (1996), pp. 235–40.
28. See Anthony Atkinson, 'The Case for a Participation Income', *Political Quarterly* 67 (1996), pp. 67–70.

29. See Mickey Kaus, *The End of Equality* (New York: Basic Books, 1992), esp. pp. 81–5, and James McCormick, *Citizens' Service* (London: Institute for Public Policy Research, 1994).

30. See Van Parijs, *Real Freedom for All*, p. 231.

31. Dore envisages basic income being phased in for youths and carrying corresponding 'duties of unpaid community service, duties which are compulsory and universal, though widely flexible in form'. See Ronald Dore, *Taking Japan Seriously: a Confucian Perspective on Leading Economic Issues* (Stanford: Stanford University Press, 1987), p. 223.

32. See Andre Gorz, *Paths to Paradise: On the Liberation from Work* (London: South End Press, 1985), esp. theses 17–19, pp. 40–7.

33. Personal communication.

34. Two other forms of selective basic income are the universal child benefit and the universal citizen's pension, both of which are already established policy in some welfare states. I put these to one side here simply because they do not directly address the problems faced by working-age citizens who are disadvantaged in the labour market.

35. See Bruce Ackerman and Anne Alstott, *The Stakeholder Society* (New Haven: Yale University Press, 1999), pp. 155–77.

36. But if some children are labelled as having had underprivileged childhoods might this not be stigmatizing to the parents concerned? I am not sure how much of a problem this is likely to be, but I would caution against dismissing it.

37. One can imagine a variant of the scheme in which those who have had underprivileged childhoods receive special earnings subsidies rather than unconditional flat-rate income grants. To the extent that the aim is specifically to redress inequalities in earnings power, there is much to be said for this variant. But our immediate concern is with enabling disadvantaged workers to escape entrapment in poor quality, unpleasant jobs. We would need to assess whether the earnings subsidy offers as much to the disadvantaged worker in this respect before accepting it as an alternative to a selective basic income.

38. If there are general protections against underemployment, along the lines very roughly suggested in note 14, then these might also be harnessed to help prevent abuse of an occupationally differentiated state pension.

39. This proposal for a time-limited basic income does not in fact contradict the original definition of UBI given at the beginning of this chapter as an income grant paid on an individual basis to all citizens regardless of wealth/income from other sources, work or willingness to work. However, in policy debates UBI is usually conceived, in addition, as an income grant that will be paid to the individual at regular intervals throughout the course of his/her life. This is the variant of UBI that Van Parijs defends in *Real Freedom for All*, though he does not altogether rule out other variants such as one-off lump-sum endowments on maturity and/or payment of the UBI as some form of benefit-in-kind (e.g., health-care). See Van Parijs, *Real Freedom for All*, pp. 41–8.

40. I do not mean to imply here that suffering such an emergency should be a condition of eligibility for this time-limited basic income, merely that such a basic income would provide the citizen with a fund which they could keep in place to draw upon in such an emergency. Citizens might squander the fund, of course. But then they might squander an ordinary basic income.

41. For a well-worked out proposal of this sort, see Ackerman and Alstott, *Stakeholder Society*, esp. pp. 21–112. Ackerman and Alstott propose a grant of some $80,000 (in 1996 US prices) for all US citizens reaching maturity, financed from a combination of wealth and inheritance taxes. See also Robert Haveman, *Starting Even: an Equal Opportunity Program to Combat the Nation's New Poverty* (New York: Simon and Schuster, 1988), esp. pp. 168–71, and Robert Kuttner, 'Rampant Bull', *American Prospect* 39 (July/August 1998), pp. 30–6.

9
Compatriot Priority and Justice among Thieves

Hillel Steiner

Suppose we steal £100 from you. And further suppose that theft occasions a just duty of redress in the thieves. Is what we owe you *less* if you live in a different city than we do? Would it be less if an international boundary lies between those two cities? Would a just division of those spoils *among ourselves* reduce our redress liability to you? What would have to be the structure of a moral theory that sustains affirmative answers to these sorts of question?

I want to acknowledge, right at the outset of this argument, that there's a very clear sense in which it pushes at an open door. For, in advancing his powerful case for understanding justice as the universal leximinning of real freedom, Van Parijs insists that

> [F]irst, we must fully recognize the crucially important difference between a universal local leximin (or maximin) and a global one, between a leximin that applies to each country of the world taken separately and one that applies to the world as a whole. And having recognized the difference between the two interpretations, we must unambiguously opt for the latter. When speaking of real-freedom-for-all we must mean it: for *all*.
>
> (pp. 227–8)[1]

Notwithstanding the fact that sub-global localities can be a good deal more local than only countries – a fact to which I'll eventually return – Van Parijs is clear that the scope of redistributive justice extends globally.

> [W]e must pursue the objective of introducing substantial redistributive mechanisms on a world scale, indeed ultimately an individual basic

income at the highest sustainable level for each human being ... as there is no morally non-arbitrary boundary to our equal concern, save the limits of mankind itself.

(pp. 228–9)

I take this to mean that the total funds raised within each country, from all the various basic income sources so painstakingly identified in *Real Freedom for All*, are justly amalgamated with those of every other country. Justice demands that each such national fund be treated as part of a global fund. And hence the unconditional basic income for each individual that leximins real freedom is a globally uniform one.

Why, then, should a leximin that 'applies to each country of the world taken separately' be regarded even as an 'interpretation' of leximinning real freedom? We know that the attainment of the aforesaid global leximin requires substantial transnational redistribution (cf. pp. 228ff.). Let's call those nations to whom such redistributive transfers are justly owed *Creditors* and their owing counterparts *Debtors*.[2] A portion of each Debtor nation's basic income fund justly belongs to (the members of) Creditor nations.[3] In view of this fact, would not a leximin that applies to each Debtor nation, taken separately – a local leximin – simply be tantamount to *justice among thieves*?[4] Under that dispensation, each person's unconditional basic income in Creditor nations would be lower than it should be only because its counterpart in Debtor nations would be higher than it should be. Can that distributive state of affairs really be just? Can such *compatriot priority* be justified?

One sort of theory that returns an affirmative answer to these questions does so essentially by denying the very possibility that nations can stand in the sort of Debtor–Creditor relation to one another that I've sketched above. (This is evidently not the view embraced by Van Parijs.) On this view, it may be possible to say, for instance, that one nation justly owes redress to another for initiating an aggressive war against it, or for imperialistically exploiting it, or for confiscating its property, and so forth. It may also be possible to say that nations justly owe debts to other nations for resources loaned or sold to them by the latter. All of these forms of owing have their individualistic counterparts in types of debt that compatriots can incur to one another, either contractually or created by some prior rights violation. But, on this view, it is *not* possible to claim that nations can justly owe debts, one to another, on *all* the same kinds of grounds that compatriots can. More specifically, they cannot owe debts entailed by such demands of redistributive justice as are implied by leximinning real freedom. Why?

The broad answer offered by such theories is that the duties of justice owed by nations, one to another, are strictly limited to *negative* ones.[5] Whereas compatriots can owe positive redistributive duties to one another – justice can require local leximinning – the only (uncontracted, uncreated) duty that nations can owe to other nations is to respect their legal sovereignty: a duty of non-interference. The reasons offered for this restriction vary considerably, not least in their cogency. Many invoke considerations of *realism*, arguing that, since compliance with such owed positive duties would – as a matter of fact – be neither voluntarily forthcoming nor systematically enforced, there simply are no such duties.

Others, understandably unmoved by this heroic leap from solely factual premises to normative conclusions, argue more fundamentally that moral norms themselves are inherently local in scope. Deriving their very meaning only from the particular distinct (national) cultures in which they're saliently embedded, they consequently can possess validity only within those confines.[6] This cultural relativization of all moral norms, this rejection of globally valid norms, is held to extend even to the demands of justice – at least in respect of its positive demands.[7]

Such accounts, it seems to me, are beset by several serious difficulties, to which they can offer no definitive solutions. We'll have occasion to consider some aspects of these presently. Among them are: (1) why the negative demands of justice, at the international level, are presumed to be exempted from such cultural relativization;[8] (2) why the presence of numerous prominent sub- and supra-national cultures – each with its own distinctive norms – is nevertheless presumed to permit distinct *national* conceptions of justice to exist saliently intact; and (3) how the very jurisdictional domains, of legally sovereign nations, can even be identified unless there is some globally valid moral norm demarcating them.[9]

Suffice it, for our present purposes, simply to emphasize that the justification for compatriot priority afforded by these accounts is *not* the one deployed by Van Parijs. As we've seen, he finds no problem in the claim that the demands of justice – positive as well as negative – have globally uniform validity. Indeed, he explicitly endorses it. So why, then, the suggestion that local leximinning can be, and in the current state of the world *is*, the just thing to do? (pp. 229ff.) For what sort of reason could Debtor nations be justified in retaining a larger portion of the global fund – and conferring a higher unconditional basic income on their own members – than would be the case under global leximin?

To address these questions properly, we need to assess the structural status of the core idea deployed in this part of Van Parijs's argument: *solidaristic patriotism*. Solidaristic patriotism is, first and foremost, a strong emotional commitment to the well-being of one's compatriots simply because they are one's compatriots. As such, there are many forms of conduct that can express it, and many policies and ways of organizing social life that can foster such conduct. These are plausibly said to include the common use of the same schools and hospitals by all social groups so as 'to erode the barriers that tend to form between social categories and to maintain a sufficient level of social cohesion'. And, more pertinently for our present subject, they may also include the non-exporting of investment capital and the non-emigration of skilled labour, despite the prospects of their enjoying more lucrative returns abroad. Moreover, restrictive institutions may permissibly be shaped so as to promote some of these forms of conduct (pp. 230–1).[10]

There are, I think, two quite different structural positions which solidaristic patriotism could alternatively occupy, within a broader moral theory, that would enable it to justify the aforesaid compatriot priority of local leximinning. The first of these is as follows. Solidaristic patriotism could be one amongst several basic or primary values in a pluralistic moral theory – one which also includes items like justice, utility-maximization, etc. among its other primary values.[11] In such theories, conflicts between primary values – situations where their respective demands are disjunctively but not conjunctively satisfiable – are resolved by reference to the weightings or rankings assigned to those values: weightier or higher ranked values override or constrain the pursuit of lesser ones.[12] Accordingly, to say that local leximinning should enjoy priority over global leximinning would, in this context, imply an assignment of greater weighting or higher ranking to solidaristic patriotism than to justice. The just entitlements of all individuals – everywhere – do indeed matter, but the well-being of one's compatriots matters more.

This is *not*, I think, the sort of view that Van Parijs embraces. For although he argues that real-libertarianism can (and should) sponsor solidaristically patriotic conduct, and that

> it can thereby consistently take on board at least some of the anti-individualistic concerns commonly associated with contemporary communitarianism,

he is very clear that this sponsorship cannot be justified directly, but only instrumentally (p. 231). Indeed, here and elsewhere he comes close to insisting on the lexical primacy of justice:

> A society is not, by definition, better if and only if it is more just. But I honestly doubt that there is much to be gained along other

dimensions I care about … at the cost of a loss in terms of social justice.

(p. 232)[13]

So if we're to find the justification for compatriot priority – for favouring local over global leximinning – we'll have to look elsewhere than in moral theories so structured as to allow justice to be overridden, whether by solidaristic patriotism or any other value.

How, then, can a theory that licenses and even mandates compatriot priority nevertheless be one that understands justice as sustaining a demand for global leximinning and that precludes its being overridden? How can awarding our Debtor nation compatriots an unconditional basic income, part of which justly belongs to the members of Creditor nations, *not* be a flagrant violation of that demand? To repeat my earlier question: wouldn't we, in doing this, be – at best – securing justice among thieves?

The underlying justificatory structure, sustaining Van Parijs's belief that we would *not* be doing so, seems closely to resemble some aspects of what Nozick has called a 'utilitarianism of rights' whereby the rights of some are traded off against those of others in order to reduce the overall amount of rights-violations: to reduce what we might call a *justice-deficit*.[14] In the present case, the prospective entitlements of members of Creditor nations are traded off to secure those of their counterparts in Debtor nations. In such a theory, solidaristic patriotism is thus not a primary value but rather an instrumental one, the pursuit of which facilitates this trade-off. Hence it can be justice-promoting rather than justice-constraining. So what we need now to consider are the reasons for thinking that this trade-off actually would reduce a justice-deficit.

But, before doing that, we should reflect on why there would be *any* justice-deficit in the first place. What exactly is the problem here? It can't be one of not knowing who justly owes what to whom. For if we suppose that the amount of basic income funding yielded by each country is assessable, and that the aggregate global yield is thereby computable, then the per capita entitlement generated by a global leximin is also computable. And if that's so, there doesn't seem to be any computational obstacle to determining which nations are Creditors and which are Debtors nor, therefore, to determining how much is owed by each of the latter to the global fund and how much is owed by that fund to each of the former.[15] Provided that Debtor nations and global fund administrators comply with those payment duties, it would be difficult to imagine how any justice-deficit could even arise.[16]

So, at first glance, it very much looks like the only story that could be told to underwrite such a possibility would have to be one that invokes considerations of non-compliance. And, indeed, part of Van Parijs's account here essentially addresses that problem and offers plausible suggestions as to the sorts of development its solution depends upon. But, obviously, solidaristic patriotism itself cannot be one of those developments: partiality, it's generally agreed, fosters rather than redresses injustice. A Debtor nation's non-compliance with its payment duty to the global fund is definitely *not* going to be remedied by solidaristic patriotism.

However, such patriotism might begin to look somewhat more promising as an instrument of justice when we consider the fact that the magnitude of a nation's owed payment to the global fund, far from being fixed, is some positive function of its wealth: increases, or averted decreases, in the latter yield their counterparts in the former. So if solidaristic patriotism operates over time to conserve or enhance the wealth of a Debtor nation, it appears that it must eventually make for a larger global fund contribution and hence a higher global leximin than would otherwise be the case. And the difference, between that higher global leximin and the lower one, represents the justice-deficit that is reduced by the trade-off fostered by solidaristic patriotism. *Real libertarianism in one country*, so to speak, thereby becomes a means, rather than an obstacle, to justice. Are there, then, reasons to suppose that solidaristic patriotism would have this effect?

Van Parijs offers a number of arguments along these lines. All of them have, in one way or another, to do with the difficulties of securing substantial basic income funds in the face of globalized market forces. For these forces currently generate powerful incentives, for the owners of those very factors of production (investment capital, technology, skilled labour) whose financial returns form the tax-base for basic income, to export them to lower-tax localities where they can earn a higher net return. Even nations strongly committed to redistributive policies find themselves drawn into an accelerating downward spiral of competitive tax reduction – and correspondingly reduced redistribution – in order to prevent this factor flight.

As with other *public bads*, one solution to such factor haemorrhage would presumably lie in the creation of institutions to constrain the anti-redistributive effects of this global competition which national governments, as the competitors, are themselves incapable of controlling. Thus Van Parijs suggests that *popular sovereignty*, the institutional form historically credited with harnessing redistributive policies to market forces, needs somehow to be established at the international level. And he notes that

> [I]n this respect, there is a world of difference between institutions that amount to mutually advantageous bargaining between nations and institutions that approximate one-man-one-vote democracy on a world scale ... Transnational democracy, not international bargaining, is the institutional tool for real-freedom-for-all.
>
> (pp. 228–9)

But the trouble with this 'democratic scale-lifting' strategy is simply that

> it will take a long time to create political entities of the right sort at the right level, to equip them with appropriate democratic institutions and to build both the political will and the concrete instruments without which substantial international redistribution will remain a utopia. *But we cannot wait that long.* The competitive pressure against existing intranational redistribution is mounting, and it would, therefore, be good if there were another strategy which would enable us to keep and regain at least part of the required leeway.
>
> (pp. 229–30, italics added)

Solidaristic patriotism is this other strategy. For the kind of conduct it fosters would counteract the 'purely opportunistic motives' of owners of highly productive assets to seek higher net rewards abroad.

> Consequently it would provide a sturdy protection against competitive downward levelling and a firm basis for the viability of high solidarity on a local level long before it becomes possible on a global level.
>
> (p. 230)

The question we need to address, I think, goes something like this. Acknowledging that democratic scale-lifting is bound to be the protracted process Van Parijs fears, are there good reasons to see national asset retention, of the sort aimed at by solidaristic patriotism, as promoting or inhibiting the attainment of an individual basic income at the highest sustainable level for each human being? Would its contribution to reducing our justice-deficit be negative or positive?

Obviously, a question of this sort can be convincingly answered only by detailed empirical projections of alternative economic futures. The scope for conclusive a priori reasoning here is severely limited. Yet some useful theoretical argument can be brought to bear on this matter, insofar as it may draw attention to considerations that have not figured in this analysis. Some of these, I suggest, tend to indicate that national asset retention is *not* the high road to justice. Why?

It seems clear – indeed, trivially true – that a global practice of national asset retention would work to the benefit of asset-rich countries and to the disbenefit of asset-poor ones. The latter have every reason to try to attract productive assets from abroad to raise their own levels of productivity. And they have the principal means to do so, inasmuch as they can offer the owners of such assets the higher net rates of return that are standardly available in low-wage economies. This, indeed, is precisely what solidaristic patriotism – as a brake on factor mobility – would counteract.

Yet from the standpoint of leximin justice, it's unclear why it should be counteracted. For it's plain that, for the most part, asset-rich countries are Debtor nations and their asset-poor counterparts are Creditors. The entry of productive assets into the latter must, *ceteris paribus*, tend to raise their wage levels and general living standards by introducing competitive pressure into markets where local landlords, employers and professionals otherwise reap the exploitative benefits of being insulated from such rivalry. People do not generally opt for the often dangerous working conditions of a multinational corporation's sweatshop, unless they think that doing so will make them better off than would scratching a precarious living out of tenant farming. What national asset retention would do is deprive them of that option. A solidaristically patriotic Marks & Spencer shareholders' meeting would vote to build its next clothing factory in Macclesfield rather than Marrakech.

Globalisation and the factor mobility it entails allow the increasingly successful bidding, by the labour forces of poorer countries, for greater access to international capital and technology. In so doing, they tend to bring about a narrowing of international inequalities. Of course and as Van Parijs's analysis suggests, this occurs at the cost of eroding the tax-base for basic income in wealthier countries. Conversely, however, it must thereby also enlarge that tax-base in poorer ones and thus proportionally reduce their net claims on the global fund. Indeed, some Creditor nations might become sufficiently wealthy to cease being Creditor nations altogether.

Clearly, it's a matter for empirical investigation as to whether these two processes – of tax-base erosion and enlargement – would both be likely to occur at the same pace and on the same scale. But that, surely, is the point: there is no a priori reason to suppose that the former would exceed the latter in these respects and, hence, no such reason to assign justice-promoting status to the national asset retention that would be induced by solidaristic patriotism. An enlargement of the Moroccan tax-base may more than offset an erosion of its British counterpart.

There is yet another reason to doubt that solidaristic patriotism is an appropriate instrument for the achievement of a high global leximin. And this has much to do with the uncertain *scope* of the commitment it is supposed to engender. That commitment, as described earlier, is one to the well-being of one's compatriots simply because they are one's compatriots. Now one does not have to be a close observer of recent events in the Balkans and elsewhere to appreciate that the reference of 'one's compatriots' can be profoundly contestable. I previously referred to the presence of numerous prominent sub- and supra-national cultures, each with its own distinctive norms. Members of many of these cultures are actively engaged in secessionist and irredentist movements aimed at revising the world's current array of nation states and other forms of legally autonomous jurisdiction. *Their* views, of who their compatriots are and to whose welfare they should thus be committed, are not invariably inferable from the lines drawn on current maps.

Nor, it has to be said, are those views likely to have been entirely untouched by perceptions of the differential distribution of productive assets among different groups within existing nation states. It seems unreasonable to suppose that the movement seeking the creation of an autonomous Croatian republic within Bosnia was utterly oblivious of the fact that Bosnian Croats are, in general, much wealthier and better educated and vocationally trained than are the members of the majority Bosnian Muslim community. Nor was it oblivious of the still higher per capita level of productive assets held by the Mostar Muslims whose desired independence from that Croatian republic was forcibly opposed by that movement. Similar phenomena have been observed in Nigeria, the former Soviet Union, Eastern Europe, Britain, Ireland, Canada, northern California, Lombardy, Belgium, Hong Kong and other parts of East Asia.

In short, Van Parijs's suggestion that solidaristic patriotism works to counteract 'opportunistic' asset-exporting behaviour must contend with the fact that it also creates significant incentives for opportunistic secessionist behaviour. For the plain fact is that there are two ways, not one, for asset-rich groups to escape high redistributive taxation: one is to export their assets and the second is to export their *countries*, that is, create new ones. And since there can be no moral principle that says international boundaries must be whatever they are shown to be on maps published before the year *xxxx*, the availability of a moral theory constraining solidaristic patriotism to reduce – rather than increase – the justice-deficit must be open to serious doubt.

I'm thus led to conclude that compatriot priority is not a serviceable vehicle for reaching the goal of global distributive justice. Although it may plausibly address some central concerns of contemporary communitarianism, it seems to do so at the cost of leximinning real freedom on a world scale. While the processes of globalization can obviously not be expected to achieve that goal, they can help to move things in that direction. For whatever else they do, they operate to redistribute wealth from asset-rich to asset-poor societies. And in so doing, they shift the international balance of claims and duties in the global fund, reducing the aggregate debt of Debtor nations and enabling Creditor nations to fund a greater proportion of their members' basic income entitlements themselves. Of course, democratic scale-lifting may also be necessary, to ensure that those claims – ultimately the claims of each individual person – are fully met. But compatriot priority's contribution to this process does not look promising.

Notes

1. Philippe Van Parijs, *Real Freedom for All: What (if Anything) Can Justify Capitalism?* (Oxford: Clarendon Press, 1995). All page references to this work are parenthesized in the text, as above.
2. For clarity's sake, it's worth emphasizing that this *moral* nomenclature is more or less the exact opposite of the *legal* nomenclature currently used to describe the location of international financial claims and duties, whereby creditor nations are mostly wealthy ones and debtor nations are mostly not.
3. Thus, assume a world of five nations – Red, White, Blue, Black, Pink – whose respective per capita basic income funding yields are 10, 7, 6, 5, 2. Since this entails a global per capita entitlement of 6, Red and White are Debtors owing 4 and 1 respectively, Black and Pink are Creditors owed 1 and 4 respectively, and Blue is neither a Debtor nor a Creditor; cf. my *An Essay on Rights* (Oxford: Blackwell, 1994), p. 269.
4. I don't want to suggest that the oxymoronic notion of 'justice among thieves' is entirely paradoxical. We can sensibly ask, for instance, whether judges should deal more leniently with gangs of thieves who divide their ill-gotten gains justly. Perhaps so. That is, what our (not infallible) intuitions may tell us is that, in gangs where such gains are divided unjustly, those who secure an excessive share should receive less lenient treatment than their colleagues. But what those same intuitions also tell us is that the aggregate leniency owed to gangs who divide justly is not, *ceteris paribus*, greater than that owed to those who don't.
5. Such theories can, and often do, acknowledge that nations have positive duties to other nations. But these are conceived as duties of charity or humanity, rather than as demands of justice. They do not entail correlative

rights in recipient nations, their fulfillment is not *owed* to them and, consequently, failures to fulfill them occasion no duty of redress.

6. The literature advancing this view is vast and growing. A prominent recent account is David Miller, *On Nationality* (Oxford: Oxford University Press, 1995), ch. 4.

7. Cf. Miller, *On Nationality* and his *Principles of Social Justice* (Cambridge, MA: Harvard University Press, 1999); also John Rawls, *The Law of Peoples* (Cambridge, MA: Harvard University Press, 1999), esp. s. 16.

8. This is particularly problematic in view of the fact that some cultures reject, or considerably truncate, such negative rights at the inter*personal* level.

9. On this last issue, see my 'Hard Borders, Compensation and Classical Liberalism', in David Miller and Sohail Hashmi (eds), *Boundaries, Autonomy and Justice: Diverse Ethical Views* (Princeton: Princeton University Press, forthcoming).

10. Van Parijs raises, only to reject, the possibility of deploying protectionist trade measures as yet another means of fostering local solidarity. These are rejected due to the risk they counterproductively foster, of retaliatory similar moves by other countries (p. 230).

11. A value is a primary one if its desirability or normative force is *underived* from that of another value: that is, if the former neither instrumentally subserves the latter nor is conceived as a form of it.

12. Cf. *Essay on Rights*, ch. 4.

13. In his introduction, Van Parijs characterizes his theory as ascribing 'soft lexicographic priority' to justice (p. 27). Hard lexical priority would here entail that a society is necessarily (rather than only probably) morally worse if its gains along other valued dimensions are purchased at the cost of a loss in terms of social justice. This allows that gains in such dimensions do make society better, but only if they are not so purchased: that is, 'maximally just', rather than 'more just', is a necessary condition of 'morally better', whereas 'more just' is a sufficient condition of it.

14. Robert Nozick, *Anarchy, State and Utopia* (Oxford: Blackwell, 1974), pp. 28–30.

15. See n. 3, above.

16. I here assume that Creditor nations, being net beneficiaries of the global fund, have no reason for non-compliance with their payment duties to it – or (what comes to the same thing) that their claims on it are correspondingly reduced by any such non-compliance.

10
Is Democracy Merely a Means to Social Justice?
Thomas Christiano

10.1 Introduction

Democratic decision making has two very different evaluative aspects that sometimes collide and usually complement each other to some degree. On the one hand, we tend to evaluate democratic decisions from the point of view of the quality of the outcomes. We concern ourselves with whether the outcomes are just or whether they are efficient or protect liberty and promote the common good. This is sometimes called the substantive or outcome dimension of assessment of democratic procedures. On the other hand, we evaluate the decisions from the point of view of how they are made or the quality of the procedure. We are concerned to make the decision in a way that includes everyone who by right ought to be included and that is fair to all the participants. Here we may think that the method by which the decisions are made be intrinsically fair.

In my view these two dimensions of assessment are irreducible. But this is not the way everyone sees it. Some, who I shall call reductionists, think that there is only one form of assessment and that other assessments are reducible to it. For example, instrumentalists or best results theorists like Philippe Van Parijs think that the way in which democratic decisions ought to be made is entirely a matter of what will produce the best outcomes.[1] On their view, the only question to be asked in evaluating democratic procedures (or any political procedures) regards the quality of the outcomes of these procedures. Pure proceduralists, in contrast, see outcomes as essentially evaluable solely in terms of the procedure that brought them about. There are two versions of this kind of view. One version of the view is attributed to some American legal theorists who wish to justify a rather strong form of judicial restraint with regard to the decisions of the American Congress. They argue that the Supreme Court of the United States ought to defer to virtually all the decisions that Congress makes except in the most obvious cases of violation of the literal words of the Constitution.[2] Some theorists of deliberative democracy, for quite different reasons, appear to hold to a kind of pure procedural view as well; they seem to think that if a process is one that is genuinely deliberative and democratic, then it justifies the outcome or the fact that the outcome results from the procedure constitutes its justice.[3] Instrumentalism and pure proceduralism are two forms of what I call *monism* but there are other forms as well.

I shall defend a different kind of view here from those described above. I shall call it a form of evaluative dualism with regard to the assessment of democratic institutions. It is dualistic because it regards democratic institutions as evaluable from two distinct and irreducible points of view that may sometimes conflict. In this paper, I set out to complete two main tasks: first, attack a version of instrumentalism advanced by Philippe Van Parijs. Second, I defend the idea that democratic decision making is inherently just while preserving the instrumental importance of democratic decision making.

10.2 Instrumentalism

Instrumentalism is the view that the value of a democratic procedure (or any procedure) consists entirely in the quality of the outcomes that it produces. Collective decision-making procedures are designed to decide matters that are usually of great moral significance. The laws and policies of a society can be evaluated as just or unjust, efficient or inefficient, violating liberty or promoting it and so on. The instrumentalist urges us to evaluate the procedure solely by considering the quality of the outcomes. The instrumentalist then tells us to choose that procedure which produces the best outcomes. If a monarchy would produce a better set of outcomes than a democracy, then there is no reason whatsoever for resisting the move to monarchy. Who cares how the decision is made as long as the right decisions are made?[4] There are many arguments for this kind of approach.[5] I shall only argue against one particular set of arguments in the literature. And I shall attempt to give a general argument against a certain kind of instrumentalism.

It is important to note that there are a number of different kinds of instrumentalism. There is what I call *fixed-end instrumentalism*. This view merely asks whether the procedures in question tend to produce a particular kind of outcome. It starts by assuming an account of what would be desirable outcomes of decision procedures and then evaluates the procedures in terms of their tendency to produce these outcomes. For instance, a view of collective decision-making procedures that begins by specifying an account of social justice (independent of the decision procedure) and then ranks decision procedures in terms of how well they achieve just outcomes, is a fixed end approach. The views discussed in the following sections of this paper are members of this class of instrumentalism.

There is also what we may call *open-ended instrumentalism*. The clearest illustration of this view is the use some have made of the Condorcet theorem. This theorem states that as long as certain assumptions hold of citizens in the democratic process, if a majority of citizens agrees on the rightness of an outcome, there is a very high probability (nearing 100 percent in very large populations) that the majority is right. If the assumptions stated in the theorem hold for a particular population, then this theorem can tell us that we have good reason to believe that the outcome of the process is right even if we have no idea what the outcome will be in advance. The procedure of majority rule has great epistemic value under certain circumstances; it can help us discover the truth, according to this theorem.

For what it is worth, my hunch is that open-ended instrumental arguments must ultimately rely on fixed-end arguments. The reason for this is captured in the maxim that one person's *modus ponens* is another person's *modus tollens*. For any democratic process, those who think that the democratic process has great epistemic value under certain conditions but disagree strongly with a particular outcome can infer that the conditions did not hold in this circumstance. Among the open-ended theories available, the only way to tell whether the conditions specified by the theory hold is to determine that the outcomes are generally desirable ones. So, in effect, the only way to determine that a particular procedure has great epistemic value is to show that it generally leads to good outcomes. I do not have the time to flesh out this argument here. The instrumentalism I criticize in this paper will be the most prominent one: fixed-end instrumentalism.

10.3 The rationale for instrumental evaluations of democracy

Before I begin my discussion of instrumentalism, I want to start by saying why instrumental evaluations of democracy make sense. By instrumental evaluations, I mean evaluations of democratic institutions in terms of outcomes. To say that instrumental evaluations are part of the evaluation of democratic institutions does not commit one to instrumentalism. The latter says that instrumental evaluations are the only cogent evaluations of democracy. My purpose in this paper is to argue that in addition to its instrumental worth, making decisions democratically is in itself just under a wide variety of circumstances.

First, it seems clear we can evaluate decisions independent of how they are made. We have views about what are just and unjust distributions of income and about what rights individuals have. Because of this we have a sense of the justice or injustice of laws and policies. And we think that laws and policies can be just or unjust whether they are made by a monarch or by a democratic assembly. We think that collective decisions can violate the rights of individuals in a whole variety of ways. For instance, if a democratic assembly votes to enslave a minority of its population or if it simply severely restricts the rights of a minority, it seems clear that this is unjust. To the extent that we have process-independent standards for evaluating legislation, we have some reason to structure collective decision-making institutions so that the decisions generally accord with these standards.

In addition, arguments for and against laws and policies within the democratic assembly as in non-democratic assemblies are often made in terms of the justice or injustice of the proposals. We cannot understand democratic discussion without seeing it as in part a contest of views about justice and the common good. Hence, citizens evaluate laws and policies in terms of standards independent of the democratic process. Again, to the extent that citizens do evaluate laws in these terms, it is clear that they can evaluate democracy or any system of decision making at least in part in terms of standards of legislation that are independent of how it is made.

Indeed, I would argue that a large part of the function of collective decision-making institutions is to bring about justice among persons and advance the common good. These aims cannot be achieved without collective decision-making institutions because they require that individuals coordinate on laws and policies (as well as institutions to adjudicate and enforce these) as a means to their realization. There are many possible coordination points. And there is disagreement among persons as to which coordination point to choose. Some people's aims are better realized by some coordination points than others, while others' aims are better realized by different coordination points. Some method for deciding on the same rules for everyone is necessary.[6]

Finally, an account of some particular method of collective decision making that asserts that it is an inherently fair method of decision making but denies that standards of justice apply to the outcomes of the method seems either arbitrary or incoherent. For instance, some have argued that the disagreements among citizens about justice are merely a matter of clash of subjective preference. They argue that since there is no true answer to the question of what the best preference or true conception of justice is, it is legitimate to treat the disagreements as mere clashes of preference and then allow the majority preference to have its way. Indeed they argue that it is unjust for any particular preference to predominate since all preferences are equal and ought to count for one and no more than one. They argue that to impose any severe restraints on democracy or to evaluate it in terms of some particular conception of justice is unjustly and arbitrarily to favor one preference over others. So here we have a quick defense of why democracy is good and ought not to be instrumentally evaluated.

This view is either arbitrary or incoherent. On the one hand, the proponents of this view might say that there is something special about democracy. They might argue that while democracy is objectively just, all the other standards of justice we normally apply are mere preferences. It is hard to see what argument can be given for this position and I have never seen one. The proposed distinction seems completely arbitrary. On the other hand, suppose we acknowledge that the standards for evaluating collective decision-making methods and their outcomes have the same status. In this case, we either get a view like the one I am defending or we must accept that the fairness of democracy is a mere preference which ought to be treated in the same way that other preferences are. Each counts for one and no more than one. So it is hard to see how there can be a principled defense of democracy on this account that does not end up in infinite regress or that does not defeat itself.

Let us consider the position that the only legitimate way of evaluating collective decision-making institutions is instrumentally.

10.4 Social-justice-guided constitutional engineering

Philippe Van Parijs's program of 'social justice guided constitutional engineering' exemplifies fixed-end instrumentalism. Its main aim is to answer the question: 'Suppose we know what social justice is, what political institutions should we attempt to put into place in order to achieve it as closely and safely as possible?'[7] 'Political institutions' here refers to society's set of collective decision-making arrangements. These are the generally followed rules by which the society makes law and policy. Hence majority rule, universal suffrage, plural voting schemes, judicial review and their alternatives are political institutions. They define the 'rules of the political game'.

On the one hand, political institutions contrast with the basic individual liberties and economic justice as defined by the leximin opportunity principle and intergenerational justice.[8] These are the standards by which law and policies are to be evaluated. Realization or not of the basic liberties or economic justice are the outcomes of the political institutions by which the latter are judged. On the other hand, political institutions contrast with other institutions such as the economic institutions that realize distributive justice and the civil and constitutional institutions that embody the basic individual liberties.

It is not the fact that political institutions are institutions or involve procedures that leads Van Parijs to evaluate them purely instrumentally. The basic liberties are at least partly defined in terms of procedures or institutional rules that define the rights and duties connected with self-ownership.[9] One must not cause physical harm to others without their informed consent, one must not kill others, and so on. These rules are not defended in terms of their consequences for justice, they are key parts of justice; indeed they are lexically prior to the other principles of justice, for Van Parijs. So Van Parijs is not opposed to procedural justice whose value is independent of its consequences. It is the political part of 'political institutions' that marks these institutions out for a purely instrumentalist evaluation. The idea is that this 'approach to political institutions … aims to shape them in such a way that those acting within them will end up generating the "right" collective outcome … '[10] As he puts it, this is 'an uncompromisingly consequentialist approach to political institutions in which democracy itself, however thinly defined, should not be taken for granted and in which anything goes, as long as the expected outcomes are the best we can hope for.'[11] It is not, however, an uncompromisingly consequentialist approach to institutions generally.[12]

Van Parijs argues for this approach by showing that its implications can survive the test of reflective equilibrium. He asks, 'whether the ruthless consequentialism inherent in the program generates any outcomes which one should be embarrassed by.' For should it be 'prone to make recommendations inconsistent with some of our considered moral judgments,' the program would 'make us deny it our support.'[13] Here we might wonder why the denial of democracy itself is not inconsistent with considered moral convictions. But it may be worthwhile to pursue Van Parijs's argument before we discuss its weaknesses.

10.5 Disenfranchising the elderly

Let us explore a line of argument Van Parijs suggests in the spirit of his justice-guided constitutional engineering with the purpose of evaluating

Van Parijs's instrumentalism. I will focus on those aspects of the argument that most strongly recommend the abandonment of equality in political institutions for the sake of alleged gains in the justice of the outcomes. The first premise is that intergenerational justice requires at the very least that each generation makes sure that the socioeconomic situation of the following generation is no worse than its. The second premise is that the way of life of the industrialized countries is not sustainably generalizable to the whole of mankind. In particular major changes are now required or will soon be required to plausibly ensure that as good is left for the next generation. Third, current political institutions are not able to prevent serious declines in the standard of living of future generations. Van Parijs argues that the aging of the population is a significant element in the explanation of this phenomenon. As the population gets older, the costs of pensions and health care go up. Van Parijs supposes that there is a considerable degree of age differentiated self-interest in the behavior of voters. And since the elderly have a shorter time horizon in which to advance their interests, they are less concerned with the future, and so they vote increasingly for their short-term self-interest. This cohort of elderly, therefore, becomes increasingly powerful and the political system responds to its needs more than to those of others. The taxes needed to pay for care of the elderly increase, while the number of people able to pay for the health care decreases. So the willingness of the employed to work diminishes as a result of higher taxes. As a consequence, the productivity of society overall diminishes and less is left over for future generations.[14]

From these claims Van Parijs concludes,

> we cannot reasonably expect such action [prevention of intergenerational injustice] from their democratic systems, because of the growing weight of increasingly selfish elderly voters. If we care about intergenerational justice, what should we do? Reshape our democratic institutions in such a way that older members of the electorate either possess less power or exercise it less selfishly.[15]

10.6   The Machiavellian approach

Van Parijs focuses mainly on the redistribution of power in political institutions to achieve the goal of social justice. This is connected with the Machiavellian aspect of his project. The Machiavellian approach to constitutional engineering, according to him, recommends constructing political institutions on the assumption that people are almost entirely self-interested (although they may display concern for their children and some even for their grandchildren). Hence, his proposals concern mainly the distribution of power. He considers three possibilities. One set of proposals directly diminishes the relative political power of the elderly. He considers disenfranchising the elderly or giving plural votes to the younger. He considers proposals for public campaign financing that disable the elderly from contributing as much to political campaigns as others. He considers various schemes of group representation that diminish the voting power of the elderly by disproportionately representing other age groups. These are baldly inegalitarian proposals: they reduce the political power of each elderly person to less than that held by others.

A second kind of proposal gives parents of dependent children proxy votes for their children. A similarly motivated proposal would lower the age of eligibility to 16 or 14. The purpose of these proposals is to lower the age of the median voter. These proposals have the merit of at least appearing to promote democracy. They seem to include more of the population in the democratic process. This kind of proposal does not diminish the power of each elderly individual relative to other individuals; it diminishes the power of the elderly as a group by increasing the total size of the electorate. A third kind of proposal establishes an independent agency, called a *guardian*, that has as its function to defend the interests of future generations. It is not directly accountable to the voters but it has a role in the making of legislation. In effect, it is an independent agent in some ways like the United States Supreme Court. Its function is to protect future generations from unjust treatment by contemporary generations.

Van Parijs also considers population policies that are designed to increase the number of people who have children in the society. Incentive programs such as tax credits and subsidies to families that have children are defended as ways of encouraging people to have children. The basis of this particular idea is the supposition that since people care for the futures of their children, having children will extend their time horizons beyond the limits of their own lives. If more people have children, more people will have extended time horizons.

Some of these ideas do not challenge the idea that political equality is itself a basic requirement of justice. Population policies do not attempt to affect the distribution of power at all. The second kind of proposal extending the suffrage to younger people or giving proxy votes to parents in the name of their children could be defended on political egalitarian grounds. Also, this kind of proposal does not obviously diminish the power of individual elderly persons relative to anyone else. So constitutional engineering that uses these methods does not seem straightforwardly in tension with the ideal of political equality. Even if these proposals are acceptable, they do not provide much by way of support for a purely instrumentalist approach to political institutions. On the face of it, these constitutional proposals are even compatible with assigning lexical priority to political equality over other concerns of justice.[16]

The first kind of proposal does, however, test our commitment to political equality. And it seems to me that these proposals are deeply problematic. Here, I do not appeal to the intuition, that I am sure many share, that the various forms of diminishing the proportion of power of the elderly are inherently repugnant. I do have that intuition but it would be unhelpful merely to assert it in this context. I will show why these proposals are problematic, and thus vindicate the democratic intuition.

10.7   A puzzle about political equality

It may be objected that in fact the first proposals do not fully test our commitment to political equality. The reason for this is that these proposals do not deprive individuals of power relative to other individuals. Even if the elderly are fully disenfranchised, individuals still face the same lifetime prospects of political power. All persons have equal votes until a certain age and then lose power after that age. In effect, they are given the same lifetime prospects for power. Hence, perhaps these proposals do not challenge the ideal of political equality. Let us call this the *broad conception* of political equality. When Van Parijs considers the possibility that one of his proposals might actually tend to undermine the political power of members of racial or ethnic minorities, he pulls back from the proposals.[17] He gives little reason for this restriction except to speculate that such a policy will not boost maximin policies. One senses that the underlying reason is a residual concern for at least the broad conception of political equality. Van Parijs seems to be willing to consider proposals that exclude people from participation for parts of their lives but he is not willing even to entertain proposals that exclude persons altogether (or even that diminish the power of persons). Let us call the conception of political equality that requires equality across all minimally competent age groups the *narrow conception* of political equality.

In what follows I shall proceed as if the disenfranchisement of the elderly does violate democratic principles as much as, or nearly as much as, the disenfranchisement of persons who are minorities. I believe that Van Parijs's sense that disenfranchising the elderly violates democratic principles is essentially sound. But it does raise an interesting and important question. I will return to this question later. I will show how the principles I defend support the narrow (age-segmented) conception of political equality over, or in addition to, the broad conception of political equality.

10.8 A critique of Machiavellian instrumentalism

What I propose to do is to redescribe the situations Van Parijs envisions so as to display them from an angle that brings out what is disturbing in his program. The redescription of the situation of the constitutional engineering project puts it in the context of actual politics where individuals and groups disagree about what justice demands in the case of future generations. It abandons the gods-eye point of view that Van Parijs adopts and attempts to see the situation from the points of view of the various members of the society. It sees the supporters of these proposals and the elderly as participants in a democratic process who offer different views about what to do. The relationship between them is one of equals who disagree on the best course of action. It attempts to bring out the idea that there is something quite unjust in excluding or diminishing the power of those who disagree with us when the disagreement is among equals. It suggests, in effect, that Van Parijs's approach is incompatible with treating one's fellow citizens with equal concern and respect. In the last part of this chapter, I will argue that this is the right way to think about political questions.

When we consider Van Parijs's proposals from our perspective as ordinary citizens, what we see is a person or group of persons who are trying to take away the power of another group of persons because they disagree with them. They wish in effect to give less than equal power to the others.

The constitutional engineers and their supporters are not just theorists; they are participants in the democratic system and in the society. From this angle we can see that they have biases against some positions and in favor of others. We can see that they are fallible; indeed we recognize these people as having been mistaken in the past about certain issues, however earnest and in good faith their efforts have been. We can also see that however sophisticated their understandings are, there are gaps in their arguments and there are unsupported premises. They display some blindness for certain kinds of problems and tend to be a bit overly enthusiastic and sometimes quite dogmatic about other issues. We also see their positions and arguments as some among many reasonably well-defended positions. They are not the only ones who are capable of drawing on expert knowledge. Many positions have the backing of various experts. Disagreement amongst the defenders of these positions and the experts they call on seems to be nowhere in abeyance. Most importantly we recognize that they have their own interests and those interests can conflict with others' interests. Those interests can bias their views of matters. In these respects, they do not differ much from others; indeed they are quite similar to other citizens. The differences between them and others lie in their disparate interests and distinctive views.

The constitutional engineers and their supporters claim that the elderly are selfish and will ruin everything for the next generation if they are given the same power as the rest of the members of society. Of course, the first thing that many of the elderly and their representatives will say in response to this is that in fact they are rather poorly treated by society for the most part. The minimal social security apparatus that is in place (say in the US) is just barely enough to hold a large proportion of them out of dire poverty. And they are subjected everyday by calls to eliminate or 'privatize' the social security system ostensibly because the system is not working well. Of course, the trouble is usually that the social security system is being constantly raided by other parts of the government to pursue other purposes. They are segregated from the rest of society, often not permitted to work; sometimes they receive no help from their families, and are subjected to an increasingly expensive and unresponsive health care system. They might also argue against Van Parijs's anti-elderly party of constitutional engineers that there should be little surprise that they organize into unions and demand a bit more than they have had in the past because they constitute a larger proportion of the population than in the past. So why shouldn't their interests get a bit more of a hearing than when they constituted a smaller proportion of the population? They will also argue that their actions do not threaten justice for future generations properly understood. They will disagree with Van Parijs's proposals and the basis for them. And not without reason.

The Van Parijs party may argue that the elderly are merely acting as Machiavellian engineers would expect. They are providing self-serving arguments to cushion their own nests. And they do so to the detriment of future generations. Therefore, they must be reined in in the name of justice to future generations. We must devise institutional rules that deprive the elderly of an equal say in the process of decision making.

At first, disputes on these matters look like disagreements. Some argue that the elderly receive more than is consistent with justice. Others argue that the elderly receive too little or at least not too much. But Van Parijs's strategy is to turn what appears to be a disagreement into a relationship between a group of irresponsible, selfish adults and a kind of impartial and judicious agent that is concerned only with bringing about justice. The constitutional engineers and their supporters reason that the members of society are selfish and unconcerned with justice and that impartial and rational individuals must structure their political environment so that they don't ruin everything. The situation can be characterized in part by the metaphor once offered by Benjamin Barber of 'politics as zookeeping.'[18] The zookeeper is charged with the task of making sure that the animals in the zoo are provided with an environment that is suited to their flourishing. The animals cannot be trusted to do this; they have no concern with the other animals and they cannot be expected to reflect on their actions and revise them in the light of their effects on others. The animals act in accordance with motives that are given in advance and more or less unchangeable. The zookeeper must take into account how they act and arrange things so as to produce the harmony the animals are incapable of devising for themselves.

I will discuss a number of ways in which one might get out of this apparent implication but let us note a few difficulties with this way of thinking about politics. The main difficulty here – one that is well brought out by the zookeeping metaphor – is that the social-justice-guided program of constitutional engineering ignores the central fact that the constitutional engineers and their supporters are part of the very same political process as those whose power they are trying to curtail. There are two difficulties associated with this fact.

First, as good Machiavellians, they should look at themselves as being motivated by the same kind of concerns as the others. What justifies the radical disjunction between the selfishness of the elderly and the impartiality of the engineers? Here it may be useful to see how different Machiavelli is from these Machiavellians. Machiavelli does not assume that the prince is much different from most of his or her fellow countrymen. He assumes that the prince is primarily self-interested and concerned with his own glory and well-being. Indeed the point of Machiavelli's argument in *The Prince* is to stop princes from trying to act justly and impartially or virtuously and exhort them to act in their self-interest.[19] The thesis is that among self-interested persons, only a self-interested prince is likely to achieve his aims. Indeed, he argues that only ruthlessly but prudently self-interested princes can really make their communities thrive. In other words, what makes Machiavelli's theory work is a kind of invisible-hand theory of politics. As long as the right people are in the right place, when everyone pursues their own interests rationally, everyone (or almost everyone) will be better off.

Van Parijs's approach is, in contrast, of doubtful coherence. He obviously rejects the invisible-hand approach; the constitutional engineers introduce a very visible hand into the process, attempting to guide it in the right direction. He says that citizens are deeply self-interested. He must suppose that this holds for the constitutional engineers, in which case they will in effect attempt to feather their own nests and will not be particularly concerned with future generations. Or he must suppose that there is some strong reason for differentiating between the constitutional engineers and the rest of society. We might call this a kind of *quasi-Machiavellianism*. It is hard to see how this disjunction between the motives of some participants and those of others can be justified. Of course, some people are more selfish than others, but we hardly have reason to think that the engineers will be the less selfish in general. Another possibility is to reject the Machiavellian approach at least as a general approach to politics and attempt to see conflicts of view as genuine disagreements among fallible and biased citizens.

10.9   Instrumentalism and inequality

Let us consider how the claim that there is a real disjunction between the motives of the engineers and those of the rest of the members of society plays out in the context of politics. It seems to express a commitment to a deeply and publicly inegalitarian approach to politics. Van Parijs's approach presupposes the idea that some are mostly incapable of attending to matters of the common good while others have a handle on the truth of the matter and are willing to act accordingly. This is incompatible with the principle of equal respect for individuals and, as I will argue in what follows, with the underlying principle of equal concern for the interests of persons. The easiest intuitive way to see this at the moment is to recall the zookeeping analogy. There is no equality of respect between the zookeeper and the animals. Only the zookeeper's judgments are respected. And there is no sense that the interests of the animals are being treated on a par with those of the zookeeper's either.

What about the above treatment implies that the constitutional engineers fail to treat their fellow citizens with equal concern? I shall develop this thought later in the chapter. For the moment, I want to identify the basic reasons. If the constitutional engineers treat the others as merely self-interested, they will rely on their own moral judgments to make decisions about their shared environment and ignore those of the others. Thus their actions will clearly fail to display equal respect for the other individuals on morally important matters.

Moreover, we must suppose that the engineers are fallible, their judgments controversial and biased towards their interests and by their backgrounds. We must conclude that their attempts to control the environment by partially excluding the others from the process of collective decision making cannot but have the effect of advancing their interests to the detriment of others. To the extent that these facts are all reasonably well understood by citizens generally, the quasi-Machiavellian program of constitutional engineering must publicly express an unequal concern for the interests of citizens.

Now think of the situation as one of disagreement about justice and its implications in this context. Once we see the issues relating to treatment of the elderly and justice towards future generations as matters on which people have serious and longstanding disagreements, we can see the approach of the social-justice-guided constitutional engineer in a different and less favorable light. The constitutional engineers note the difference of view of a group of people in society and decide that, were this group to participate on an equal basis, their own favored view of justice would be less likely to be implemented. So they decide to deprive the other group of some of their political power. Instead of debate and discussion on the merits of the issues among equals and instead of voting among equals when discussion comes to an end, this approach recommends that their opponents be deprived of some of their power.

From the point of view of the elderly who disagree with the views of the engineers, the actions of the constitutional engineers is either a naked grab for power in the service of a view about justice they disagree with or it is an assertion of moral superiority they reject. When they take into account the fallibility and bias of the engineers, they must conclude that the engineers and their supporters do not have an equal concern for their interests.

Van Parijs's approach ignores this dimension of the problem because he starts by saying that we should assume that we know what justice is. The supposition suggests either that there is agreement on what justice is or that there is a kind of expert knowledge about what justice is which knowledge is to be deferred to by rational agents. The problem is that there is disagreement about justice and reasonable people disagree on it. There is in my view likely to be an objective fact of the matter on the subject of justice. But no one can claim to have sufficient knowledge of it to exclude others from having a say. So when the elderly disagree on what the appropriate trade-off is between concern for future generations and concern for the present, Van Parijs will frame the issue as justice versus the elderly. In fact we ought to frame the issue as Van Parijs's view of justice versus the different views that the elderly have. And instead of thinking of constitutional engineering as the discipline that attempts to secure what we know to be justice, we must think of it in part as the inquiry into how to treat individuals as equals when they must make decisions about which they have deep disagreements.

10.10   Constitutional engineering as precommitment

Let us consider a way to overcome this difficulty that Van Parijs does not discuss. Think of the actions of the constitutional engineers as involving a kind of precommitment strategy of society for achieving intergenerational justice. Such an analysis of the situation may avoid the inegalitarian implications of the initial analysis. Individuals sometimes engage in strategies of precommitment because they think that they may encounter situations where they will not make rational decisions and they wish to make sure that they do not act stupidly in those situations. The standard example of this kind of strategy is that of Ulysses and the Sirens. When told that the song of the Sirens is so beautiful and alluring that it makes men take leave of their senses and jump into the water never to be seen again, Ulysses devises a plan that allows him to hear the Sirens without losing his mind. He has his shipmates bind him to a mast and instructs them not to heed his orders to let him go when the Sirens begin to sing. His shipmates of course are instructed to put wax in their ears. Ulysses recognizes the imperfection of his reason and its susceptibility to failure under particular circumstances. He has a clear aim and asks his shipmates to engage in fairly clearly described actions to help him pursue his aim.[20]

Can we think of society as engaging in a strategy of precommitment when it attempts to deprive the elderly of an equal proportion of power? If we can, we might be able to say that the elderly are not themselves irrational but that they may find themselves in a situation where they are peculiarly susceptible to make irrational or at least unreasonable choices. Hence, they, along with the rest of society precommit themselves to institutions that disable them from acting contrary to their most important aims. Unlike the situation of constitutional engineers acting on the thought that others are too selfish to devote themselves to justice, this new analysis suggests that everyone recognizes in himself or herself the capacity to act foolishly. They set up institutions to stop themselves from destructive action. And they do so as a means to pursuing their own rationally determined aims.

In order to conceive the Van Parijs approach as a case of precommitment, we must suppose that every clear thinking moral person more or less agrees on what justice requires here. We must also suppose that they can see that the mere appearance of disagreement in this context is due only to momentary selfishness or irrationality. Furthermore, the actions to which they are precommitting themselves must be reasonably clearly discernible for those who must carry them out. Only in this way does it make sense to say that society precommits itself through an institution in order to avoid undermining its aims.

The trouble is that it is not the case that everyone agrees on what justice requires in this context. Disagreement on matters of justice and the means to achieve it is ubiquitous. Van Parijs himself is non-committal on any of the particular claims he makes about the elderly as well as the strategies he proposes to solve the problems. He is also non-committal on the question of what justice is. For though he says that later generations must be at least as well off as earlier ones, he does not commit himself to any metric of equality. He acknowledges the plurality of well-defended metrics and refuses to take a stand for one. This is an area full of controversy among moral and sensible people, and these disputes are not likely to go away. An uncharitable observer of these proposals might think that it is precisely because there is disagreement on what justice requires and how to bring this about that there is a felt need to reduce the power of some of those who would support the opposing programs.

Let us consider the idea of having a non-elected guardian of the rightful interests of future generations in the legislature. This is meant to counteract the power of the elderly by having decent, knowledgeable and morally minded individuals veto proposals or perhaps modify proposals so as to ensure justice towards later generations. As a precommitment strategy, this proposal is highly problematic. First of all, these people are likely to disagree amongst themselves about what justice requires. In the light of this disagreement the clarity required of the instructions to the guardian will be entirely missing. In addition, though, they will have the power to override the deliberate aims of the legislature. Surely, this is not precommitment.[21] The strategy that best describes the Van Parijs approach is not precommitment, it is a kind of preemption and, in my view, it is usurpation.

In any case, though the digression concerning precommitment is instructive, Van Parijs cannot have recourse to this kind of approach. Reliance on such an approach would compromise the 'uncompromisingly consequentialist' approach he takes. The limitations on the power of various groups in society are to be imposed even if they cannot be agreed upon or democratically decided upon.

10.11   A dualistic account of democracy

There are two sorts of reasons that can be given for democracy. And these reasons can give conflicting recommendations. This is the reason why moral reasoning about democracy and democratic outcomes has the complex structure that we normally see in it. On the one hand, we clearly do think that political institutions are important because of the ends they serve. We value political institutions because they make justice in society possible, because they advance the common good.

10.12   Democracy and the equal consideration of interests

On the other hand, we think that the democratic process has an intrinsic fairness. Here, I lay out the basic conception of justice which is the principle of equal consideration of interests. Second, I articulate and defend principles of respect for judgment and publicity on the basis of this principle. Thus, justice demands the public realization of equal consideration of interests. Third, I argue that democracy is required by justice understood as the public realization of equal consideration of interests. These theses will permit us to answer the questions about the dual nature of the evaluation of democracy and the questions about its authority and its limits.

The basic principle of justice from which my argument proceeds is the principle of equal consideration of interests. It has two parts. First, it is a welfarist principle. It states that justice is concerned with the advancement of the interests of persons. Interests are understood as parts of what is good overall for a person.[22] Second, justice strikes an appropriate balance between the interests of individuals when they conflict. It gives each person a *claim* to his or her share in that appropriate balance of conflicting interests.[23] The appropriate balance between these conflicting interests is given by the idea of equal consideration of interests. The interests of individuals are to be advanced equally by society. This equality proceeds from the importance of interests as well as the separateness of persons. No one's good is more important than anyone else's. No one's interests matter more than anyone else's. Each person has a life to live and the interests of each person are combined into a special unity within that life. Thus the principle of equal consideration of interests requires that the interests of individuals be equally advanced in terms of lifetime prospects.

Since justice concerns the kinds of claims people can make against each other in determining the appropriate balance of well-being, justice is essentially a weakly public principle. That is, principles of justice must spell out ideals that people can appeal to in criticizing their relations with each other and they must be able to provide, at least in principle, concrete guidance as to how to legitimate them. While other values such as aesthetic and purely welfarist values may be and indeed are obscure even in principle to those who pursue them, they are not usually the basis of claims that people make on the social world they live in. Justice, by contrast, is a set of principles by which people make claims and can be satisfied or not in a way that can be publicly argued. Claims are not like scientific hypotheses which are about obscure matters for speculation. So, principles of justice ought not to require knowledge of society that is in principle inaccessible to people. A principle that requires that we go beyond our cognitive limitations is not able to provide this guidance. So the principle that requires that the basic institutions of society equally advance the interests of the members of society must do so in a way that is compatible with this inevitable ignorance. It must be given an interpretation that satisfies publicity. It is a weak notion since it does not require agreement on principles of justice within a community: it simply demands that the principles be ones that people can in principle see to be in effect or not.

10.13   Responsiveness and weak publicity

Here, I shall provide a substantive argument for this conception of weak publicity. A political arrangement is responsive to individuals to the extent that the arrangement takes seriously the complaints of members regarding the basic principles of the arrangement. It also implies that the complaints be in some way accommodated by the scheme at least to the extent that such accommodation is compatible with the basic idea of equal consideration of interests. Each person has a kind of correlative right to appeal in matters that concern the basic justice of the arrangements and his or her fellows must in some way listen. The principle states that the arrangements ought to be responsive to anyone who has at least a kind of minimum ability to understand, elaborate and critically reflect on principles of morality. Those who have the right of appeal must satisfy this minimum requirement.

The right of appeal that each citizen has is limited only by the basic principle of equal consideration of interests. Any citizen may make any kind of appeal regarding the basic principles of the society including appeals against the inclusiveness of the principle of responsiveness. And the principle of responsiveness is limited only by equality of interest.

What this means is that citizens have a right to dispute interpretations of equality as well as interpretations of interest that enter into a specification of equal consideration of interests. The society has a correlative requirement to respond to these complaints, either by persuading the citizen of its interpretation or by in some way accommodating the citizen's complaint if possible. This is a principle of respect for the judgment of each citizen who satisfies a minimum of competence in moral reflection. It treats each person as having something to say and of being worthy of being listened to when they do say something. What is there to be said in favor of such a principle? The basic right of appeal and the requirement of response are supported by any principle that takes seriously the idea that the interests of individual persons ought to be advanced. Three fundamental kinds of facts about human societies link the interests of individuals to the interests of individuals in having a right to appeal to the principles of their societies. Call them the *facts of judgment*.[24] The first and most straightforward kind of fact includes the fallibility of judgment and the facts of disagreement. The second kind of fact relates the judgments of individuals to their interests. The third type relates the abilities to appeal and reflect on judgments about the justice of one's society to the interests of individuals.

(1) The fallibility of moral judgment is pervasive, even when confined to the parameters set by a principle of equality. Since the principle of equality requires one to compare and weigh the interests of persons who are quite different from oneself and who have lived their lives in parts of society that are quite different from one's own, one is likely to be quite often mistaken about what those interests are and how to compare them to one's own. Indeed, individuals are rarely able to give as much as rough sketches of their *own* interests in social life and most often individuals find themselves in the process of continually adjusting their conceptions of what is good for themselves and others. Furthermore, the principles by which to bring together all these varied, complex and obscure interests are likely to be quite often very difficult to discern and assess. Common sense and the ubiquity of controversy among intelligent persons on these matters are sufficient to underscore these points. Under these circumstances it would be perverse and often self-defeating to rule out of court the judgments of those who disagree with one on matters of justice and thus it would be wrong to deny them a right to appeal to the principles underlying their social life.

(2) There are two facts that connect individuals' judgments to their interests. Individuals' judgments are usually cognitively biased towards

their interests in various ways, and, as a consequence, controversy over principle often reflects conflict of interests. Individuals' judgments of what is just or unjust are in various ways more sensitive to their own interests than to those of others. They are of course better acquainted with their interests and they assign some account of their interest's special significance to the extent that they think that it tracks the good. And since judgments about what is fair or just are affected by judgments about what is good, a number of disagreements will reflect the interests of those who disagree. Such judgments may reflect interests in other ways as well. Since individuals are more sensitive to the harms they undergo than to those of others, they may inadvertently unduly downplay losses to others. This will distort their judgments about the proper distribution of good things to the detriment of others. None of this is meant to suggest that individuals generally intentionally mould principles to their own advantage or use such principles as a mask for their own interests. Individuals simply have natural cognitive biases towards their own interests.

There is another crucial link between interests and judgments. Individuals' judgments often reflect modes of life to which they are accustomed and in which they feel at home. To live in a world governed by the principles one adheres to as opposed to someone else's is often, in Michael Walzer's apt analogy, like living in one's own home furnished by one's own familiar things and not in someone else's or in a hotel.[25] To the extent that there are interests related to this sense of at-homeness, and their judgments about justice reflect this sense, individuals have interests in the world they live in conforming to their judgments.

These two facts linking judgments to interests strongly imply that a political theory devoted to the advancement of the interests of individuals ought to take their judgments seriously and assign them a right to appeal to the principles of their own society. If the judgments of some particular person or group of persons are not taken seriously, these considerations suggest, the interests that are connected with their judgments also will not be given much weight. And since the facts of cognitive bias and at-homeness are not changeable, it is a permanent feature of the political landscape that if one excludes a person or group of persons from having a say, their interests will not be properly taken account of. These facts favor such a right to appeal particularly when they are coupled with the fallibilism noted above. Indeed, they point to particularly important sources of fallibility that uniquely support the right of appeal and the requirement of responsiveness.

(3) There are also facts linking the right to appeal and the interests of each individual. First, the right of appeal and the consequent respect shown for each person supports each person's interest in learning about their own interests as well as justice. This is because each person must learn about his or her interests as well as justice partly through discussion with others. But if others deny that person a right of appeal, those others have far less incentive to listen to that person's complaints and less incentive to respond to them. As a consequence, the person is less likely to reap the benefits of social discussion about these matters; in particular, that person will likely not be able to hear responses to his or her own views. To the extent that a person is able to learn new ideas principally when that person's own standpoint is addressed and responded to, such a person's right to appeal will be a powerful support for learning.

(4) The denial of a right to appeal would constitute a serious loss of status for a person in a society. A person whose judgment about that society is never taken seriously by others is treated in effect like a child or a madman. Others deny such a person the recognition of his or her moral personality. If, in addition, the other facts of judgment such as the facts of fallibilism and cognitive bias are taken into account by citizens, it should be clear that those minimally competent persons who are denied the right of appeal are being told that their interests are not worthy of equal or perhaps any consideration. This is a disastrous loss of status. This suggests that a person is not considered worthy of just treatment. Since there is a deep interest in status, such a denial of the right to appeal must be a serious setback of interests.[26]

The above account of the relation between interests and judgments is neither Machiavellian nor is it quasi-Machiavellian. These latter principles assert that individuals are motivated by self-interest nearly exclusively. In my view there is little or no evidence supporting such contentions. Indeed, the evidence suggests that individuals' political behavior can be explained by a concern with justice and the common good as well as their own interests.[27] The above principles do not make claims about motivations; they assert that individuals have a variety of interests in having their judgments paid attention to. Partly this is because their judgments reflect their interests in a number of ways.

The right of appeal and requirement of responsiveness give substantive support for a weak principle of publicity. The idea is that the members of the society ought, at least in principle, to be able to see that justice regulates their society. By 'in principle' I mean merely that individuals, with limited, highly fallible and biased cognitive capacities, should be able to see that their society treats them with a concern for justice, as long as they put in some effort and understand the facts of judgment.

The argument for weak publicity is as follows. A society ought to be responsive to its members' complaints about justice, for the reasons given above. The idea of responsiveness implies that either society persuades its citizens that they are being treated justly or it accommodates their concerns. So a society is *fully* responsive to its citizens, only if they have been persuaded or society has changed in accordance with their judgment. It follows that in a fully responsive society the citizens must be satisfied because they can see they are being treated in accordance with the principles of justice.

Remember however, it is not necessary that they agree to the principles that are publicly embodied. The reason why this is so is because this would impose an impossible burden on principles of justice. Theories which require agreement on principles themselves as a condition of justice simply cannot get off the ground. They push the respect for judgment to a point that undermines justice and eventually defeats itself. A theory of justice must rely on the truth or legitimacy of its central claims as well as the strength of its arguments. A theory of justice of the sort that I am defending here is able to do this while avoiding self-defeat because it states that respect for judgment is based on consideration of interests; respect for judgment is not something that is of rock-bottom significance. Its significance is explained by a deeper concern for well-being.[28] It is also this basic concern for equal consideration of interests that explains the limit on the respect for judgment so that such respect does not undermine the possibility of justice.

Finally, it is clear that no society can fully publicly embody justice. This is because citizens are bound, as a consequence of the facts of judgment, to disagree about what justice requires in a society. Hence, the requirement of publicity will need to be modified to take into account the impossibility of full publicity. The only way it can do this is publicly to embody justice in a way that is compatible with a wide range of disagreements about what justice requires. This, in my view, is where democracy comes in.

10.14 Equality and democracy

The institutions of society must publicly express the equal consideration of interests in a way that can be clear in principle to its members. Here I shall sketch an argument to the effect[29] that democratic decision making is a generally necessary condition for satisfying this principle in a public way.[30] The basic argument starts from the premise that equal consideration of interests provides a just solution to conflict of interests. When we consider that there are deep conflicts of interests in how we ought to organize our common world we see that justice ought naturally to apply to these conflicts of interest. We have interests in shaping our common world but since our interests are deeply intertwined and since they differ in many ways, they conflict. Hence, the principle of equality ought to apply to our common social world.

But we cannot divide up that world into pieces and then distribute them. Our common social world in many ways constitutes an indissoluble unity. The system of property, the systems of criminal and civil justice, the legal apparatus for protecting the environment and other collective goods as well as the system of taxation and so on are all unified. We have to shape them in one way rather than another. Now of course, we could try to do this by trying to make everyone equally happy or in some other direct way. The trouble is that we have no clear ways to measure our own or others' happiness or how to compare them. Mostly this follows from the facts of judgment that I listed above. This would imply that no effort at somehow equalizing well-being among participants with regard to these common features of society will be publicly defensible even to those who accept equal consideration of interests.

We might try to realize publicly equal consideration of interests by distributing economic resources equally. But this approach faces the same difficulty as equality of welfare. The principle of equal distribution of resources is extremely complex.[31] Once we take into account talents, handicaps and dispositions to experience pleasure and pain, we must either reject equality of resources or the principle itself will turn out to be as difficult to embody publicly as is the principle of equality of welfare. We should expect the same level of disagreements about what this principle actually implies and how it should be implemented as in the case of equal welfare. Another difficulty arises once we think of the common world as essentially a non-divisible good; we cannot divide it into resources and then distribute them. There are interests associated with diverse ethnic and cultural affiliations as well. These interests cannot be so clearly handled in an egalitarian way by dividing up resources amongst citizens.

In addition to these difficulties, these two conceptions of equality are highly controversial interpretations. Many others have been offered such as the principle of equal opportunity for welfare, the principle of equal access to advantage, the principle of equality of capacity and many others. I do not wish to say that these principles are useless or that one of them cannot be the correct principle. What I do wish to say is that in the light of the continuing and unabating controversy about these principles, none of them presents us with a public expression of the equality of all citizens. In my view, these kinds of principles are best thought of as parts of contributions to egalitarian democratic discussion. Only when they are offered in the democratic forum will the equal concern for the interests of all citizens be given a public expression, or so I shall argue.

Yet we can distribute resources for participating in collective decision making such as votes, as well as resources for bargaining and coalition building as well as deliberation in reasonably clearly equal ways. These resources can be used to advance the interests of the citizens who hold them. And the equal distribution of these resources publicly realizes the equal consideration of interests in the light of our ignorance about how to understand and compare our interests. So it is by distributing equally the resources for making collective decisions about the common social world that the equal consideration of interests can be publicly realized to all citizens. Hence, democracy is a just solution to conflicts of interests with regard to the common social world.

I have spoken of conflicts of interests being justly resolved by democratic means. But what of conflicts of judgment regarding what is right in matters that pertain to civil and economic justice? Surely, these determine much of our common world together. The systems of property, the package of rights of association and expression as well as privacy play a large role in defining our common world. We wouldn't say that disagreements about the contours of these rights are per se conflicts of interests. But, in fact, because of the facts of judgment, we can see that important conflicts of interests underlie these disagreements. In the light of the facts of judgment and of the deep disagreements about interests and equality implied by the controversies about civil and economic justice, it should be clear that merely imposing principles of economic or civil justice would amount to treating the interests of some as of an inferior worth than those of others. If we can see that equality in the economic and civil spheres is inevitably a subject of controversy, then we can see that a society cannot hope publicly to embody equality by means of implementing equality in these spheres. In the light of these disagreements and the facts of judgment, the only way to give expression to equality is to give individuals an equal say in the process of debating and collectively deciding on how the economic and civil spheres are to be organized.

Of course democracy only gives partial satisfaction to the principle of publicity. In view of the disagreements that citizens have over what constitutes equality in society, even when collective decisions are made in a way that takes everyone's interests equally into consideration, the outcomes will be thought to be unjust and inegalitarian by many. This follows from the fact that there is disagreement. But these disagreements are inevitable. The adherence to democratic decision making constitutes a kind of final resort in the public realization of the equality of citizens in the light of disagreement. Democracy is the only way to resolve disagreement that remains faithful to equality. This is what makes democracy a uniquely just solution to political conflict and disagreement. It is what ensures that democracy legitimates outcomes even when they are unjust in the eyes of some.

10.15   In defense of the narrow conception of political equality

Let us attend briefly to the question of broad and narrow political equality. The principles above support the narrow conception of political equality. The reason for this is that the very same problems that usually arise between persons are also likely to arise (although in a slightly attenuated form) between age groups. People have distinct interests at different stages of their lives. People's lives form wholes wherein the different stages are distinct parts of these wholes. The interests associated with the stages are themselves parts of the good on the whole of a person's life. Individuals' lives are structured in part in terms of how they wish to live this sequence of stages of life.

At the same time, in a democratic society, laws and policies can change at any stage in life whether one plans for it or not. Changes such as these have important effects on whether one can carry out one's life in the way that one thinks best. This is not something for which one can insure oneself entirely since even the rules governing insurance can also change over time. In a society governed by law that can be changed, it is not the case that individuals can make choices in earlier parts of their lives that guarantee outcomes at later stages of their lives. Hence, if individuals' interests in organizing their lives and being able to depend on (or adjust) that organization over time are to be recognized, they must have a right to have their interests considered whenever the conditions on which they depend are subject to change.

Furthermore, the facts of judgment apply as much, or nearly as much, to different age groups as to different classes of persons. The judgments of younger individuals regarding what is good for older individuals are fallible and cognitively biased towards their own interests.

The problem of inequality arises when we consider that different individuals assign very different relative weights to the later parts of their lives and assign different roles to that part of their lives in the overall structure. Those who assign a more significant role to it are likely to do worse in a regime that does not allow them a say in collective decision making later in life than those who assign a much less significant role. This is because they will not have a say in whether and how the laws, on which their plans depend, change. For those who assign little value to the later parts of their lives this will not matter.

To give equal consideration to the interests associated with all these different forms of life in the light of disagreement over what laws are best, it is necessary that each person have a say in whether and how the laws are changed at the different stages of their lives. These considerations are such that individuals can see that if the elderly are disenfranchised, it will be a publicly clear expression of unequal concern for the interests of at least many persons for whom the later parts of their lives are very important. To give public, equal consideration to those persons it is necessary to give power to persons at all stages of their lives. Therefore, the arguments that support the broader notion of political equality also support the narrower conception.

10.16 Conclusion

I have argued that the 'uncompromisingly consequentialist' approach to political institutions ought to be rejected in favor of what I call a dualist conception of the value of democracy. Democratic institutions that accord with the ideal of political equality are, on my account, intrinsically just. They can also be evaluated in terms of their outcomes. I have not said much about the problem of how to weigh these values against each other. In my view, democratic decision making ought to have authority as a matter of justice when there are disagreements about the justice of laws and policies. That authority does have limits, but in general it is a duty of justice for individuals to comply with the directives of a properly functioning democracy. I have not argued for these claims here; such an argument requires more space than I have left.[32]

Notes

1. See his 'Is Democracy Compatible with Justice?', *Journal of Political Philosophy* 4 (1996), pp. 101–17, and more recently his 'The Disenfranchisement of the Elderly, and Other Attempts to Secure Intergenerational Justice', *Philosophy and Public Affairs* 27 (1998), pp. 292–333.

2. The view is attributed to Robert Bork. See his 'Neutral Principles and Some First Amendment Problems', *Indiana Law Journal* 47 (1971), pp. 1–35.
3. This view seems to be expressed in Iris Young, *Justice and the Politics of Difference* (Princeton: Princeton University Press, 1991), and Benjamin Barber, *Strong Democracy: Participatory Politics for a New Age* (Berkeley: University of California Press, 1983). Joshua Cohen has argued recently that the idea of democracy really comes down to the idea of *collective authorization*. A set of arrangements is collectively authorized when free and equal citizens can reasonably agree to those arrangements. Collective authorization, he argues, includes both the dimensions of procedure and substance. For Cohen, this notion inevitably implies a commitment to a kind of consensus on both procedure and outcome. Reasoned consensus is the fundamental norm in such an approach because it is the only way to ensure that individuals are treated as free and equal citizens when they must submit to the powers of a coercive state. See his 'Substance and Procedure in Democracy', in Seyla Benhabib (ed.), *Democracy and Difference* (Princeton: Princeton University Press, 1996), pp. 95–119.
4. For a particularly striking illustration of this view, see Philippe Van Parijs, 'Is Democracy Compatible with Justice?' See also the arguments of Richard Arneson, 'Democratic Rights at National and Workplace Levels', in David Copp, Jean Hampton and John Roemer (eds), *The Idea of Democracy* (Cambridge: Cambridge University Press, 1993), pp. 118–47.
5. There are purely moral arguments such as the arguments for consequentialism, which directly entails instrumentalism in democratic rights as well as for justice in general. I shall not discuss this kind of argument in this chapter. Suffice it to say that the one version of instrumentalism I attack in this chapter is not consequentialist generally though it is consequentialist about political institutions. There are arguments from the incoherence of democratic ideals such as those found in social choice theory as well as those found among economic theorists of democracy. I have argued that the results of social choice theory do not provide any argument against the intrinsic worth of democracy; on the contrary, they argue that certain kinds of assessments of outcomes are incoherent. See my 'Social Choice and Democracy', in *Idea of Democracy*. I have argued that the worries of economic theorists can be overcome once we get a clearer view of what democracy is all about in my *The Rule of the Many* (Boulder, CO: Westview Press, 1996), ch. 5.
6. See Jeremy Waldron, *Law and Disagreement* (Oxford: Oxford University Press, 1999), ch. 5 and throughout for a discussion of the coordination and disagreement elements in the rationale for collective decision making.
7. Philippe Van Parijs, 'Disenfranchisement of the Elderly', esp. p. 294.
8. See Van Parijs, *Real Freedom for All* (Oxford: Clarendon Press, 1995), for a defense of these principles.
9. See *Real Freedom for All*, p. 26.
10. Van Parijs, 'Disenfranchisement of the Elderly', p. 299.
11. Van Parijs, 'Disenfranchisement of the Elderly', p. 301.
12. As for instance is Richard Arneson's in his 'Democratic Rights at National and Workplace Levels'.
13. Van Parijs, 'Disenfranchisement of the Elderly', p. 301.
14. Van Parijs does not give his full endorsement to the premises of this argument but he does think it has plausibility. His main purpose is to use this at least plausible scenario for illustrative purposes.

15. Van Parijs, 'Disenfranchisement of the Elderly', p. 299.
16. In my view, there are objections to lowering of the age requirement on the grounds that young people in general do not have the kinds of moral capacities that enable them to reflect on moral issues in politics. There are also objections to conferring proxy votes on parents to advance the interests of their children. Here the objection is simply that the whole point of democratic participation is that the individuals who are to be given power are given power. The proxy vote merely gives more power to parents with their own characteristic concerns and biases. But these are arguments that require a lot more work and the proposals do not obviously violate a concern for political equality. So they do not provide good test cases.
17. Van Parijs, 'Disenfranchisement of the Elderly', p. 306.
18. See Barber, *Strong Democracy*.
19. Niccolo Machiavelli, *The Prince* (Harmondsworth, UK: Penguin Books).
20. See Jon Elster, *Ulysses and the Sirens* (Cambridge: Cambridge University Press, 1983), for incisive discussion of precommitment strategies.
21. For a much more detailed and thorough discussion of the problems of applying the idea of precommitment to politics, see Waldron, *Law and Disagreement*, ch. 10.
22. See Larry Temkin, *Inequality* (Oxford: Oxford University Press, 1993), for this distinction.
23. See Dennis McKerlie, 'Equality', *Ethics* 106 (1996), pp. 274–96, for this idea of equality being the basis of claims of persons.
24. The facts of judgment are very much like what Rawls calls the *burdens of judgment*. See John Rawls, *Political Liberalism* (New York: Columbia University Press, 1993). There are two main differences. The idea behind the facts of judgment is designed to bring out the important interests individuals have in being able to think and act in accordance with their own judgments. The facts of judgment, as I conceive them, apply to questions of justice as much as to questions about the good life.
25. Michael Walzer, 'Interpretation and Social Criticism', in S. McMurrin (ed.), *Tanner Lectures on Human Values VIII* (Salt Lake City: University of Utah Press, 1988), pp. 1–80 (14). Walzer overplays the significance of this consideration by turning it into the central idea of his political theory and he seems to allow thereby deeply unjust societies to be just. But it clearly ought to have some weight, and a theory that takes the interests of individuals seriously can give it a modest significance for justice.
26. Hence, institutions that realize equality of well-being, for example, but make their members feel like superiors and inferiors are failing in their task. I claim that the ideals of equality of welfare or equality of opportunity for welfare and all the other complicated epicycles that have been devised as candidate conceptions of equality are simply not appropriate as conceptions of social justice. The information required to see whether any of these ideals is in place is beyond the capacity of the human mind to grasp. See Richard Arneson, 'Equality and Equal Opportunity for Welfare', *Philosophical Studies* 56 (1989), pp. 77–93, and G. A. Cohen, 'The Currency of Egalitarian Justice', *Ethics* 99 (1989), pp. 906–44, for brilliant but misguided efforts to develop the idea of equality. I criticize them in my *Rule of the Many*, ch. 2.
27. See the essays in Jane Mansbridge (ed.), *Beyond Self-interest* (Chicago: University of Chicago Press, 1993), for evidence of this sort.

28. The publicity constraints that Rawls and Joshua Cohen impose on justice require a great degree of consensus on values in society. They do this because they take something like respect for judgment to be at the basis of justice. Without consensus, a society cannot regulate the lives of citizens without contravening their judgments. I argue for this point more fully in chs 1 and 2 of *Rule of the Many*.

29. In *Rule of the Many*, ch. 2.

30. Democracy is *generally* a necessary condition because it is overridable in circumstances of extremely unjust outcomes. When outcomes become so unjust that they override the normally legitimating function of democracy is as yet unclear to me.

31. See Ronald Dworkin, 'What Is Equality?: Equality of Resources', *Philosophy and Public Affairs* 10 (1981), pp. 283–345, and Cohen, 'Currency of Egalitarian Justice', for illustrations of the enormous complexity of this principle and its potential for generating controversy.

32. I have argued for this in 'Justice and Disagreement at the Foundation of Political Authority', *Ethics* 110 (1999), pp. 165–87, and in my book *Democratic Equality* (Oxford: Clarendon Press, forthcoming).

11
Hybrid Justice, Patriotism and Democracy: a Selective Reply

Philippe Van Parijs[1]

'A hundred years before the expression took hold, Condorcet was an *intellectuel engagé*. His whole life was shared between thinking about principles and striving to turn them into reality.'[2] Over 200 years after Condorcet's death, this model is still worth emulating. Part of a political philosopher's job, as I conceive of it, consists in elaborating and vindicating a coherent set of principles that firmly formulates an ideal worth fighting for. But another part, no less important, no less strenuous, is to make oneself available, as opportunities arise, to support and help shape attempts to move closer to this ideal, local and global, direct and indirect.

As I have now completed the first half century of my existence, I need to make sure – if I want to live up to this model – that my life does not end up having been much thinking and little striving, as perhaps my fascinating Brussels predecessor Joseph Charlier (whom I discovered thanks to the instructive contribution by John Cunliffe, Guido Erreygers and Walter Van Trier)[3] may have felt his had been. I must therefore allow the balance to gradually drift from one of these poles to the other. As compelling opportunities to do so have not been lacking, one unfortunate consequence is that I have been left with less time than I expected to perform various more abstract tasks, including giving a detailed reply to each of the exceptionally stimulating essays included in this collection. Some of what I would have said with more time available is contained in various replies already published in response to earlier criticisms,[4] including ones by some of the contributors to this volume, and indeed in the reaction to Brian Barry by my old accomplice Robert van de Veen which is included in this volume.[5] But some of what I would have liked to say in order to do full justice to the painstaking job of several of my critics will remain unsaid. This is the price to be paid for avoiding a further postponement of the completion of this reply, but it is one I much regret paying.

Consequently, I shall concentrate on two tasks. First, I shall restate what I regard as the fundamental contentions of *Real Freedom for All* in a way that, I hope, will eliminate a number of misunderstandings. In the course of doing so, I shall allow myself to refer to several recent articles in which various points are developed more fully. Next, I shall deal at some length with two important issues which occupy only a very marginal place in the book but constitute the main focus of two contributions to this volume: the scope of social justice and its relationship to democracy.

11.1 A hybrid conjecture in the form of three principles

Real Freedom for All is an exercise in 'reflective equilibrium'. Essentially it consists in formulating and testing a conjecture about the content of social justice that aims to be consistent with my considered judgements and hopefully those of some of my readers. The challenge consists in working out a coherent set of principles that simultaneously captures, as simply and fully as possible, the importance we intuitively attach to freedom, equality and efficiency, to empowering the weak, and to condemning free riding, as well as countless other firm convictions, from the quite general to the very specific.

The conjecture I make in *Real Freedom for All*, as the provisional outcome of this quest, can be rephrased as the ordered conjunction of three principles: (1) universal self-ownership, (2) undominated diversity of comprehensive endowments, and (3) sustainable maximin distribution of the value of external endowments. The first principle means that every member of the society considered owns her own body (and soul). The second principle requires that what is given to one person over her lifetime, whether as internal or external resources, should not be unanimously preferred to what is given to another. The third principle requires that the amount of external resources given to those who are given least of them should be as large as it can sustainably be, with resources measured by their opportunity costs, as approximated by their competitive market values. The fact that the three principles are ordered means that the first enjoys a soft priority over the second, and the second over the third. The softness means that a major improvement of the satisfaction of an inferior principle can justify a minor deterioration of the satisfaction of a superior principle.

It is worth emphasizing that I made no claim to deriving this ordered set of principles from some logically prior set of natural rights to human and non-human entities, or from some more fundamental notion of equal or maximin real freedom (as Peter Vallentyne[6] and Brian Barry,[7] respectively, suggest that I do). The formula 'real freedom for all' is simply offered as a convenient compact summary for the combination of the three principles. It has been chosen because it highlights the claim that distributive justice is a matter of distributing possibilities, or freedom, rather than results, and that one should focus upon the *real* opportunities available to *each* individual. But what constitutes a fair distribution of these real possibilities is not captured by some prior notion of equal real freedom. It is given by the conjunction of the three principles, whose validity is a matter of joint optimal fit with one's considered judgements.

Real Freedom for All does not make much of an effort to elaborate the condition of self-ownership and the priority rules. Its main focus is on the specification of what it means to distribute real possibilities in maximin fashion. As such, it aims to improve upon the specifications of the same fundamental idea that are to be found, in sketches or in full, in the works of Rawls, Sen, Dworkin, Rakowski, Arneson, G. A. Cohen and others. What it proposes can be viewed as a hybrid combination of undominated diversity and value equalization. Opting for this hybrid has the odd consequence of justifying an unconditional basic income for all, whereas each of the two ideas it combines, if allowed to cover indiscriminately both the external and internal component of one's endowment, would justify no more than a transfer system targeted to the comparatively less talented – stingy if undominated diversity of comprehensive endowments were all that mattered, massive if the maximin distribution of the value of what one is given applied to one's talents as well as to one's external resources.

11.2   Undominated diversity, and why it is not enough

Doubtless it is possible to improve upon my conjecture regarding the best way of capturing my own considered judgements, quite possibly along the lines adumbrated by some of the contributions to this volume. But prospective improvers should be aware of what led me to make my specific proposal. Perhaps a helpful way of rephrasing that underlying motivation is as follows.

In a pluralist society, people reasonably disagree about what matters in life, and hence about which abilities it is most important to have. Full acknowledgement of this situation does not make it impossible to judge that person *A* is less well equipped than person *B* and is therefore entitled to a transfer from *B*. But it would make it odd to decree that *A* is entitled to a transfer from *B* despite the fact that both *A* and *B* find, in the light of their respective conceptions of the good life, that *A* is better equipped than *B*. And it would also be odd to decree, in the name of equality, that *A* is entitled to a transfer from *B*, while *C* is not entitled to a transfer from *D*, in a case in which *A* and *C*, and *B* and *D*, respectively, are identically endowed. Reducing the requirement of justice to the elimination of all cases of universal preference of one endowment struck me as the only way of ruling out simultaneously these two possibilities.

It is worth emphasizing that the motivation for undominated diversity, thus restated, is not – as, judging from Andrew Williams's comment,[8] I must have suggested – that undominated diversity can be understood as potential envy-freeness, in the sense that, compared to the endowment of every other person, each person would prefer her own endowment if she used as a standard a conception of the good actually adopted by at least one member in society. The 'availability' of envy-freeness in this sense is an interesting way of reformulating undominated diversity. But the fundamental motivation behind it has nothing to do with the elimination of envy: it is simply the respect for a diverse set of conceptions of the good life.

Note, too, that once preferences are trimmed so as to eliminate ill-informed or incoherent ones, the gap between this criterion and one based on a conception of the good, which is, as is Arneson's for example,[9] fairly plural, and which is therefore associated with an ordering of endowments that is only partial, is not that wide. Nonetheless, as our societies become more pluralistic, or as the level at which issues of fair distribution arise starts encompassing more diverse societies, undominated diversity might become so easy to satisfy that very little redistribution will be justified in this way. This implication would seem particularly unwelcome as growing pluralism is going hand in hand with expanding inequalities, themselves the joint outcome of technological change and globalization.

The reason why undominated diversity is of little help as a basis for addressing these inequalities is not only that in pluralist societies, in which some people might give little importance to earning power, great income inequalities are consistent with the absence of dominance. In addition, and more fundamentally, in our increasingly complex knowledge- and communication-based economy earning power cannot be identified, as it is in elementary microeconomics, as a feature of an agent's endowment: how much a person, with given talents, will manage to earn is heavily dependent on what productive slots her connections, her training, her citizenship, her place of residence, her mother tongue, the fluctuations of her temper, and sheer luck will enable her to occupy, and on how well she fits in, in that slot, with co-workers, bosses, and clients as well as local culture and technology. Consequently, it is wrong to imagine that one could address the growing inequality of earning power by identifying and correcting inequalities in people's internal endowments.

11.3   The maximin distribution of the value of external endowments

A far more promising option arises if one retains undominated diversity as a weak background constraint, while asking how a fair distribution of external endowments should be characterized in the sort of environment I have just sketched. Even those who feel most uncomfortable with the idea of an unconditional income, such as Stuart White[10] or Elizabeth Anderson,[11] are willing to admit the legitimacy of a dividend scheme of the Alaskan type. If there is a jointly owned natural endowment, such as oil, instead of giving each member of the society concerned an equal and untradable volume of oil, it makes far more sense to give everyone a cash equivalent.

It is important to note that what this cash equivalent gives people actual access to will vary from one person to another, depending on each person's conception of the good life. How much a person will manage to get of what she wants will be affected by the preferences of others, because equal cash means, in the absence of discrimination, access to equal market value, itself the outcome of the interaction between the supply of factors of production and the tastes that underlie consumer demand. This interaction determines how precious external resources are at a particular time, as reflected, at least roughly, by the price they command in a properly functioning market. Equality of cash endowments therefore means external endowments that are equally precious, equally valuable, in terms of how much others would like to have them. It is this intuitive notion that guides the choice of a competitive price metric to articulate my third principle, rather than – as, judging again from Andrew Williams's remarks,[12] I must have suggested – any connection there might be, under some conditions, between competitive equilibrium and the achievement of envy-freeness.

According to the criterion of value equalization, just as with undominated diversity, each individual's eventual entitlements depend on everyone else's preferences. But the nature of this dependence is very different in the two cases. In particular, as regards the implications of value equalization there is no reason to expect that growing pluralism will lead to less redistribution. At the same time, it must be conceded that there is something more institutionally contingent about the plausibility of value equalization. The fairness of giving everyone the same cash equivalent is conditioned by the non-discriminatory nature of the market in which this cash is to be spent. If some goods or services can be bought, some flats rented, some jobs filled, only by people of a particular race or gender, the notion that cash distribution provides an appropriate way of achieving a fair distribution of external resources loses a great deal of its appeal.[13]

The key step in *Real Freedom for All*, however, involves lending considerable muscle to the principle of value equalization by incorporating jobs amongst the resources to which it applies. This massive extension of the scope of the principle is the positive side of the insight that feeds deep scepticism as to undominated diversity's capacity to handle the challenge of capturing the injustice of mounting inequalities. What determines people's earning power and actual income is not only their endowment in skills and in material wealth, as in elementary textbooks, but no less a complex set of opportunities, some structured, some unstructured, which enable people to tap – very unequally – society's tremendous income-generating power. Of course, to tap this source of material benefit, some work usually needs to be done, just as in order to inherit from one's old aunt it may have helped to pay her a few visits. By no means does this invalidate the fact that most of what the 'tappers' receive must be viewed as a gift – as should be clear when comparing the yield of paying the same number of visits to a rich aunt and to a poor one, or the payoff of a given physical and mental effort in Manhattan and in Peshawar. In the language adopted by Peter Vallentyne, effort and option luck operate on the background of very unequally distributed brute luck.[14]

Accommodating this insight massively expands the legitimate base for Alaska-type redistribution, far beyond natural resources and the transfer of wealth through donation and inheritance. *Real Freedom for All* does not defend the *equalization* of the value of this enlarged base, but only its sustainable *maximinimization*. This can be operationalized, *Real Freedom for All* argues step by step, by maximizing the yield of efficient, comprehensive and predictable income taxation, and distributing this yield equally to all, irrespective of their earnings. Like Rawls's difference principle, this may appear to be some outcome-equalizing programme, but is not.[15] Instead, it formulates an opportunity-egalitarian approach that means business in a sophisticated and messy world, in which opportunities cannot be neatly measured as the value of a person's raw 'human capital' but are the product of an untraceable interaction between innate talents, education trajectory, family connections, lucky hirings, smooth complementarities, etc.

With this comprehensive gift-maximinimization principle firmly in place, undominated diversity can still play a modest limiting role in the background, but the risk that neutrality might make equality shrink into insignificance, very serious if we had nothing but undominated diversity to fall back on, has now been effectively defeated. No need to rely on any particular conception of the good – neither pro-market, nor anti-market, for example – in order to justify the maximin distribution of the market value of external endowments in a broad sense that encompasses employment and other market rents.

11.4 The proper place of solidarity

Unlike undominated diversity, this maximin principle cannot be said to give some interpretation to a notion of reciprocity or solidarity, at least as most intuitively understood. Like several of my critics,[16] I am sensitive to the idea that free riding is ethically wrong.[17] Yet, I am unimpressed by the critique that the unconditional basic income justified by my maximin principle is a form of free riding, or indeed, in Gijs van Donselaar's version of the critique, a form of parasitism.[18] Let me briefly explain.

It is bad enough to be a free rider, that is, to benefit from a good while leaving others to bear the full cost of its production. But it is even worse to be a parasite, that is, to benefit from the good while thereby increasing the cost borne by those who produce it. Unlike those whose work benefits mere free riders, those whose work benefits parasites would be materially better off if the beneficiaries did not exist. And this is the case, van Donselaar says, for those who get their basic income without doing any work towards it.

I am not impressed by this critique because what turns the basic income consumer into a parasite is simply the fact that she takes her fair share of what is there for everyone to share. If there is something to be shared among any given number of people, it is self-evident that if one of these did not exist there would be more for the others. Now, as mentioned earlier, those of my critics who are most sensitive to solidarity concerns concede that in the case of the proceeds of Alaskan oil, for example, equal sharing irrespective of people's contribution, or willingness to contribute, makes ethical sense. And they have provided no decisive ethical reason for establishing a discontinuity between the fair sharing of the value of natural resources and the fair sharing of the value of other external resources to which we are given very unequal access, in particular the rents incorporated in our jobs. For example, the value of natural resources is determined by the use others have made, make and will make of them. A ton of oil would be just as worthless as a job would be if there were not, or had not been, other people to invent techniques, produce and consume. And it is, of course, the object's having a value, rather than its sheer existence, that provides a potential for cash redistribution.[19]

Or take the following suggestion as to where the discontinuity may lie. It is no doubt true that some jobs, even if fully available, would be declined by certain individuals. It is even conceivable that some people may turn down all existing jobs. But this cannot be a reason for considering that the value of jobs, in the sense of the employment rents associated with them, is not fit for distribution to the voluntarily unemployed. If an individual lacks what van Donselaar terms an 'independent interest' in some natural resource, such as a plot of land, and thus attaches no value to it other than as an item to exchange in return for compensation from others, is this a compelling ground to exclude her from any share in its value? Surely those of us who covet everything are not entitled, as a matter of justice, to a greater share of the value of a collective inheritance than those whose 'independent interests' are less extensive. It seems far more sensible to take land values as generated by the interaction of the more or less focused desires of all, and to distribute its aggregate value equally to all. And if job rents are added to the stock of resources spontaneously distributed in very unequal fashion, there is similarly no reason to restrict their fair redistribution to those who have an 'independent' interest in them. The modest income afforded to the voluntary unemployed by the taxation of employment rents is therefore no more – and no less, in a sense to be discussed very shortly in connection with global justice – stolen income than that derived from natural rents. What justifies either is not solidarity but fairness. Fairness is not a substitute for solidarity. But it must shape the 'basic structure' against the background of which cooperative ventures governed by reciprocity and solidarity can meaningfully operate.

A legitimate concern for reciprocity and solidarity in a wide variety of contexts should therefore not inhibit our efforts to empower the more powerless by providing everyone a modest unconditional, individual and universal income. In most places, many steps are still needed to get there, and many compromises, different in different places, will need to be struck. One will need sometimes to settle for less than subsistence, sometimes for the household rather than the person as the relevant unit, sometimes for some sort of participation or willingness to work as a strict condition, very often for some sort of means test, and occasionally, perhaps, for everything at once. Never mind. This is not an all-or-nothing affair. Progress, however modest, is worth welcoming and supporting. But to determine whether a reform constitutes progress, and how significantly, it helps to be clear about the direction in which concern for a fair distribution of what we are given should take us. For clarity and coherence about the destination will enable us to confront unabashed the arrogance and hypocrisy of the privileged. They will also help us counter the oppressive instinct of those control freaks who dream of an 'active social state' that will bend the weakest to their will by compelling them to do what they themselves would never dream of doing. From step to step, in many variants and through countless detours, we must instead build an emancipatory 'active social state'.

Even those most concerned to make benefit claimants professionally active may see the point of a system that integrates into a single universal basic payment the bottom part of the welfare state benefits and the fast expanding patchwork of refundable tax credits, and other advantages restricted to earners. Such a floor is not a substitute for more restrictive provisions based on solidarity, insurance, or direct reciprocity. It is rather a condition for their fair and efficient operation.

11.5   Patriotism in the service of global justice?

After this global reaction to the pieces that address the central themes of *Real Freedom for All*, I turn to a more focused response to the two pieces that address important issues that it hardly touched at all.

Hillel Steiner endorses the cosmopolitan view of social justice sketched in the final section of *Real Freedom for All*, and hence the appropriateness of 'scale lifting' from the national to the global level as the first-best strategy to bring about whatever redistribution justice requires.[20] But he does not think much of the second-best strategy I felt I had to offer because of my conviction that vigorous scale lifting would take too long.

Steiner does agree that 'it will take a long time to create political entities of the right sort at the right level, to equip them with appropriate democratic institutions and to build both the political will and the concrete instruments without which substantial inter-national redistribution will remain a utopia'.[21] The alternative instrument I proposed was to build up and use 'solidaristic patriotism', characterized by Steiner as a 'strong emotional commitment to the wellbeing of one's compatriots simply because they are one's compatriots'. But such patriotism, Steiner claims, would not make things better but worse, as regards the trans-national leximin which justice requires. It amounts to greater justice among thieves at the cost of greater theft.

The core of Steiner's argument is straightforward. Suppose redistribution is not or only very partly globalized, and that against this background each sovereign country endeavours to maximize its own basic income, in all likelihood much higher in richer countries than in poorer ones. Steiner and I agree that this is worse, in terms of worldwide maximin, than a basic income administered and maximized on a global scale. But whereas I claim that solidaristic patriotism would improve things using this standard, Steiner believes that it would worsen them. 'Compatriot priority is not a serviceable vehicle for reaching the goal of global distributive justice.' Why not?

First, it would inhibit the movement of capital, physical and human, from richer to poorer countries, and would thereby make the highest sustainable basic income higher in the richer countries, and lower in the poorer countries, than would otherwise be the case. Greater justice in some place perhaps, but only among thieves, among people who enjoy a national basic income higher than the (weighted) world average, and hence higher than what the basic income would be if it were organized, as first-best justice would require, on a world scale. Justice will not be fostered, but hindered, as a result of Marks & Spencer's patriotic owners choosing to invest in Macclesfield rather than in Marrakech.

This first case against 'compatriot priority' is afflicted by two crucial weaknesses. First, it is by no means 'trivially true that a global practice of national asset retention would work to the benefit of asset-rich countries and to the disbenefit of asset-poor ones'. When the United States keeps for good half the post-docs it attracts, this contributes to a flow of human capital from asset-poorer to an asset-richer country. Had 'compatriot priority' been stronger, relative to the attraction of a better pay or a more stimulating working environment, this further impoverishment of the asset-poor countries would have been prevented. True, the net flow could still be positive, as profit-seeking investments find their way to a less productive but also less demanding labour force. However, in a world in which technical and organizational talent is ever more crucial to a country's economic success, the creaming off of the world's human capital may amount to a plundering of the asset-poor countries by the asset-rich of a magnitude which dwarfs the earlier plundering of their natural resources.[22] That the absence of a global practice of national asset retention works to the benefit of asset-poor countries and to the disadvantage of asset-rich ones is, therefore, not 'trivially true' at all. It may prove disastrously false.

Moreover, even if it happened to be true, even if a global practice of national asset retention worked to the disadvantage of asset-poor countries, it would by no means follow that it would depress the highest sustainable level of basic income achievable in these countries. My key claim in favour of solidaristic patriotism is that, in its absence, asset-rich assets present a far more credible threat, not only to move from Macclesfield to Marrakech, but also from Macclesfield to Madison, or from Marrakech to Madras, and back, depending on how favourable a deal they are offered. In this context, even if some asset-poor country would be a net asset gainer in case of asset-migration uncluttered by patriotic concerns, the lack of such concerns would by the same token weaken the country's grip on the income from these assets, and hence its ability to fund, among other things, a basic income. The central purpose of solidaristic patriotism is not to reduce inequalities between countries. Even if it increases such inequalities, it is fully justified in terms of a (second-best) world maximin if it enables countries, especially, but not only, the asset-poorest, to tax sustainably to the benefit of its asset-poorest individual members more than it otherwise could. By overlooking this dynamic dimension, and hence the key distinction between a country's wealth and its basic-income-potential, Steiner's first reason for indicting solidaristic patriotism misses the core of my (admittedly elliptical) argument for it.

Steiner's second reason for indicting solidaristic patriotism is that the latter might operate at the level of peoples that correspond to only a subset of a country's whole population, in particular to a comparatively rich subset. Whenever this is the case – Steiner mentions a significant number of plausible recent illustrations, including Belgium – solidaristic patriotism promotes a different way in which the asset rich can escape high redistribution: not by individually exporting their assets but by collectively 'exporting their countries', that is, by seceding. Even though I am sympathetic to major increases in the political autonomy of territorially distinct linguistic communities, I completely agree with Steiner that full secession would generally be a bad thing in terms of a worldwide leximin. This is so in part for the static reason he has in mind – the termination of net transfers from richer to poorer regions – but, above all, again for the dynamic reason that secession would sharpen international fiscal and social competition as a result of nations becoming smaller and more numerous, and would thereby weaken each nation's redistributive grip. I am therefore strongly opposed, not only to economically motivated secession, but also to any significant decentralization of redistributive powers.[23]

How is this to be reconciled with my plea for solidaristic patriotism? Quite easily, I think, if one heeds the motivation I give for the latter in *Real Freedom for All*: 'The competitive pressure against existing intranational redistribution is mounting, and it would, therefore, be good if there were another strategy which would enable us to keep and regain at least part of the required leeway' (p. 230). The choice of the locus of desirable solidaristic patriotism is not left to the vagaries of spontaneous popular sentiment. It must be nurtured in those places, and only in those places, in which it helps to protect an existing or emerging redistributive *patria*. This is not to deny that viable redistribution needs to be structured differently in a federation of regions with significant political autonomy and in a strong unitary state. Nor is it to deny that strong patriotism at one level may hamper efforts to lift redistribution to a higher level. But it should be clear that my advocacy of closely targeted solidaristic patriotism is a long way from a general endorsement of any nationalistic demand. More than making sense of justice among thieves, this would have amounted to fostering theft.

11.6   Democracy, a mere instrument?

The second important issue hardly considered in *Real Freedom for All* but central to one of the pieces in this volume is the relationship between justice and democracy.[24] Thomas Christiano takes issue with the uncompromisingly instrumental approach to democracy which I only hinted at in the book (e.g. pp. 19, 224, 229 and 231), but developed more fully and illustrated at length in several subsequent essays.[25] He is particularly inflamed by the fact that, at the beginning of 'The Disfranchisement of the Elderly, and Other Attempts to Secure Intergenerational Justice', I dare to consider – even though I unambiguously reject – the suggestion that the elderly should be stripped of their voting rights, or have the weight of their votes reduced, in order to prevent an ageing electorate from adopting policies that would be unfair to the young and the unborn.

Christiano does not deny that outcomes are relevant to assess collective-decision procedures. On the contrary, he persuasively argues that a purely procedural justification of democracy – roughly defined as a collective decision-making procedure that rests on political equality – would be either arbitrary or incoherent. He defends instead a *dualist* justification of democracy, which appeals not only to democracy's instrumental value in promoting just outcomes but also to the intrinsic justice of its procedures. His essay, however, leaves open both the precise characterization of just outcomes and the way to resolve conflicts that arise when the two standards diverge, as he admits may happen.

How significant is the disagreement between us? I do agree with Christiano that democracy is a 'generally necessary condition' for the realization of justice. Moreover, the reason why I believe this to be the case is that democratic procedures show, or purport to show, equal consideration for the interests and conceptions of all citizens, which is precisely the feature of democracy which makes it (generally?) intrinsically just according to Christiano. But while I am willing to affirm that democracy – not only in the 'broad conception' of political equality for all citizens, but also in Christano's 'narrow conception' of political equality at all ages – is intrinsically well suited to produce just outcomes, I find it unnecessary, and indeed confusing, to infer that democracy is intrinsically just, and hence to swap my pure 'fixed end instrumentalism', as Christiano calls it, for his hybrid alternative.

This is not just academic knit-picking, and Christiano's challenge is therefore not otiose, for the following two reasons. First, a process which gives perfectly equal consideration to the interests and conceptions of all citizens may display a propensity to take decisions that are highly, and unjustly, detrimental to the interests of non-citizens – foreigners, children and the unborn. I cannot see why the fact that true democracy is a good tool to fight the unjust privileges of those, among (contemporary adult) citizens, who are despots or the rich should make us decree that it is intrinsically just, when it is unfit to fight unjust privileges relative to non-citizens. Hence there is nothing self-contradictory, or outrageous, about exploring deviations from democracy that may achieve greater justice towards non-citizens. Indeed, those really committed to justice would be foolish not to explore such deviations, however cautious they should be, as I certainly was, about decreeing any of them worth trying.[26]

Secondly, and far more importantly for practical purposes, the notion of the intrinsic justice of democracy induces a strong presumption that 'more democratic' systems are intrinsically more just, and hence more desirable, than less democratic ones. What prompted me to think more systematically about democracy is precisely the realization, starting with the Indian example discussed in 'Justice and Democracy: Are They Incompatible?', that more democracy – the strict implementation, for example, of universal eligibility – can be badly counterproductive in terms of civil peace and social justice. On the contrary, the 'Machiavellian' programme of investigating, in ruthlessly consequentialist fashion, the likely consequences of various more or less democratic institutional designs for the sustainable achievement of social justice,[27] is not only intellectually more exciting, but of great and urgent relevance if one is to avoid making irreversible blunders by naively extrapolating from the working of democratic one-nation-states such as France or the United States to the needs of plurinational countries or supra-national polities.[28]

Of course, all this presupposes a commitment to a specific conception of justice, and Christiano repeatedly points out that there is considerable disagreement about this. Political philosophers and the institutional engineers they might inspire are fortunately not in a position, in 'zookeeping' fashion, to impose despotically their personal conception of justice and the corresponding institutions. A democratic majority must decide. But this must not stop political philosophers from telling the majority what it should decide and why, including as regards institutions that will modify its own functioning and lead it to take decisions different from what it otherwise would. As I have tried to explain in connection with intergenerational justice,[29] this task is not self-contradictory, or possible only when it is not useful. But for it to make sense, the conception of justice to which it appeals must be defensible by arguments that embody an equal respect for each citizen's conception of the good life and an equal concern for their interests. This I claim is the case with social justice as 'real freedom for all'. No reason, therefore, to shy away from pushing for bold justice-inspired institutional reforms. Condorcet, I bet, would not disagree.

Notes

1. I am most grateful to Andrew Williams for several years of thoughtful feedback and stimulating discussions, from the 1996 conference at the University of Warwick, which sowed the first seeds of the present volume, to his careful and competent editorial comments on this 'Reply' over five years later.
2. See Elisabeth Badinter and Robert Badinter, *Condorcet: un intellectuel en politique* (Paris: Fayard, 1988), p. 60.
3. See Chapter 2, John Cunliffe, Guido Erreygers and Walter Van Trier, 'Basic Income: Pedigree and Problems'.
4. See the following: 'Social Justice as Real Freedom for All: a Reply to Arneson, Fleurbaey, Melnyk and Selznick', *Good Society* 7 (1997), pp. 42–8; 'Justice as the Fair Distribution of Freedom: Fetishism or Stoicism?', in M. Fleurbaey and J. F. Laslier (eds), *The Ethics and Economics of Liberty* (London: Routledge, 1997), pp.197–205; 'Reciprocity and the Justification of an Unconditional Basic Income: Reply to Stuart White', *Political Studies* 45 (1997), pp. 327–30; 'Reply', in J. Cohen and J. Rogers (eds), *What's Wrong with a Free Lunch?* (Boston: Beacon Press, 2001); and, most extensively, 'Real Freedom, the Market and the Family: Reply to Seven Critics', *Analyse und Kritik* 23 (2001), pp. 106–31.

5. See, respectively, Chapter 4, Brian Barry, 'Real Freedom and Basic Income', and Chapter 5, Robert J. van der Veen, 'Real Freedom and Basic Income: Comment on Brian Barry'.
6. See Chapter 3, Peter Vallentyne, 'Self-Ownership and Equality: Brute Luck, Gifts, Universal Dominance, and Leximin'.
7. See Chapter 4, Barry, 'Real Freedom and Basic Income'.
8. See Chapter 7, Andrew Williams, 'Resource Egalitarianism and the Limits to Basic Income'.
9. See Chapter 6, Richard Arneson, 'Should Surfers Be Fed?'.
10. See Chapter 8, Stuart White, 'Fair Reciprocity and Basic Income'.
11. See Elizabeth Anderson, 'Optional Freedoms', in Cohen and Rogers (eds), *What's Wrong with a Free Lunch?*, pp. 70–4.
12. See Chapter 7.
13. For further discussion, see 'Real Freedom, the Market and the Family: Reply to Seven Critics'.
14. The underlying intuition is well expressed by Herbert Simon in 'UBI and the Flat Tax', in Cohen and Rogers (eds), *What's Wrong with a Free Lunch?*, pp. 34–8.
15. For an explanation of the difference principle, see Philippe Van Parijs, 'Difference Principles', in Samuel Freeman (ed.), *The Cambridge Companion to John Rawls* (Cambridge: Cambridge University Press, 2002).
16. See, in this volume, Stuart White, 'Fair Reciprocity and Basic Income'; also Elizabeth Anderson, 'Optional Freedoms'; and William Galston, 'What about Reciprocity?', in Cohen and Rogers (eds), *What's Wrong with a Free Lunch?*, pp. 29–33.
17. See 'Justice and Democracy: Are They Incompatible?' and 'Linguistic Justice'.
18. See Gjis Van Donselaar, 'The Benefit of Another's Pain: Parasitism, Scarcity, Basic Income' (University of Amsterdam, Ph.D. thesis in Philosophy, 1997).
19. See Philippe Van Parijs, 'Reciprocity and the Justification of an Unconditional Basic Income: Reply to Stuart White', *Political Studies* 45 (1997), pp. 327–30, responding to Stuart White, 'Liberal Equality, Exploitation, and the Case for an Unconditional Basic Income', *Political Studies* 45 (1997), pp. 312–26.
20. See Chapter 9, Hillel Steiner, 'Compatriot Priority and Justice among Thieves'.
21. See *Real Freedom for All*, p. 230.
22. An increasingly important dimension of this plundering will be linguistic. As English spreads as a world lingua franca, the value of having English as the country's mother tongue increases, and the value of having another language shrinks. There follows an unprecedented specific pressure for human capital to move from countries made asset poorer by this process to countries made asset richer by it. For further discussion, see P. Van Parijs, 'Linguistic Justice', *Politics, Philosophy, and Economics* 1 (2002).
23. This is not a merely theoretical position, but is reflected in my personal involvement in Belgium's public debate. See, for example, Gérard Roland, Toon Vandevelde and Philippe Van Parijs, 'Repenser (radicalement?) la solidarité entre les regions', in F. Docquier (ed.), *La solidarité entre les régions: Bilan et perspectives* (Bruxelles: Deboeck Université, 1999), and Philippe Van Parijs, 'Philosophie de la fiscalité pour une économie mondialisée', *Bulletin de documentation du Ministère des finances* 60/2 (2000), pp. 25–48.

24. See Chapter 10, Thomas Christiano, 'Is Democracy Merely a Means to Social Justice?'.
25. Philippe Van Parijs, 'Justice and Democracy: Are They Incompatible?', *Journal of Political Philosophy* 4 (1996), pp. 101–17, Philippe Van Parijs, 'Reciprocity and the Justification of an Unconditional Basic Income: Reply to Stuart White', *Political Studies* 45 (1997), pp. 327–30, Philippe Van Parijs, 'The Disfranchisement of the Elderly, and Other Attempts to Secure Intergenerational Justice', *Philosophy and Public Affairs* 27 (1998), pp. 292–333, Philippe Van Parijs, 'Contestatory Democracy versus Real Freedom for All', in Ian Shapiro and Casiano Hacker-Gordon (eds), *Democracy's Value* (Cambridge: Cambridge University Press, 1999), pp. 191–8, and Philippe Van Parijs, 'Power-Sharing versus Border-Crossing in Ethnically Divided Societies', in Steven Macedo and Ian Shapiro (eds), *Nomos XLII: Designing Democratic Institutions* (New York: NYU Press), pp. 296–320. According to Christiano, I do not stick to this systematic instrumentalism, because of the priority I ascribe to self-ownership in my conception of social justice. But what follows from that conception, in this respect, is not merely the inscription of the key components of the protection of self-ownership in the constitution, but a consequentialist evaluation of a society's institutions – including political institutions, such as the rules that determine how the police are organized, funded and controlled – in terms of their impact on the effective protection of the self-ownership rights of all categories of citizens (against the state, and above all against each other).
26. See 'The Disfranchisement of the Elderly, and Other Attempts to Secure Intergenerational Justice'.
27. Christiano repeatedly characterizes my interpretation of the 'Machiavellian' approach as resting on the view that citizens and political agents 'are deeply self-interested'. This is a misunderstanding: 'The "Machiavelli" component, on the other hand, refers to an approach to political institutions which aims to shape them in such a way that those acting within them will end up generating the "right" collective outcome, even though they *may* be moved by little else than their own *private* concerns'; 'People need to be taken as they are or can feasibly be made to be, not as elementary economic textbooks posit they are. There is no need to assume that voters are strictly selfish ... ' See 'The Disfranchisement of the Elderly, and Other Attempts to Secure Intergenerational Justice', pp. 299, emphasis added, and 322, respectively.
28. See Philippe Van Parijs, 'Should the European Union Become More Democratic?', in A. Follesdal and P. Koslowski (eds), *Democracy and the European Union* (Berlin and New York: Springer, 1997), pp. 287–301, 'Power-Sharing versus Border-Crossing in Ethnically Divided Societies', and 'Must Europe Be Belgian? On Democratic Citizenship in Multilingual Polities'.
29. See 'The Disfranchisement of the Elderly, and Other Attempts to Secure Intergenerational Justice'.

Select Bibliography

Compiled by Jeroen Knijff

Barry, Brian. 'Real Freedom and Basic Income', *Journal of Political Philosophy* 4/3 (1996), pp. 242–76.

Couture, Jocelyne. Review, *Economics and Philosophy* 14/1 (1998), pp. 143–51.

De Wispelaere, Jurgen. 'Sharing Job Resources: Ethical Reflections on the Justification of Basic Income', *Analyse und Kritik* 22/2 (2000), pp. 237–56.

Donselaar, Gijs van. 'The Benefit of Another's Pains: Parasitism, Scarcity, Basic Income', Ph.D. Dissertation, University of Amsterdam, 1997.

Donselaar, Gijs van. 'The Freedom-Based Account of Solidarity and Basic Income', *Ethical Theory and Moral Practice* 1/3 (1998), pp. 313–33.

Farrelly, Colin. 'Justice and a Citizens' Basic Income', *Journal of Applied Philosophy* 16/3 (1999), pp. 283–96.

Fleurbaey, Marc. Critical Notice, *The Good Society: a PEGS Journal* 6/2 (1996).

Galeotti, Anna Elisabetta. Review, *European Journal of Philosophy* 5/1 (1997), pp. 88–93.

Gough, Ian. *Global Capital, Human Needs and Social Policies* (Basingstoke: Palgrave now Palgrave Macmillan, 2000).

Groot, L. F. M. *Basic Income and Unemployment* (Amsterdam: Thela Thesis, 1999).

Hamminga, Bert. 'Demoralizing the Labour Market: Could Jobs Be like Cars and Concerts?', *Journal of Political Philosophy* 3 (1995), pp. 23–35.

Hempell, Thomas. 'Freizeit als Vermögen: Anmerkungen zu Philippe Van Parijs' Konzept eines Basiseinkommens', in Jean-Christophe Merle et al., *Internationale Gerechtigkeit* (Rechtsphilosophische Hefte, Vol. 7; Frankfurt am Main: Lang, 1997), pp. 153–9.

Hunyadi, Marc, and Marcus Maenz. 'Does "Real-Freedom-for-All" Really Justify Basic Income?', *Swiss Political Science Review* 4/1 (1998), pp. 45–65.

Krebs, Angelika. 'Why Mothers Should Be Fed: eine Kritik an Van Parijs', *Analyse und Kritik* 22/2 (2000), pp. 155–78.

Langis, Georges. 'Allocation universelle et justice sociale', *Cahiers de droit* 37/4 (1996), pp. 1,037–51.

Lukes, Steven. 'Reply to Van Parijs', *Ratio Juris* 8/1 (1995), pp. 64–7.

Michel, Heiner. 'Sind Marktpreise gerecht? Eine Kritik am Van Parijsschen Ökonomismus', *Analyse und Kritik* 22/2 (2000), pp. 179–97.

Midtgaard, Søren Flinch. 'Ambition-Sensitivity and an Unconditional Basic Income', *Analyse und Kritik* 22/2 (2000), pp. 223–36.

Robeyns, Ingrid. 'Will a Basic Income Do Justice to Women?', *Analyse und Kritik* 23/1 (2001), pp. 88–105.

Schroeder, Doris. 'Wickedness, Idleness and Basic Income', *Res Publica* 7/1 (2001), pp. 1–12.

Steinvorth, Ulrich. 'Kann das Grundeinkommen die Arbeitslosigkeit abbauen?', *Analyse und Kritik* 22/2 (2000), pp. 257–68.

Sturn, Richard, and Rudi Dujmovits. 'Basic Income in Complex Worlds: Individual Freedom and Social Interdependencies', *Analyse und Kritik* 22/2 (2000), pp. 198–222.

Torisky, Eugene V. 'Van Parijs, Rawls, and Unconditional Basic Income', *Analysis* 53/4 (1993), pp. 289–97.

Vallentyne, Peter. 'Self-Ownership and Equality: Brute Luck, Gifts, Universal Dominance, and Leximin', *Ethics* 107/2 (1997), pp. 321–43.

van der Veen, Robert J. 'Real Freedom and Basic Income: Comment on Brian Barry', *Journal of Political Philosophy* 5/3 (1997), pp. 274–86.

van der Veen, Robert J. 'Real Freedom versus Reciprocity: Competing Views on the Justice of Unconditional Basic Income', *Political Studies* 46/1 (1998), pp. 140–63.

van der Veen, Robert J., and Groot, Loek (eds), *Basic Income on the Agenda: Policy Objectives and Political Chances* (Amsterdam: Amsterdam University Press, 2000).

Van Parijs, Philippe. 'Arbeid, vrijheid, basisinkomen: antwoord aan Toon Vandevelde', *Tijdschrift voor Filosofie* 59/4 (1997), pp. 698–701.

Van Parijs, Philippe. 'Difference Principles', in Samuel Freeman (ed.), *The Cambridge Companion to John Rawls* (Cambridge: Cambridge University Press, 2002), pp. 200–40.

Van Parijs, Philippe. 'Real Freedom, the Market and the Family: a Reply', *Analyse und Kritik* 23/1 (2001), pp. 106–31.

Van Parijs, Philippe. 'Reciprocity and the Justification of an Unconditional Basic Income: Reply to Stuart White', *Political Studies* 45/2 (1997), pp. 327–30.

Van Parijs, Philippe. 'Social Justice as Real Freedom for All: a Reply to Arneson, Fleurbaey, Melnyk and Selznick', *Good Society: a PEGS Journal* 7/1 (1997), pp. 42–8.

Van Parijs, Philippe. *What's Wrong with a Free Lunch?* (Boston, MA: Beacon Press, 2001).

Vandenbroucke, Frank. *Social Justice and Individual Ethics in an Open Society: Equality, Responsibility, and Incentives* (Berlin: Springer, 2001).

Vandevelde, A. 'Basisinkomen, arbeid en reële vrijheid: over het werk van Philippe Van Parijs', *Tijdschrift voor Filosofie* 59/4 (1997), pp. 666–97.

Weinberg, Justin. 'Freedom, Self-Ownership, and Libertarian Philosophical Diaspora', *Critical Review* 11/3 (1997), pp. 323–44.

White, Stuart. 'Liberal Equality, Exploitation, and the Case for an Unconditional Basic Income', *Political Studies* 45/2 (1997), pp. 312–26.

Widerquist, Karl. 'Perspectives on the Guaranteed Income: Part I', *Journal of Economic Issues* 35/3 (2001), pp. 749–58.

Widerquist, Karl. 'Reciprocity and the Guaranteed Income', *Politics and Society* 27/3 (1999), pp. 387–402.

Williams, Andrew. 'Resource Egalitarianism and the Limits to Basic Income', *Economics and Philosophy* 15/1 (1999), pp. 85–107.

Index

The editors would like to thank Will Smith for preparing this index.